ADVANCED PARAGLIDING

What I've Learned from the World's Best Pilots

By Gavin McClurg

Cross Country

In the core, since 1988

About this book

This book took shape during a chat between Gavin McClurg and Hugh Miller on the back of a truck heading up to launch in Roldanillo, Colombia, in January 2018. The pair started chatting about the success of Gavin's Cross Country columns and his Cloudbase Mayhem podcast. As they got off the trucks, shouldered bags, grabbed coffees and hiked into the thick fog and woods behind launch, they wondered whether the best of all the accumulated knowledge could be distilled into a book. The result is in your hands. It's been a three-year project, involving transcribing, re-interviewing, editing and writing new content. The aim was to produce something similar to Dennis Pagen's seminal The Secrets of Champions. We hope we've crossed the line and reached goal – do let us know.

About Cross Country

More journal than magazine, Cross Country aims to keep flyers fuelled with inspiration and information. Founded in 1988, and read by tens of thousands of pilots in over 75 countries, Cross Country is respected as independent and authoritative. Ten issues are published each year. Cross Country also publishes best-selling technique books. Find us online at www.xcmag.com, and come and join the family - you'd be very welcome.

The Publisher

Cross Country International
Tollgate, Beddingham
Lewes
BN8 6JZ, UK
www.xcmag.com

 This is not a teach-yourself manual – please learn with a qualified instructor at an approved school. Free flight is an evolving discipline, theories adapt, equipment is superseded and advice changes: please send feedback to editor@xcmag.com.

Author: Gavin McClurg
Designer: Marcus King
Production: Marcus and Charlie King
Subeditor: Andrew Craig
Proofing: Ed Ewing and Charlie King
Editor and Publisher: Hugh Miller
Front cover portrait: Jody MacDonald
Back cover photo: Andy Busslinger
ISBN: 978-1-8380173-5-4

Gavin's Dedication

This book is dedicated to my wife Mattie, who encourages my dreams, and my daughter Fallon who reminds me to make it home.

“Free flying is either in you or it’s not. And when it is, it’s not something that goes away. It’s just there.”

Jeff Shapiro

NIVIUK
AMAZING ADVENTURES
Paying attention to small details has led us to where we are today.
We are much like Gavin, who is constantly defying expectations with the challenges he sets himself to accomplish. He has achieved great feats by persevering through adversity.
We are proud to be part of his adventures, together we make them truly amazing.
Thanks Gavin
GAVIN McCLURG

www.niviuk.com
Facebook.com/Niviuk
instagram.com/Niviukparagliders

FOREWORD

When I first met Gavin, I honestly did not know what to make of him. He was certainly a nice guy - full of positive energy and with an over-the-top enthusiasm for all things free flight. Gavin's boundless ambition was combined with a big-time go-for-it attitude. I'd seen this combination many times before and it's often a classic recipe for disaster when starting a high-risk sport. I hoped he'd survive the next few years - as I am sure a few of my mentors thought about me. Surviving the learning curve, gaining experience, and reaching a more balanced place is one of the rites of passage we all must endure in the pursuit of flight.

That rite of passage came for Gavin a few years later in 2013 when he broke the North American foot-launch record. He flew a bold route through the big and remote mountains of Idaho in conditions that would have been challenging for even the most experienced of us. Gavin used advice I gave him in a way and to a level I had not quite intended, but to great effect nonetheless. This flight both inspired and terrified him, along with many of us. But as it turned out, it was not a one-off but a springboard for even bigger things. Gavin went on to fly the length of the Canadian Rockies with Will Gadd, then to fly the length of the Alaska range, starting the expedition with Dave Turner and finishing it solo. These were huge, fully committed, epic adventures. He competed in three (and counting) X-Alps races and is the first and only American to make it to the finish in Monaco. He has survived, and thrived… and along the way he's become a significant contributor to the sport.

Gavin is still pushing his limits in tireless fashion. His talent does not lie in an exceptional aptitude for sport. His talent is in his persistence and relentless determination. Calvin Coolidge, the 30th president of the United States, wrote that "nothing in this world can take the place of persistence." He continued, "Talent will not; nothing is more common than unsuccessful people with talent. Genius will not; unrewarded genius is almost a proverb. Education will not; the world is full of educated derelicts. Persistence and determination alone are omnipotent. The slogan 'Press On' has solved and always will solve the problems of the human race."

These qualities, which Gavin has in spades, have no limitations, are accessible to all, and can be applied to all things, which brings us to his creation of the podcast and hence this book.

The Cloudbase Mayhem podcast was unplanned. The seed for its eventual germination was accidentally discovered during our 500 Miles to Nowhere expedition in 2014. Of course, the true nature of any expedition is a journey of discovery. We have to remain wide-open to experience, and not become so focused on the original objective that we miss all the unexpected jewels and gems along the way. These surprise experiences are the inspiration for new expeditions, potentially leading to even greater discoveries. The book you hold in your hands is the result of one of those greater discoveries. The book's creation is an implicit reminder to us all to just be willing to start journeys outside our comfort zones, even when unsure of the destination or our ability to get there. Just press on, believe, and figure it out. Everything will be fine…

Where this journey would lead, while not obvious at first, became clearer once Gavin started down the path of interviewing fellow pilots, and committed to its continuation. I had the honor of being podcast number 1, ground zero for Cloudbase Mayhem. I had no idea at the time how much of a moment that was. Gavin recruited other voices from the North American flying scene as he sharpened his interviewing skills. The project's potential began to take form and gain momentum as he reached out to the international flying community and even more iconic voices. They saw it too. He got many of the greatest pilots of all time to participate in this grand adventure. At the time of this writing there are now more than 140 episodes on the podcast and there is no sign of slowing down. Gavin, through his persistence and determination, has made this happen. We are all now the beneficiaries.

The result is not a typical book with a single voice. This book is an international curated collection of voices, experiences, perspectives, and approaches to life and the sport that we all love. It is the undeniable power of the lead gaggle, the world's lead gaggle with the best pilots in the world sharing their knowledge. And it is not just about techniques. As a great martial artist once said, "only amateurs think that techniques are enough." This book is also about the philosophy of adventure, the value of accepting risk and managing it, and the importance of training the mind as well as the body. It is about the flying life.

The podcast and this book gives not only to the reader but to the contributors. As contributors, it is our opportunity to give back to the sport that has defined us and given us so much. We can share the moments of our greatest joys and deepest sorrows. We can have our knowledge not become lost or forgotten, but be a stepping stone to a deeper understanding, a deeper connection, and greater achievements in flight for future pilots. Most of all, it reminds us that our community, our gaggle, is the most powerful and important asset we have as it connects us, teaches us, and enriches us all.

I cannot image a greater gift to our sport than the creation of this enduring platform to collect and share our knowledge and flying experiences. Chapeau Gavin! And a huge thank you to the global flying community for their continued participation. Long live The Cloudbase Mayhem!

Bill Belcourt

CONTENTS

THE SPECIFICS

APPENDICES

USA 1

WELCOME

Thank you for buying this book. It's the result of more than 15 years of flying, and eight years of interviewing lots of the world's best pilots. I hope you enjoy it.

So how did we get here? In 2011 I was living in Morocco after a five-year circumnavigation as the captain of a large catamaran, taking kitesurfers all over the world. Freshly ashore, I suddenly had a lot of time to devote to flying. I needed a place to live, and I wanted to fly big lines.

I spent the following season in the European Alps with a single purpose: chasing airtime with my good friend Bruce Marks, who was even hornier to fly than me. Bruce won the 'Chocolate Bar' award for the most 100km flights on XContest three years in a row, starting that year. We both heard from many pilots what you hear on the show repeatedly: to learn to fly fast, you've got to fly comps.

So Bruce and I flew across the pond that July to the Chelan Open in Washington State, a place I now know to be one of the best venues for racing in the world. At the time we were both flying the Niviuk Artik 3, a mid-range EN C. The comp was a blast, and my passion for flying catapulted. Meanwhile, we heard that Matt Beechinor had flown 193 miles from Mount Baldy in Sun Valley, Idaho, deep into neighboring Montana across five huge mountain ranges. A few weeks later Matt's neighbor and mentor Nate Scales flew even further: 199 miles. These were insane distances in BIG mountains that shook the paragliding world, and they totally floored me. This wasn't Brazil or Texas or South Africa flatland flying in a lot of wind. These were big, high-altitude, hypoxia-inducing flights in huge terrain that I had no idea were possible. Decision made: I had to move to Sun Valley and fly with these guys!

That August, Sun Valley was hosting a World Cup. It was a rare US stop on the international tour. The organizer of the event heard I was moving to town and sent me an email that he would give me a wild card[1] if I wanted to compete. Oh hell yes! But I'd never flown an EN D wing, let alone a two-liner. I booked a flight back to the US and sent an

[1] Paragliding World Cup event organizers typically get five wild cards to be given to pilots that the organizer chooses if they haven't qualified through normal means.

email to Niviuk, begging them to lend me an Icepeak 6. It's a pretty tame wing by today's standards, but at the time one of the comp gliders that dominated the tour. My first day flying in Sun Valley, my first day flying a comp wing and my first day flying a two-liner was the day before the event. More exciting than that, my guide would be none other than the site record holder, the legend Nate Scales! Sun Valley has some of the strongest air in the world, right up there with Owens Valley. This would be evidenced on the last day of the comp, when the veteran World Cup pilot Guy Anderson disappeared for two days.
Nate took me around a rowdy 100k FAI triangle that day, nearly all of it without being able to see the ground (the US west was enveloped in a ferocious fire season and visibility was almost nil). It was close to the biggest triangle I'd ever flown; we flew 7,000 feet higher that I'd ever been, and considerably higher than you're supposed to go! It was the first time I used oxygen, and my water container froze solid on my back. And it was awesome. I was already well and truly addicted to paragliding, but when Nate and I cut down through the haze and landed back in town that evening, closing the triangle, my addiction turned into an obsession.

Guy Anderson was miraculously found banged up but alive after the town pulled together a whopper of a search and rescue effort. Many of the World Cup pilots then stayed around for an open distance competition. Unfortunately the weather didn't cooperate and we didn't fly a single task, but pilots who were usually out of reach to lesser mortals like myself helped pass the time by giving instructional talks every afternoon. Topics ranged from the use of oxygen to combat hypoxia; to the importance of hydration and calories; to glider design and SIV. Ozone test pilot Russ Ogden gave a talk on two-liners that I happened to record on video. I uploaded it to YouTube and it went viral almost immediately. I couldn't believe what I was learning. I had read everything I could get my hands on, watched every video. But here were the best in the world openly sharing and dissecting the mysteries of flight in long form. It was obvious I wasn't alone, there was a massive chasm of knowledge between the flying gods and the rest of us.

A year later Nick Greece, Nate Scales, Matt Beechinor and I attempted a vol-biv expedition from Hurricane Ridge near Zion National Park in Utah to Jackson Hole, Wyoming, across the Wasatch range. During the trip we stopped at Black Diamond headquarters in Salt Lake City to interview Bill Belcourt, who was the head of Black Diamond's research and development and one of the most respected pilots in the Americas. Bill has a very special way of describing free flight, and we knew that if we recorded him, we'd get some fantastic material for a documentary film we were shooting about the expedition[2]. As soon as we hit record on the cameras, Bill gave us one mind-blowing observation after another. It was unfiltered access to his 30-plus years of experience of free flight. We recorded over an hour of material, but only a tiny fraction would fit in the film.

A year later all the material Bill had given us was still sitting on a hard drive, and it was driving me crazy. I had to figure out how to get it out into the world! I didn't have a clue how to do a podcast, but that interview became episode number 1. The Cloudbase Mayhem was born. In those early days I'd release a show whenever I got around to it. There was no

[2] The short film **500 Miles to Nowhere** premiered at the Banff Mountain Film Festival and later screened at dozens of other film festivals around the world.

schedule, the sound was terrible, and it would take me a couple of days to do the editing because I had no idea how to deal with audio. But very quickly it was clear we were on to something. By episode #10 we had a solid following, my inbox was being bombarded with thank yous, and it was clear the podcast wasn't just entertainment, but was even saving lives. By episode #20 we had professional audio gear, a proper sound room and a professional editor to deal with what's always the hardest part of production. Listeners frequently tell me the shows are discussed on the way up to launch or debated in the landing field, and that pilots frequently have me in their heads when they fly, reminding them to be smart. As I say over and over again on the show, the purpose of the Mayhem is to share knowledge and make our community fly better and fly safer. Few of us have access to sky gods and mentors and hopefully the Mayhem helps bridge the gap. It's an honor and an absolute delight to bring you the show, and now this book, which I hope will help even more pilots than ever access the minds and brains of the world's best pilots.

This book is based on the distilled wisdom and insights of more than 100 pilots interviewed over eight years. Many are loaded with important advice. Some might even save your life. The result is a free-flight manual that you can read like a normal book, from beginning to end, or you can pick up and use like an encyclopedia, going directly to a specific topic. Either way works.

To write this book I had the great pleasure of going back and listening to all of the interviews again. And again, and again. It turns out that we don't talk at all the way we write, so I've had to take just about everyone's words and adapt them for print. I've gone to great lengths to do this in a way that maintains what the pilot was actually saying without changing their concepts or meaning, but I've often liberally adapted what they said to make it flow on paper.

The book has two main components. We have a 'deep dive' with 18 of the world's best pilots, whose input had the most impact on me personally. Hopefully you'll experience this as going to a bar and sitting down with a very dear friend and getting access to the stuff behind the veil. This wasn't an easy choice, and obviously the guests who had the most impact on me may not be the ones who affected you most. But I think you'll find this section fun and filled with things you might not have picked up in the actual show. We've also gone back and re-interviewed several of the pilots, in order to obtain more detail in many areas.

The other big component within the book is the 'how to' chapters – selection boxes of great advice from a wide range of pilots. Having trouble thermalling? Can't stay with the lead gaggle on glides? Can't figure out how to win? Got a fear of injury that you can't shake? Go to this section and scribble, highlight, bookmark and try it out the next time you fly.

Free flight doesn't come with a manual. You've got to figure it all out as you go. Hopefully this book will help us negotiate the journey a little more efficiently. Enjoy!

Surfing the Sierras – the author on a vol-biv expedition through the Sierra Nevada, California.
Photo: Jody MacDonald

Patagonia ambassador Gavin McClurg flies past Denali during a successful 37 day unsupported expedition to be the first person to traverse the full length of the Alaska Range by foot and paraglider. **Jody MacDonald** © 2021 Patagonia, Inc.

patagonia®

Tips for the Naturally Unconfident Pilot

ADEL HONTI

Adel Honti admits to regularly being scared while flying – something many of us can relate to. But, she argues, fear is not something that should hold us back. Adel's risen to the top of her game by using an analytical approach and an appreciation of mental processes. These, she says, have helped her understand how to operate more adeptly in our invisible world. She explains why "tasks are won and lost in the mind."

Adel thinks fear is actually crucial not only for keeping us safe but also for making flying enjoyable, and the trick is in learning to deal with it in a healthy way.

Along the way, she's also discovered her own methods for getting into that wonderful state of 'Flow' where we're so absorbed in what we're doing that all else drops away. Adel has tips on dealing with failure, learning to focus for longer periods, and paying more attention to the technical aspects of the sport to improve our speed.

We all agree that confidence and the mental side of flying is critical to flying well and staying safe, but if we aren't naturally confident people, how do we progress beyond surviving so that we really thrive in our incredible sport?

Adel describes how to set achievable goals and how to identify weaknesses and mistakes (not just in flying, but in your life) in order to tackle them head-on. This leads to flying farther and faster, and may make some surprisingly positive changes in your non-flying life as well…

Adel, tell us about a time you recently learned something in flying.

It was in Roldanillo at the Colombian Open in February 2018. I'd heard so much about the sugarcane fires in the Cauca valley, but I'd never experienced them myself. One of the last days of the competition I was in a really good position with the lead gaggle, but it was getting shaded out everywhere as we got near goal. Naturally, I was feeling a little competitive…

So – me and three other pilots in the lead gaggle decided to glide towards the smoke from a crop fire that had just been started. It was clearly a good option in terms of finding strong lift. But as we entered it, the smoke was really dark and burning leaves

> **"The one technical aspect that most people don't train correctly for or don't train enough for is the glider. SIV isn't even a requirement in most countries."**

were coming up everywhere, catching in my lines and my glider. At first it was fine, it was just a 1.5m thermal, but then suddenly I was shooting up violently and then I totally lost my glider. Wham! It was full-on SIV. It went all over the place and I couldn't even tell what to do. And I'm thinking: "What if I throw my reserve right now? I might land in the fire!"

I wish I could say it was skill that got me out of that – suddenly the glider was just ok, and the four of us all glided out unharmed and made goal. It was amazing and we were all elated, but the real lesson was when we got back to headquarters. Michal Gerlach, who was leading the comp at that point, and was only about a half a minute behind us when we went into the fire, decided to just land as the risk of going into it was too high. He said for him it was just irresponsible.

So I decided right then that at the end of the day, this is just a game and all we're doing is fighting for virtual points. We're not getting anything out of it – no fame or money or anything. I think we often take it too seriously. Or maybe it's just me!

That's the red mist for you! So, how did you get into competitions?

I'd been flying about ten years but maybe only flew about ten hours a year between 2004 and 2013. Just ridge soaring and flying with my friends – it was just a little hobby. I didn't know how to fly cross country at all. I didn't understand even how it worked. But my best friend and mentor, Koppany Beliczay, kept encouraging me to get into competitions. He kept saying if I didn't fly competitions I'd never get any good. But I always thought you couldn't do a competition unless you were good, so I never considered doing one. Koppany signed me up for the Hungarian national championship in 2013. I had a blast, but I absolutely sucked. I didn't know how to thermal or glide or really do anything. I'm a really analytical person, I'm good at figuring stuff out, and it really irritated me to be so bad! So after that comp I changed my life so I could dedicate more time to flying and more time to comps.

How have you applied your analytical approach to training? I understand you break training down into three categories?

Sports have three major components: the physical, the technical and the mental. To succeed, whether you're a business person or Olympic athlete, you have to excel in each of these.

The first step is to write down five aspects from each of these categories for yourself, that you think a world champion would excel in. For example, from the technical side, it might be how well you climb. From the mental maybe how well you deal with bombing out, etc. And then you take these points and show them to a pilot who you look up to, who then rates you in each of these categories. It's pretty terrifying to get this kind of feedback, but from these honest opinions you get to see where you need to improve. Do you need more stamina, or maybe you need more patience? Go on, give it a go – it'll help for sure (see the appendix at the back of the book).

The interesting thing for me was that when I had other pilots do this same exercise a lot of people really struggled with what to put down for the mental side. And that made me realize how undervalued the mental side of this sport is. Maybe it's because flying is so much more attractive to men than women, and men have trouble talking about feelings and fears and emotions? Some pilots are amazingly good at it, others are very instinctual and others, like me, really need structure.

What does that structure look like?
First I looked at the physical. I didn't initially value that very much, I didn't think it was important. Lots of pilots at comps are older and out of shape. But then I realized that endurance and the ability to concentrate for a long time is very strongly correlated. When I started flying in high-level ten-day long comps, by the fifth day I was just exhausted and would have a hard time waking up with any energy and enthusiasm for the day ahead.

So I realized I had to take fitness seriously. And another aspect is definitely safety. When I started flying two-liners two years ago, I realized if I was tired or had any physical pain I was really compromising my safety. If you're not fit you cannot react quickly. And finally if you aren't fit and you've got super heavy comp equipment, that's always going to be in the back of your mind when you're low and trying to decide between an easy retrieve and a more committing move. If you're fit, you don't care about a long walk. So it can literally be the difference between making goal or having a big flight and ending your day early. The same is of course true for all pilots; day one paragliding students on the training hill, pilots who choose to fly out early knowing they don't mind a walk-up if they bomb, and of course vol-biv pilots. Being fit is always an advantage.

That's so true. To fly big lines, you have to be totally comfortable with landing deep with whatever you have on your back and walking out. The physical side of our sport is radically underestimated. What about the technical side?
The technical side is something just about everyone puts on the list. Understanding your instruments, understanding how to use the data, MacCready, how well you're climbing, finding good lines, meteorology, cloud development, understanding your glider, and so on. But of course, the one technical aspect that most people don't train correctly for or don't train enough for is the glider. SIV isn't even a requirement in most countries. You can't possibly understand your glider just from flying it, you have to really understand how it stalls and how it recovers.

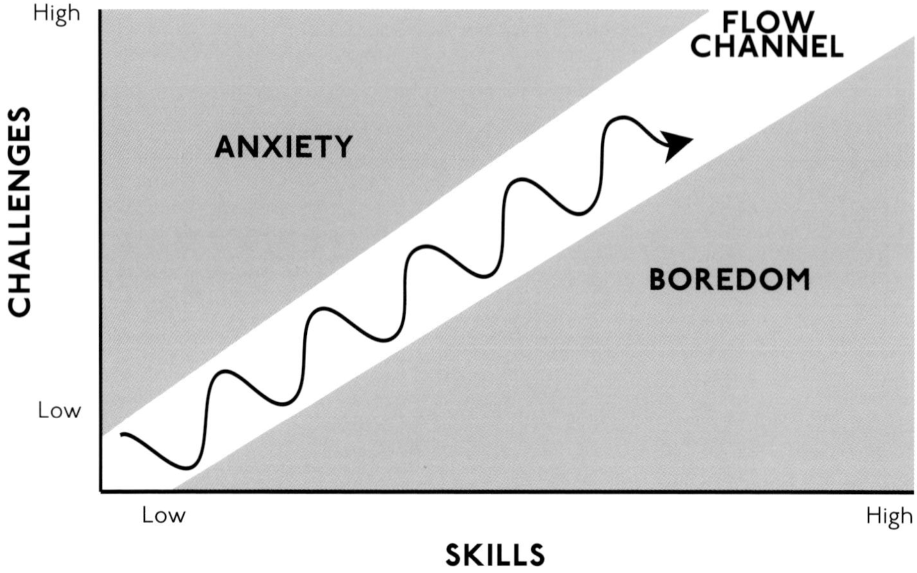

Flow isn't complicated - it's that state of absorption we all experience from time to time. To give it a chance, we need to be stimulated and challenged enough, but not overly stretched. See if you can notice a period of flow. You might be ironing, surfing, playing the guitar... anything when we're absorbed in the task at hand

The acro pilots all say the same thing – you have to do at least 300 stalls to be proficient in stalls. It has to be something you can do without thinking about it. It shouldn't even get your heart rate up.

My SIV instructor is Fabien Blanco, in Annecy, France. He told me that doing one SIV a year is better than nothing, but it's close to nothing. It needs to be something we could do when we wake up in the middle of the night. Something instinctual, using muscle memory. That's what the French team and many of the other great teams are doing. But of course, most of us don't like being scared, so we avoid SIV courses if we possibly can…

And what about the mental side? It must have been so scary to hand your list of what you thought you were and weren't good at to your peers to get their feedback! What were some of the big takeaways there that you realized you had to deal with?

Definitely the big one was that I didn't have enough self-confidence. For example, in my first Europeans in Macedonia I was all ready to take off on the launch carpet, but I just kept letting everyone go in front of me. I kept imagining myself blowing my launch, falling on my face or dumping my glider on another pilot in front of all these legendary names. I'd think: "What happens if my ballast is too heavy and I just roll down the launch?"

Then in the air in the gaggles it was so aggressive and crowded, I just let everyone cut me off. If you're self-confident it changes how people see you and how they react to you. But that wasn't me. I recognized that I wasn't confident and I had to begin with just acting more confident, and I learned to trust the skill set of my competitors.

But how did you train that? What did you actively do to get more confident?
First, I saw a sports psychologist, and read some books. The general concepts are very well understood in other sports. In flying we're all kind of teaching ourselves, but the answers are out there. The theories and training methods are available, and we can use them.

Flying is 80% mental. Whatever I improve in the technical aspect is only going to improve 20% of my game. The technical stuff only makes a very small difference in my flying. But when I learned about modeling success; visualization; using a mantra while flying; learning to deal with fears; how to set appropriate goals; dealing with failure; working on my self-confidence; meditation; choosing a mentor... when I started analyzing all these things, my flying took huge leaps. I was ranked in the top 200 in the world when I only had about 600 hours. And I'm completely average. I'm not very athletic and I'm not particularly talented as a pilot. Anyone can do this. Psychology is huge in this sport.

I also started reading a lot more about flow theory. This is a concept that the Hungarian psychologist Mihaly Csikszentmihalyi first introduced in the '60s. Flow is a high-functioning state where you're totally interested in and absorbed by the task you're doing. It's the key to all outstanding human performance.

Imagine a chart where on one axis there is the challenge, and on the other there is the skill. Beginner pilots have very little skill and a very high challenge, so there is a lot of anxiety and fear. It's impossible to enter flow from that state. But as we improve and we get more skilled we can set higher and higher challenges, and once these two match correctly, we can enter a state of flow. It's a mental state where time doesn't exist. We can work, we can play with our kids, paint, compose music or do adventure sports – it doesn't matter what we do, but we function at such a high state that we don't notice that time has passed.

Whatever we are doing, creating, or solving a problem it seems effortless. If we don't set the challenge high enough but our skill level is high already, then we experience time, it's boring, time takes forever. But at the other end, if the challenge is way above our skill level, then time is very fast – we have no recall of what has happened. Many people have experienced this when they have an accident. In a car accident or a flying accident, you just can't remember what happened second by second. When you ask a pilot who's had a major cascade and not solved the problem, they often can't remember what happened to their wing, what caused the problem in the first place. Their memory of the event is hazy at best and probably incorrect.

How does anxiety and fear play into this?
Anxiety is not something we can get rid of – it's always going to be there. I accepted it and now I welcome it because if I'm advancing, if I'm moving out of flow because I'm learning something, then anxiety and fear are normal. I just have to get better so the

skill matches the challenge again. I just need to learn more and improve. Fear is not something we should be afraid of because it's critical to have. Fear is our innate immune system. Imagine how terrible it would be if I could just switch off sensitivity in my skin in freezing weather? My fingers could freeze because I would never realize what's happening and I would never put on a glove. Or I could just put my hand on the stove and burn myself.

Jeb Corliss is one of the top wingsuit pilots in the world and in 2012 he had a near-fatal crash. It was a miracle he survived. He said: "I made a big mistake. I lost fear." Fear is super-important, because without fear you will die.

> **"Fear is not something we should be afraid of because it's critical to have. Fear is our innate immune system."**

There should be a balance, because if you are in a fear state you are not in flow and you become tense and your ability to analyze and think and fly well are crippled. Without fear you make very bad decisions, but if you have too much fear you aren't going to perform very well. You have to find the right balance.

The trick is to find ways to conquer the low-level fear and anxiety. I use music and mental exercises to help me switch off these emotions. Before launching I have very specific music I've collated, and I listen to the same thing every time. When I'm flying, I have mantras that I say over and over again to help me lower my pulse when things get tense. When I get scared, I try to welcome it, it means I'm learning. There's nothing wrong with being scared. You just have to learn to manage it. Deep breathing helps too.

I understand you recently learned about how the French have built such incredibly successful pilots at the World Cup and world championship level?

The French team coach Didier Mathurin told me that the secret to developing good pilots into world-class pilots was by building a team. In France there are tons of really good pilots, but turning them into world-class pilots is a big step. They've learned that when pilots are alone their egos get in the way of sharing knowledge. They want to keep their secrets. When they are part of a team, you can break down the ego, you can make the pilots share their knowledge, and then everyone progresses. Individuals will always hit a plateau. Hitting a plateau happens in every sport and is often why people quit. But when you get a group of excellent pilots together who push each other and get a great coach to assist them in sharing their knowledge freely, the level rises.

In Slovenia they don't have financial backing and they don't have a dedicated coach like the French, but even though it's a very small country they have several world-class pilots. They've learned that by being friendly, by sharing knowledge, and just having a good time together, they can all excel.

Of course, we can all easily adopt this approach, by forming a good group with friends where we all help and support each other.

Finally, let's talk about wanderlust...

This subject has always fascinated me. Why are some people so drawn to adventures and crazy sports like flying and others are not? When you look at society as a whole, we have different types of roles for people, and most people are happy and they feel comfortable if their future seems stable.

But there is a smaller group of souls who feel restless. If everything is too stable, and you can see your path these people feel even a little suffocated. These people want challenge. These people enjoy risk, and these are the people who can move society forward. We need a big group of people who can keep society stable, but we need a smaller group of people who are willing to jump off cliffs, are willing to go to the Moon, willing to explore new lands and follow their insatiable curiosity.

Of course, the mortality rate of this smaller group is much higher. And it's a good thing that they are the minority in society! Each group needs the other, just like a working democracy - you need balance. But both groups are essential. You just have to figure out where you belong. If you're stuck in your nine-to-five job and you hate what you do because you keep dreaming about doing something more, doing something bigger, then don't be afraid to make a change!

ADEL'S TIPS ON DEALING WITH FEAR

First, get the fundamentals right: learn to take off in all conditions, even with ballast; do SIV training every year; practice PLF landings by wearing your harness and jumping off a high table to a gym mat, rolling off the energy. To admit vulnerabilities is not a weakness but a strength.

Fear is always present when you're outside your comfort zone. It's not something that will ever go away altogether. Pilots often treat it as a macho thing and would never admit being scared at certain situations. Very few people can actually lose the feeling of fear completely, but that's a ticket to a body bag. It has the same dangers as a person whose skin loses all feelings and can't tell when he's freezing or burning. Instead, you need to learn to deal with it. I use many tips from Seven Steps to Dealing with Fear in Paragliding, written by Heike Hamann, in Fifty Ways to Fly Better.

MODELING

If you want to be able to fly for six hours, but you're not sure if you can do it, then practice driving for six hours without stopping, and understand what helps you keep focused.

VISUALIZATION

Imagine the task before taking off. Imagine what the thermal we are in looks like (is it a raindrop, or a fried egg?). Imagine the wind like a river flowing up and around objects.

MANTRAS

See what works for you! I like to say things like: "well well well, the sea is rough today!" or: "I've done this before, I'm a good pilot." Mantras should help you reframe the situation, so for example, if you are on a committing glide and notice yourself tightening up and thinking: "Shit I'm low", instead tell yourself: "This is a good bit of research I'm doing here."

MINI GOAL SETTING

If I'm feeling unsettled, but there's no objective reason for feeling afraid, I just say to myself I'll let myself land after 10 minutes more flying. Often this is enough for some transitory anxiety to pass.

KEEPING A DIARY

Write down in a bullet-point diary what you do well and what mistakes you have made during a task, and you will see a pattern – mistakes you often repeat.

DEALING WITH FAILURE

There's always a next task, a next comp; every single comp is just a training for the next one. Comp flying is not a destination, it's a constant journey of learning and getting better. As long as I can learn to do things that I never believed myself capable of, I'm proud and happy.

SELF-CONFIDENCE

Don't get intimidated. You have the full right to be in the air just like everyone else. Don't let better pilots cut-in in front of you at take-off or in a thermal. Don't let yourself be bullied.

FOCUSING

Learn to concentrate on lots of inputs at once (instruments, weather, other pilots around you, birds, clouds, dust, etc). An exercise that F1 drivers use to help with this is Fit4Race – you have to do lots at once, like kneeling on a fitness ball while throwing different sized balls against a wall with different hands. It feels like training for the circus!

If you've committed yourself to glide in somewhere low, then reframe any negative thoughts. Say to yourself, "I'm gliding in deep here", or "this is a useful piece of research and practice." Never, ever tell anyone on the radio that you're really low. It's an external confirmation of an internal narrative. Don't do it!
Photo: Jody MacDonald

HOW TO BUILD A SOLID FOUNDATION

Most accidents could be eliminated if we maintained the margin that matches our skill level. The key is never to close that gap. We're all beginners at the beginning, we all go through intermediate syndrome, and some of us will become experts and experience the 'expert halo'. At every level flying is dangerous, but for different reasons. If we build a solid foundation of frequent ground handling, regular SIV, weather knowledge, solid decision-making skills, fitness and health, and keeping within our limits, we can enjoy a lifetime of injury-free flying. Solid houses are built on good foundations. So are good pilots.

"You need a coach or a mentor. You'll always screw it up if you do it yourself. You need someone you're accountable to."
Ben Abruzzo

"My father got me into flying very young, and taught me that the foundation is everything. I see a lot of people jumping up to more demanding gliders because they want to be fast and compete before they have all the necessary skills. It was frustrating sometimes, because I wanted to be fast and compete, too. But now I'm thankful I took my time. I spent years perfecting stalls, spirals, backfly and glider management skills, so when I started flying comp gliders they weren't scary, and I could fly them confidently using a lot of bar."
Aaron Durogati

"Planning and having a goal encourages trying, and leads to more distance. It draws you forward. Think about the route in advance, get the lie of the terrain, work out the most efficient way through by looking at previous flights online – all these things add up to efficiency and speed. Plans can always be abandoned, but having a plan keeps you in the air when things get tricky and keeps you from giving up."
Tom Payne

"In my early years I was mesmerized by the simplest flights, and hanging out with the flying community. I competed in my first acro comp six years after learning, and during those years I pretty much flew every day. Acro is like drinking a beer – it's going to affect you in a positive way!

"Everyone can fly acro. And everyone should. There's no secret. You have to start with the basics and get really comfortable with stalls. You should do hundreds and hundreds, in every condition. Then you should get into negative maneuvers, and once you have really good wing control you should do wingovers. It's hard and takes a lot of control and understanding of the dynamic forces, weight shift and brake. If you can do good wingovers, you're well on your way to being a good pilot."
Veso Ovcharov

"Landing posture is really important. When you're coming in to land, you should look like Kilian Jornet running down a mountain. You need to be in position to take an impact. Your shoulders and chest should be forward, your legs should be bent and ready, and you should flare with your hands behind you in the torpedo that we use to launch. Most pilots just sit back with their feet out of their pod and are in a seated position when they land. If you get in sudden sink or miss the flare, that's not an athletic position to take an impact.

Straight and stable flight with a good flare into a tree or bush or rooftop or really any object is a lot safer than a last-minute hard turn with a bunch of pendulum force to try to avoid something.

"For pilots on C wings or lower, if you have a collapse the input should almost always just be hands up. Gliders these days have a ton of passive safety, and they'll recover if you just put your hands all the way up. Even better is hands up and lean towards the collapsed side if it's a really big collapse, and a lean towards the open side if it's 50% or less. I see a lot of pilots do way too much when they have a collapse, and get themselves into more trouble. When you have a collapse, you fall, and human instinct is to put your hands down. Just about every cascade event I've ever seen is from pilots not letting their wing fly because their hands were too low."

Mitch Riley

"The important thing that most XC pilots don't have down is the acro full stall. It's the only way to reset certain situations, and done correctly, you lose almost no altitude. For safety it's critical. The other thing missing is practice throwing the reserve. You have to be able to throw correctly and know when to use it without hesitation, automatically. If you fly XC, you'll get into difficult situations; guaranteed."

Théo de Blic

"Problems come from the ground. When pilots get into acro and start learning, if they get into trouble it's because they try moves too low. Acro is safe as long as you give yourself plenty of margin and don't push things when you're low."

Max Marien

"Something that isn't drilled into us enough when we're learning is the importance of air speed. A wing has to be moving through the air, or you're in a stall. This is emphasized when you learn to fly an airplane, hang glider or sailplane, but not enough with paragliding. Low airspeed is dangerous. Coastal soaring pilots are used to low groundspeeds because of the wind; I see some come to the mountains and land with way too much brake. Speed is your friend. Fly with only enough brake to feel the glider and react to a potential collapse. Become hyper-aware of the air on your face. If you don't have airspeed and get hit with a dust devil or sudden sink, you'll have no energy to react."

Reavis Sutphin-Gray

The Analyst

ALEX ROBÉ

If you want to fly big Alpine lines, Alex Robé has written the manual. Along with his friend Primoz Susa, Alex is always right at the top of XContest on the big days in Europe. The Austrian won XContest outright in 2015 and 2017. When we chatted in 2019, he was lying in third place, with a 260km FAI triangle as his **lowest value flight**.

What makes Alex's consistent success even more impressive is the fact that he flies on only about ten days a year. Like many of us, his time is constrained by family and work commitments.

An engineer by profession, Alex analyses every day he flies – before, during and after – to maximize his personal skills development. Some of what he does is incredibly detailed, and may be beyond the motivation of many of us. But his knowledge consistently leads him to be on the right launch, at the right time, ready to fly the right route on the right day.

Alex has views on wing selection that might be at odds with yours. His approach to building endurance may be something you'd never consider. And your computer may not be fast enough to hold all the windows that Alex has open when he does his forecasting. But what is for sure is you will learn something from this true master of XC flying.

Alex, again and again on XContest on the really big days there'll be a huge list of massive flights all over the Alps, but it's pretty much guaranteed you'll be right at the top of the list, with one of the highest average speeds. You fly an Enzo 3, and that's certainly part of it, but so do a lot of other pilots. How are you doing it?
The answer is actually pretty unspectacular. With my job and limited spare time, I've just learned to fly the right place with the right conditions. The key to flying far for me is to figure out what the best option is in my area. I live in the Eastern Alps, and I want to limit myself to four hours of driving or less. Where I live is very good for big FAI triangles, but there are a ton of options and you have to choose which will be ideal on a given day.

Years ago I really went into a deep analysis of weather forecasts, and luckily for us the forecasting systems have really improved. Over time when you look at a lot of forecasts

> **I go flying on days that are close to perfect. Choosing the right days eliminates a lot of risk.**

and then you go fly, you begin to get a feel for which models work the best when certain variables are present. I don't have a single source – it's a compilation of many models, and then deciding which one should be weighted more heavily on a given day. All of them have their advantages and disadvantages; on some things they're a little bit too conservative or a little bit too aggressive or just wrong. So I really focused on finding the right models.

And understanding weather is also a big part of how you mitigate risk – correct?
This is also key to me for risk management. I'm not a pilot who just focuses on passive safety and hopes for the best. I've always focused on being responsible for myself, and having an intimate understanding of the weather helps you understand what you're getting into. I don't go flying on scary, windy days. I go flying on days that are close to perfect. Choosing the right days eliminates a lot of risk. Of course all days have a few surprises, but I try to fly on days where I can stay in the air for ten hours or more, and by definition those are really good days.

Tell me about wing choice.
When it comes to wings, I think a lot of pilots fly wings that have a lot of passive safety, because they think the wing will take care of them. I have a totally different approach. I don't want to give control away to the wing. I want to feel everything. I think it comes down a lot more to attitude than ability. What type of pilot are you? What approach do you have? Are you the kind of person who can take full responsibility for your actions or do you like to give some of that control away? I want the balance where I can feel enough to thermal efficiently but where my wing isn't nervous. Two-liners give the pilot a lot more feel and control, and they are much more collapse-resistant.

Yes, absolutely. But you have to know how to keep them open, because they bite hard when they do collapse. I think to fly a two-liner safely you have to have a lot of hours and a lot of training, because there's actually very little passive safety. If it goes pear-shaped, you aren't going to get out of it by just putting your hands up, you have to act fast and act correctly.
I totally agree. But it's not just the feeling you have on a two-liner. It's the control. The construction of a three-liner from a design perspective is pretty radically

different. It's just much harder to fly fast on a lower-level wing, and you can't be as well connected to the wing as you are on a two-liner. Rear riser control is so effective, and makes flying fast safer for me.

Let's get back to weather, and how you identify the big days.
I have a pretty simple approach that I've developed over the years. First of all, I disregard any predictions longer than seven days ahead. Things get interesting for me five to two days ahead. We have a really great service here in the Alps called soaringmeteo.org. It's a GFS (Global Forecasting System) model, which isn't very precise, but it gives you a quick look at the day's quality one week ahead, so you can begin knowing if you should start paying attention. Then we look at Windy.com to look at other meteo models, so you can compare and look at what kind of air mass is coming, and especially what kind of cloud cover you can expect. I also love the meteograms of Meteoblue. There you see how good the cloud base will be, how thick the clouds will be, will there be precipitation, etc. Then, if things are still looking good two to three days out, I'll start looking at the Austrian Meteorology Institute ZAMG, which has a really good cloud and overcast forecast and a particularly good rain forecast. And then finally what's especially important if the weather is coming from the south is to look at the dust forecast, which often isn't picked up on the other models. The south winds can pick up a lot of dust from the Sahara and totally kill the day's thermal index.

One day ahead I'll look at Austrocontrol to see the thermal quality, cloudbase height and if there'll be any overdevelopment. There are other models like meteoparapente – that's really good on the day if it's humid, because it's precise at predicting where thunderstorms will be. If thunderstorms are isolated rather than widespread, you can still have a really productive day. And finally I use XCSkies quite regularly, because it's very optimistic with the wind and nearly always calls the wind lower than the other models.

Alex, how much of your success do you credit to learning the weather?
60%. Definitely. Just imagine if you are on the wrong hill on the right day. You won't get those hours. It's also for me a huge safety factor. I would not dare to fly my Enzo 3 or a "hot" wing with my abilities if conditions weren't nice. What you guys do in the X-Alps I would just never consider. I don't have the ability to cope with those kinds of conditions.

You've mentioned you're quite restricted in the time you have to pursue flying.
I have a job where I have a really restricted amount of vacation time. I also have a family that I want to take care of. So I have to be really picky about the days I choose to fly. Typically it's about ten days per year.

If you're only getting ten days a year, there are obviously big long gaps sometimes between flying days. What are you doing in the days before and the night before to get tuned up? I often feel pretty rusty if I haven't flown in a while.
Maybe you go flying on the wrong days! When I see a good day coming, my passion for flying totally overwhelms me. And on those long, big days, we usually start really early in the day when the air is smooth and conditions are weak. You

have to be really sensitive and calm, and it's like that for a good portion of the morning, you're just cruising along making distance. That gives you plenty of time to get comfortable and get back into the groove, so when the day starts turning on and it starts to get more rowdy, you're nicely warmed up.

Are you doing anything to prepare mentally and physically for these really long flights? Ten hours is a long time in the saddle.

Everything comes from setting a goal. I'm an engineer, I like goals and I'm goal-oriented. For example, the two days we just flew in Grente, I wanted to fly two days in a row and be in the air 12 hours or more each day. I need to be able to hike two hours to the Antholz launch with a 25-30 kilo backpack and fly 12 hours, then get only a few hours of sleep, drive three hours to Mayrhofen and do it again. And I want to be able to do all this and not get hurt through being tired. To do all that I have to work backwards and look at what I have to do to achieve this. For me that's two to three days in the gym each week listening to your podcast, so I can also be training my mind and have that training in parallel. My workouts aren't particularly hard, but I want to make sure my core is strong, my shoulders are strong for carrying all the gear and flying on the B handles all day, and my legs are strong enough for the big hikes and pressing a lot of bar all day.

On the mental side, what I hear from my wife all the time is that I'm not normal. I'm kind of a nerd when it comes to analysis. My preparation starts immediately after the flight I've just done. I compare my igc files to the pilots I flew with, using Ayvri to see where they maybe climbed better, or found a better line, or were able to fly a particular section faster than I did. Then I blog about the flight, which is my way of keeping a visual journal of my feelings and experiences. Then as the next day nears and we've chosen the launch, I'll have waypoints stored for where the thermal triggers are and routes already mapped out that have worked in the past, either from myself or other good pilots. For every launch I go to, I write myself a guide about everything – photos from previous flights, of clouds, what we experienced with the weather, and things we learned. Over the years this guide for each launch gets bigger and bigger, and even if I've used that launch a dozen times in the past, I'll go through the guide. This helps me bring confidence to the day and it helps me be efficient.

Are you using Skyways to decipher the lines and thermal triggers, or is that too general?

Skyways is totally irrelevant because it covers all the tracks. It's not selective. I am only concerned about the best lines, not the average ones. I'm only interested in the really exceptional flights.

Tell me about two things. Your gear – what are you flying and why? And when you're in the air, do you have any specific check-in moments? Mantras maybe, or anything specific for food and hydration?

I fly the X-Rated 7 harness, and I upgraded this year from the Zeno to the Enzo 3. For instruments I use the XCTracer with the FLARM, and the Oudie 4 for navigation purposes. I put the XCTracer next to my ear on my shoulder strap and put the volume down low, and I leave the Oudie up pretty loud. Between the two I find it perfect for finding the core and understanding what's going on with the air. On the XCTracer I adjusted the tone settings from the default, but I prefer to have almost no dampening so I know immediately if the air is going up or down. But the Oudie really averages it out, and so with the two I get a much better understanding of the sky. I use an InReach for safety and a Flymaster tracker that I just put in the back of my bag, which makes uploading your track log to XContest easy, and it also makes it really fun for my friends to watch my flight in 3D while it's happening.

> **"When I go flying I really, really want to be the last one to land. I want to squeeze out every single minute of the day."**

When I'm flying I just have carbohydrate bars for eating, and I always enrich my water with electrolytes. I always drink at least two liters during a big flight and I pee very regularly.

The key for me to having a good day is to start way before I launch. I like to have a lot of time. So if it's a hike to launch I like to arrive way before we plan to launch so I can set up all my gear, check my radio, check my instruments, pee tube, water, check all my lines, eat enough, have some relaxed chats and just be really ready.

You mentioned that you've got a "recipe" for going big?
My recipe begins with a checklist. I never want to forget anything. So first in the recipe is a checklist for all my gear. My balaclava, extra battery, charge cables, sunblock and this kind of thing. I never want to be at launch and realize I don't have something.

Next is to make sure I have good pilots with me. Days before I have identified a good possible day, I post on social media and reach out personally to pilots I like to fly with who are fast and plant the seed and begin a discussion. I ask: "What do you think about using this launch, how big do you think we can make it?" and so on. When I get to a launch I'm hoping there'll be a lot of pilots there to share the fun. I do everything I can to spread the word - everyone should get the chance to know a big day's on the cards.

You mentioned earlier that you are a paragliding "nerd". What does that mean?
I suck up everything I can when it comes to flying. As I live in Austria, most of the time the weather is bad, so I try and read everything I can. I've read every book there is on free flight several times. I think a lot about how I can fly more efficiently all the time. How can I get a little bit faster? I take a lot of video and pictures every time I fly, and then at the end of every year I make a wrap-up of the year. In the video I speak about exactly what I'm thinking at the time – why I'm taking this route, what I'm seeing in the air, where I've maybe made a mistake. Then I can look back on all this data

regularly and learn for the next season. When I go flying I really, really want to be the last one to land. I want to squeeze out every single minute of the day.

Why are there so many engineers like yourself in this sport?
Engineers are analytical. They are used to questions like: "Why is that? How far can you go?" We engineers are confronted with problems all the time, and it's up to us to solve them. And that's exactly what flying cross country is. Solving problems. You can't see anything, but you have to figure it out. Engineers are used to working on their own, which is just like flying. Nobody is there to help you.

Tell me about risk management in your flying.
I've noticed that when I get scared or nervous, it's usually because of uncertainty. Uncertainty leads to fear. Suddenly there might be a strong wind I didn't expect, or something in the forecast that I hadn't anticipated. My approach to reducing fear is to try to keep everything systematic and simple. First, I always try to keep the beauty in mind. Take a look around, breathe, relax. Second is to work out whether it's shitty because I've missed something in the forecast, or it's just something local that I have to press through. And last I want to be connected on the radio to really positive, good pilots. If it gets nasty I can check in with them, and if they aren't that bothered by the conditions then I shouldn't be either. Sometimes it's just you who doesn't feel great. And finally I'll reduce my speed a little bit, and then really try to dissect why I'm experiencing this fear. Is it fear because of the conditions, or is it a mental thing? I'll try to break it all down into facts. If the thermals are disorganized and rowdy but I'm high, I can tell myself that I'm not actually in any danger and I just have to accept the challenging conditions and fight for a bit.

You have to be careful not to let your feelings get control of your mind. A lot of things need to go wrong to have an accident most of the time. Your ability and your state of mind can usually overcome most dangerous situations if you stay in problem-solving mode, instead of panicking. And even then you can still have luck. So most of the time fear isn't warranted and can be reduced.

Do you ever show up to a launch and just feel like you don't have it that day?
Never. I can never remember once. When you only fly on really nice days, there is no reason to have these kinds of frustrating thoughts. When I'm forced to land, it's because I've misjudged a situation and haven't found a thermal, but I've never landed because I've been forced out of the sky because of anxiety. What gets people in trouble is almost always wind. I'm living proof, I've been flying for over 20 years now and I've never had an accident. Be wary of the wind. It's a really simple recipe – fly the good days!

What's the number one thing that you see that leads to accidents?
Listen to the type of person you are. If you're the type of person who prefers to give away a little responsibility, then maybe big cross-country flying isn't for you. There are so many ways you can enjoy flying, but if it's not really in your blood or you're doing it for recognition, remember you are playing with life-threatening risk. If you really feel comfortable flying and you really enjoy it, you will be a good, safe pilot.

FLYING DECISIONS

Recipe to never miss a good day in the Eastern Alps by Alex Robé

> 7 DAYS

Do nothing ;-)

5-7 DAYS

soaringmeteo.com - Thermal index 'ThQ', Föhn tendency

Windy.com - ECMWF: wind and thunderstorms

Meteoblue.ch - Meteograms for wind and cloud distribution

2-5 DAYS

Soaringmeteo

XCSkies.com - Average wind

ZAMG.ac.at - Cloud cover and rain animation

Skiron - Dust nucleus > solar radiation

Windy & Meteoblue

Phone with flight buddies

BOOK VACATION DAYS!

DAY BEFORE

Austrocontrol

Soaringmeteo, XCSkies, SAMG, Windy

Meteo-Parapente
Rain location and covnvergences

Phone - Final check & travel arrangements

EARLY IN THE MORNING

Austrocontrol - best thermal heights, cloudbase

Webcams - Panomax, Foto-Webcam

Meteo-parapente - winds

Local meteo stations - detail

THE DAY AFTER

Compare screeshots with own experience to develop better understanding

HOW TO THERMAL BETTER

Climbing consistently faster than others is an art form that few pilots have perfected. A handful of truly great pilots thermal 2-3% better than the rest of us on the World Cup circuit. The less time we spend thermalling, the more time we spend going where we want to go, so our aim should be to ace this critical and magical aspect of our sport.

"When you're turning in a thermal, rest your mind. Just observe. Look at the clouds, listen to your vario, but relax your brain."
Willi Canell

"Learn to sample a lot of air. I'm always searching, looking for better pockets of air, when I'm climbing and gliding. I'm never satisfied with my rate of climb; I know there's always a little more to be found. I also turn really flat – I very rarely bank it up hard. Often I push out on my outside riser or apply a little bit of outside brake to keep my glider really flat."
Nick Greece

"If you're in a column above other pilots climbing, keep looking down to check if anyone's coming up faster. Move over them as soon as you see it happen. You can keep above a stack of ten pilots pretty easily just by doing this.
If you're flying in a light thermal, or getting to the top of the climb and it's

"Climbing speed is one of the keys to flying faster and further. We need to be always climbing efficiently in the strongest thermals throughout the day. An important way to become better at thermalling is learning to do big, proper wingovers. Wingovers teach pilots to control their gliders in a lot of different situations. When we get pitched out of the thermal and when our gliders get into odd positions, it teaches us when we can and can't turn the wing, and how to get it back to where we want it to be relative to a thermal.

Wingovers are one of the few moves that combine the three movements of our glider: pitch, roll and yaw. To do them in one fluid movement is really challenging. Wingovers should always be learned in the right environment – first under instruction over water, because wingovers are incredibly dangerous. You're learning to build and dissipate energy in the glider. Through brake input and properly timed weight shift, you can either kill energy or build energy in the glider. Through that you can put your glider wherever you want while thermalling, and get into the core."
Matt Beechinor

"If you want to climb well, you have to ALWAYS search for a better climb. Listen to the feedback from your glider. Constantly search and be sensitive for where you need to tighten or loosen your turns to find the stronger lift.

To feel more in climbs, open the waist strap on your harness. This will make you much more sensitive to your wing. Hammock harnesses (without a seat board) are a compromise. You save weight, but you're giving up safety and control. You can't give your wing as precise an input using a hammock harness.

If you want to fly fast, you have to learn to climb fast. Thermalling is a lot more important than gliding well or using your speed bar efficiently. Your average speed towards any XC objective when you're thermalling is zero. And you have to know when to leave. If you're in a 4m/s climb and it drops to 2m/s, GO. Don't spend one more second in that climb unless you're low and don't have the height to get to the next climb. Newer pilots frequently stay in slower climbs way too long."

Marko Hrgetic Hrga

getting weak, experiment with flying with no outside brake and just a bit of inside brake. This works particularly well with higher aspect wings. By allowing your outer wing to fly at trim speed, the profile seems to be more efficient at surfing up the small nudges of lift you get. You also get more feedback as the core moves. Try it out when you're circling with someone who's flying more conventionally, and see who ends up on top!"

Hugh Miller

"Firstly, never be satisfied with what you have. Explore constantly to find a stronger core. Secondly, move quickly to a better climb. Don't hesitate unless you are low and at risk of bombing out. Newer pilots consistently stay way too long in their thermal when someone nearby is climbing faster. Third, make a game of every thermal - NEVER let someone below you outclimb you, and ALWAYS find a way to outclimb those above you. Fourth, listen to the air and feel for warmth. Let the glider pull you into a thermal. Trust your instincts.
And change gears often. If the day is 'on' and you've been finding 4m/s climbs and yours drops to 2m/s, don't hesitate, leave. Equally, be vigilant for signs the day might slow down with cirrus arriving, or the sun dropping. Don't get stuck in top gear when you need to change down."

Gavin McClurg

"Turn off your sink alarm! I hate its sound and when you're in sink you can fly faster, but you can't optimize sink, so it's distracting. We have to optimize our climbs. I find the vario's thermal centering function valuable in the flats, but not very useful in the mountains. If you have too many things to think about or look at, you're borrowing from your ability to observe. Keep the tech simple and easy."

Chrigel Maurer

HERO3
FLYSURFE
KITEBOARDI

How to Fly the Flats

ARMIN HARICH

Armin astounded everyone by flying over 300km with an ultra-safe EN B wing, the Skywalk Tequila. It was a German record – in fact, Armin was the first to fly 300km in Germany with any kind of wing! Armin began flying in 1989. He's one of the co-founders of Skywalk Paragliders, and is revered as a flatland sky god. Armin has also managed to fly nearly four decades without a single accident.

Armin, you've never had an accident in flying – that's a rare thing! What do you chalk that up to?
I have plenty of fear. I don't get excited when conditions get dangerous, like some people do. And I'm not a competition pilot, so I don't fly around using a ton of bar low or in bad air. I prefer to fly in nice conditions on good days. If it's shitty, I go do something else.

Fear is a good thing.
Yes – fear keeps you alive!

Tell me about the genesis of your flying, and specifically flatland flying.
When I was 17 years old, I was the German national canoeing champion. I entered a contest that was a combo of canoeing and paragliding. The guy I raced with taught me how to fly, and I taught him how to canoe. In the next few years I really pursued flying and became, I guess, a professional, although back then that didn't mean much! In 1995 the longest flight on a paraglider was 71km, which was done in the Alps. That year I flew 166km in the flatlands and broke the record, which at the time no one thought was possible. The flight was from a tow launch, but back then we would only get up 150m before coming off the tow, so it was pretty exciting to get up and fly all day!

Isn't airspace really difficult to negotiate in Germany?
It's very tricky in Germany, and it has gotten quite a bit worse since those days. When I did the 300km flight there was a NOTAM[1] that allowed me to fly through a particular

> **In the flats all those features and triggers are still there – they're just softer.**

area that day, otherwise I wouldn't have been able to do it. But when you have a dream to fly far in the flatlands here in Germany, airspace is part of it, and you just have to figure it out.

What advice can you pass along about flying the flatlands[2]?
There are a ton of tips and tricks to flying the flats. For example, in the mountains the sun angle makes it much easier to understand where the thermal will be. As the day advances we track the sun angle and try to fly aspects that face the sun. In the flats, the signs are much more subtle. There aren't big surfaces like mountains that directly face the sun, so our visual cues change. In the flats, the thermals track with the wind, and if there are clouds we can get cloud streets that really help us. But on blue days we have to look for other potential triggers like fences, tree lines, changes in field colors, tractors or other things that alter the landscape.

Let's take it step by step. What weather forecasts are you looking at before you head out to the tow paddock?
Topmeteo.eu is the first thing I check to see if cross country is possible. This gives you the day's potential for flight distance. Then I check the cloud potential to make sure there won't be any overdevelopment, and then I check the wind. If we're doing a one-way flight, we want at least 15km/h and up to 20km/h.

What I find myself doing a lot is, after studying a forecast and deciding it's a good day, I'll make a plan using flyxc.app, say for example to do a big FAI triangle. But as much as I tell myself that it's just a possible plan and of course I'll just fly the day, I get locked into that idea when I'm in the air. How do you stay flexible?
Especially in the flatlands, you have to stay really flexible. I make plans because you have to, especially with all the airspace, but I try to give myself a lot of options. So if the wind is a little different or the stability is not what we expect, I can alter the plan in the air and not be caught too off-guard.

[1] A notice to airmen is a notice filed with an aviation authority to alert aircraft pilots of potential hazards along a flight route or at a location that could affect the safety of the flight.
[2] Armin has excellent videos on how to fly flatlands and advice on all kinds of flying at arminharich.de

Tell us one of your key strategies to achieving long flights.
The most important thing to learn is to recognize when you're coming to a tricky area. An example is when you're climbing up to cloudbase and you know you're going to cross a difficult section ahead without clouds or obvious triggers, or maybe there's cirrus and the sun is being dampened. When you're low you don't have many options, so when it's tricky you have to stay as high as possible. The goal when flatland flying is to stay in the air the entire day. That sounds obvious, but it's not so easy and it's tempting to fly too fast. When you recognize you're coming into a difficult area, slow down, get as high as you possibly can and glide very efficiently without using too much bar; then you can survive. Survival is the key.

How do you approach flatlands when you're not flying directly downwind?
The most important thing to understand in flatlands is to know how the thermals are structured. Cloud streets, for example, follow the wind direction. Even if you have no clouds, we still have cloud streets – the physics of the thermal are the same; we just can't see them. So if you have to fly crosswind or upwind to a waypoint in a competition or to get around airspace, you have to always make upwind progress whenever you can, because when you're low your only option is to go downwind. If you're following a cloud street that will take you downwind of your goal, you have to jump to an upwind cloud street. The best way is to fly directly perpendicular to the cloud street that you're on and get as high as you possibly can before you try.

What are your thoughts on avoiding sink in the flatlands? What most of us learn when we're in sink is to turn 45 degrees and use a lot of bar, but in the flatlands I've found that sometimes isn't aggressive enough.
Cloud streets have the updraft portion and the downdraft portion. Both are oriented with the wind. The downdrafts trigger thermals. So if you're flying downwind and you're in the downdraft, it makes sense to fly 90 degrees to the wind immediately to get over to the updraft. But it can be tricky to find. Less experienced pilots can simply turn around and fly directly into the wind and the thermal they just left, but this isn't a very efficient way to fly far!

Armin, this year I chased big distance in the Sertão in Brazil. It became really obvious after a week there that success depended on recognizing well in advance when to shift gears and slow down. It would often go blue quite suddenly in the middle of the day, for example, and if you didn't recognize it quickly enough you would be on the ground.
I've never flown in Brazil, but I think one of the keys to flatland flying anywhere is to know what areas are difficult so you can fly more conservatively.

How do you identify those areas? Is that just experience gathered from flying through the same terrain a bunch of times, or is it something you can identify in advance?
The best resources are the flight databases, like XContest. If I'm flying a new area, I study all the previous big flights from a launch I want to use and see where pilots ran into trouble. I try to guess what time of the year it was done. Was it spring, fall or

In the flats the differences in terrain are more subtle, but no less important.
Photo: Burkhard Martens / Thermikwolke.de

summer? If it was spring, the fields will be green and there will be a lot more water. If it was fall, they'll be brown and much drier. Then you can analyze what you expect to be similar or different and plan accordingly.

Talk to me about finding that first thermal and getting established. There's nothing more frustrating than getting off tow and going 10km and bombing out.
For me that's not frustrating. As long as I've landed safely, I've had a great day! The weather is almost always at least a little different than what we think it will be, so that's also something I don't get frustrated about. If the day doesn't align with what I hoped it would be that's fine, I just go do something else. The only thing that maybe frustrates me is when everyone else is getting up and I'm not, but then getting frustrated probably doesn't help!

But the advice I would give is to arrive at launch at least an hour before the first thermal starts. That gives you time to prepare your gear, to get a feeling for the day, to watch the sky, talk to other pilots and get your head in the game. Then I always try to be the first one in the air. I like to be early, because if you want to fly far you need as many hours as possible. But often, I'm the first one on the ground because I try too early, but I can get right back to launch. I've already felt the air and have a good sense for what the day is doing, so if I bomb out I don't care.

Any cross-country tips you can pass along after more than three decades of flying?
One of the best tips I got was from a sailplane pilot. He said: "Don't try to find the thermal, try to find the area where the air should rise up the most." It's a lot easier to find generally rising air than an actual thermal. The key here is that it's not just finding places where the ground is hot. Often rising air can be found, for example, over a dark, dense forest that's very cold. You'd think there would be no thermals, but it works because of the difference in humidity of the surrounding air. If the air has more humidity, it's lighter. Or when you get a bunch of shading, you can often find thermals where there's humidity on the ground, because water doesn't cool as easily and there will be more humidity in the air which makes it lighter. Understanding the physics of water vapor and how the sun's energy affects packets of air helps you stay in the air.

> **"Don't try to find the thermal. Try to find the area where the air should rise up the most."**

I think pilots who haven't flown in the flats much find them quite devoid of features and triggers, and finding thermals isn't nearly as obvious as it is in the mountains.
In the flats all those features and triggers are still there – they're just softer. You just have to look for any change. Something that is just a little different is usually a trigger, whatever it is. The flats are a lot more silent. It's not screaming at you like it is in the mountains.

Let's imagine you're flying a cloud street, flying downwind and you're getting ready to leave a climb and go on glide. What angle should you exit the cloud?
You have to understand how the thermals are structured. If there's no wind, the theory is you should leave the thermal 60 degrees right or left to find the next thermal. If you have wind, the next thermal should be directly downwind, but when you're following a cloud street you should usually turn right or left as soon as the lift runs out when going on glide, but there's no hard rule.

WHEN TO MOVE UP

Pilots on wings above their skill level is one of the main causes of accidents in our sport. Time and again, pilots say that if they could rewind the clock they'd stay on mid-range wings for longer. And as Jeff Shapiro says, "you are the pilot you are, not the pilot you want to be. The wing isn't going to make you a better pilot." But this view wasn't shared by all pilots. Alex Robé believes wing choice depends on the kind of person you are and what kind of days you choose to fly. Regardless, this sport is best played with an eye on the long game and wing choice plays an important role in that decision.

"Paragliding is dangerous. Are comp gliders any more dangerous? Maybe a little, but I'm a middle-aged guy with two kids and a wife. I'd like to go paragliding every day, but it doesn't happen. So to stack the odds in my favor, after 15 years on comp wings, I now fly an EN C. For pilots who get a lot of hours, train hard and want that extra performance, it's totally suitable to fly a hot glider. But I'm not that guy. When I hear people bitching about common gliders, I really think that's inappropriate, because you can do amazing things on a lower-end glider."
Nate Scales

"Of course the glider makes a big difference, but I think people are taking risks by flying gliders too demanding for their skill level that they don't really know how to control."
Tom De Dorlodot

"Move up when the wing you're on is holding you back. There's a point in your flying when you want more. That's when you step up. You should not move up because the glider you're on is tired and it's time for a new wing. It's much better to fly a glider at 100% than to have a racy

"The **risk homeostastis theory**[1] is good to think about in flying. If you put a helmet on a cyclist, they just increase their speed to compensate. It's the same reason we didn't see accidents decrease when the Open Class was banned – we actually saw an increase. A lot of pilots who would have never flown an Open Class glider jumped on an EN D wing before they had the skills to keep it open. For all intents and purposes the skill needed to fly an EN D and an Open Class glider are the same, but that lower classification gave a lot of pilots false confidence."
Tom Payne

[1] If the perceived level of risk in one part of a person's life changes, they will compensate by either reducing or increasing the amount and severity of risks they take, in order to maintain an equilibrium of perceived risk.

"You can't cheat aspect ratio. The higher the aspect, the harder it is to control, especially when things go wrong. If you're looking to move up, the first thing you need to ask yourself is: what's holding you back? Is it really the wing, or is it your ability? If you can't stay in the air for seven hours on your EN B, you won't be able to on a more demanding wing either. Your brain only has so much bandwidth. If you're using much of it to fly your wing, you're going to miss all the important things that keep you in the air. You won't be looking around; you won't see the birds; you won't see a cloud developing; you won't see another pilot climbing better; you won't be relaxed. So perversely you move up to a higher performance wing, but you fly worse. As you progress and get to know the sky, you start to let the wing do a lot of the work for you. You can't rush it; flying is a huge apprenticeship."
Hugh Miller

one that you can't fly as well. The hot gliders are brilliant gliders to fly, but you have to be current and you have to have the hours. When you start dropping off the currency and you don't have the hunger, you should gear down."
Jocky Sanderson

"Every time I've stepped up to a more demanding wing, I've had an episode. So now every time I get a new wing, I try to give myself a ton of height and a lot of margin until I feel really comfortable on the wing. Don't move up to a hotter wing until you feel the wing you're on is really holding you back."
Cody Mittanck

"I think a lot of pilots fly wings that have a lot of passive safety because they think the wing will take care of them. I have a totally different approach. I don't want to give the control away to the wing. I want to feel everything. When we [the flying culture] push the passive safety approach, people take less responsibility for their flying. I think it comes down more to attitude than ability. What type of pilot are you? Are you the kind of person who can take full responsibility for your actions, or do you like to give some control away? Two-liners give the pilot a lot more feel and control, and they're much more collapse-resistant. It's not just the feeling you have on a two-liner. It's the controllability. The construction of a three-liner from a design perspective is radically different. You can't be as well connected to the wing as you are on a two-liner."
Alex Robé

"The more relaxed you are, the better you fly. Flying relaxed trumps flying a hotter wing every time. If you're relaxed, you can observe everything."
Marko Hrgetic Hrga

"In my opinion, if you're flying an EN D wing, you need to be doing 300 hours a year and regular SIV training. You need that to be current and connected. If you're having frontals on the wing you're on, you're probably on a wing that's beyond your skill level. But lower aspect and lightweight gliders will frontal with much less warning."
Greg Hamerton

The Engineer

BRUCE GOLDSMITH

Where to start? Bruce Goldsmith has pretty much done it all. He flew competitions at the very top level for over 25 years, first as one of the golden boys alongside John Pendry and Rob Whittall in the often-unbeatable British hang gliding team, then later in paragliding. His successes include winning the World Paragliding Championships in 2007, and being British champion three times. Bruce started the paragliding design side of Airwave, and was a principal founder of Ozone in 1998. He moved on to design for Advance for a period, before creating his own company, Bruce Goldsmith Design (BGD). Bruce is president of the Swiss-based APPI education system, author of the best-selling techniques book Fifty Ways to Fly Better and a columnist for Cross Country since 1991. When I spoke with Bruce, he was working with his then 17-year-old son Tyr on nailing his first 100km flight.

Let's start off with your son, Tyr. I understand he's 17 and getting pretty good. How long has he been flying, and how did he get into it?
Tyr's been around flying all his life, but he really started seriously three years ago. How he actually learned to fly is a funny story. He grew up and learned to read and write near Gréolières, near the Ozone offices in southern France. I used to fly down and land after testing and pick him up after school. One day he said to me: "Hey, dad, why don't you do something cool like ride a motorbike?" For him paragliding is just normal. Riding a motorbike was something different. Paragliding is in his blood – it's nothing unusual.

How have you approached teaching Tyr?
I've actually never been an instructor. I've been in comps for a long time and I've coached some elite pilots, but I've never taught pilots from the beginning. So when Tyr wanted to become a pilot he went to a traditional school to learn. Nowadays it's pretty hands-on. I have the feeling I know what he's capable of and what he's not capable of, so I make sure the challenge of the situation suits his ability.

> **Observation is the most important thing to develop. Your neck should get chafed and tired from looking around so much.**

Bruce, you won the world championships in 2007. Was that when you hung up comp flying?
I was obviously very happy about that win. My own style is very tactical, and it doesn't suit the full-on smash-the-bar sprints that we have these days. The paragliding competition scene has become more and more what I call fishbowl racing. Small tasks that are less than two hours. And often the final glide is the critical part. I was more interested in big tasks, technical ones that took six or eight hours and required a lot of endurance. To me the best tasks were the ones with only 10 or 20% of the pilots in goal. The 2007 championships had very difficult tasks, and the reason I won was very simply because I was the only pilot to get into goal every day! That fashion of flying has been on the decline over the last decade.

Why do you think there are so many engineers in free flying? There seems to be something about having a mathematical mind and flying.
One thing that comes to mind is people who are dyslexic are often engineers. People who are dyslexic often have good spatial awareness and a feel for three-dimensional space. That's why they're good at engineering. When you're in a thermal and you've got this whole mass of gliders whirling around in three dimensions, people who have great spatial awareness can take a lot more in.

Can you tell me more about the process of designing a wing?
Normally you're not creating a glider from scratch. You're usually building on a previous design. You know what an existing glider's weak points are yourself, or you've heard from customers or dealers, or perhaps you're comparing it with what other brands have made that improve on what you've done. You start with the weaknesses, try to solve them, and of course you'll try to incorporate some new ideas. There's always a list of 10 or 15 new ideas up your sleeve, things that you'd love to develop, but time and resources will limit most of them. We'll then build a prototype to see what ideas worked and which ones didn't and compare it with what we have – always tweaking little things and testing new ideas. The test flying process is like an investigation. Each time you tweak something and go flying, you're picking up clues as to what's working and what isn't. Some ideas you just have to drop, even if they seem sensible.

"If you're ever in doubt, do the safe thing." Photo: Bruce Goldsmith

Have you stayed passionate and motivated to fly all these years, since you began flying in the mid-'80s?

I was extremely passionate about competition flying all those years. I was always flying the top competition wings, always pushing the absolute limits of performance and safety of the gliders, which was really fun and exciting. When Open Class gliders were banned, that was a major shock for me. That had been my world for a long time; pushing the development of gliders had always been an intrinsic part of competition. Over the last six years, since I stopped flying top-level competitions, I've been more focused on intermediate gliders, because it's very difficult to make money on competition gliders. But I'd say I've stayed extremely enthusiastic this whole time about flying.

Have you ever had an accident?

Yes. My first was in the hang gliding world championships in the Owens Valley, in California, in 1993. I tumbled my glider over the peak of White Mountain (14,242ft) and came down under reserve, but luckily I landed in soft snow and I was uninjured. There was no helicopter rescue back then. I slept that night wrapped up in my reserve, and then walked down the mountain the next morning. I got to a road about 11am and someone from the organization picked me up and drove me to the take-off, where my mates on the British team had already rigged another glider for me. An hour later I was back in the air competing again! The only place I know of in the whole world

"The hardest thing in paragliding is to learn to fly automatically." Bruce thermals out of one of his local sites; Col de Bleine, France. Photo: Martin Lifka

that absolutely lives up to its reputation is the Owens. Everything there is bigger, stronger, the cloudbase is higher, the winds are stronger – everything is double what it is anywhere else.

That's a hell of a story! But you said that was your first. Have there been others?
Interestingly, I quit hang gliding competitions after that accident because I felt paragliding was safer. Hang gliders in that period were very dangerous and very prone to tumbling. In that competition three of the six pilots on the British team tumbled. Two of us hit the ground and one flew away, but I didn't feel it was safe enough.

In 2009 I hit a lamp post while doing a spot landing. I just misjudged it and hit the post and fractured a vertebra, but nothing too serious.

What's your favorite place to fly?
My favorite place to fly competitions is St André in the southern French Alps. Tasks there can go in every direction – most places we fly comps you'll go up and down a ridge or out into the flats. In St André the options are endless. And it's gorgeous!

What are the most common things you see that lead to accidents?
People not appreciating their own level and what they're capable of doing. Everybody

needs to push the limits sometimes, but to push beyond your limit is what leads to accidents. If you're in doubt, take the easy option and do the safe thing. I think people get overconfident and push the limits usually in two ways: they fly in too much wind and that catches them out; or they fly a glider that's beyond their skill level. I think people tend to have a good understanding of what their own level is, and if they listen to their inner voice, listen for the doubts, they can more easily avoid trouble and accidents. What you're always trying to do is put the odds in your favor. You don't want to get surprised by your glider. If you're in doubt, err on the safe side. If you're honest with yourself and your own abilities and limits, and fly a glider that you can manage in conditions that suit your skill level, you're a long way towards being safe.

> **"What you're always trying to do is put the odds in your favor. You don't want to get surprised by your glider."**

You said earlier that you used to pretty regularly fly 300 hours a year and you're now flying less than half that. Have you noticed any change in your intuition or ability in the air because of that cutback?
I don't think the reduction in hours has altered my enjoyment or ability to fly well, but something I've noticed is the effect of age on my flying ability and flying skill. I'm now 56, and I definitely feel I'm not able to do the same things that I could 10 or 15 years ago. I have to increase my safety margins because of my age.

Are you talking about reaction time, or things like seeing birds, or something else?
Well, for instance if I had to land in an area with rocks 15 years ago, I would just pile in there and jump from rock to rock and get away with it. Now if I went into the same rocks, I'd hurt myself for sure. I'm less agile, more fragile and I'm probably a bit slower in reaction time as well to be able to cope when things don't go the way you want them to.

Can you tell me the three most important things to focus on in order to progress?
Number one: if it's not working, do something else. This is a very simple idea, but quite often people try to do something and, if it doesn't work, they persistently keep hammering away and come away defeated. This simple rule works really well for me. If it isn't working, change it. For example, perhaps you're trying to reach a landing field and you've got a headwind and can't get there. Instead of just hammering on, switch your mentality and do something else. Be flexible in your mind and don't get fixated on something.

Number two, especially in competitions, but in all flying: observation is the most important thing to develop. Especially looking at what other pilots are doing in the air, because they're showing you what's working and what isn't. And then of course observing all the natural features that affect us – the wind in the trees, birds climbing, smoke in the valley, etc. Your neck should get chafed and tired from looking around so much. In a competition, you have to be aware of what every single pilot in your visual range is doing. If someone is doing something different, you have to assess as soon as possible whether it's working or not.

Number three: the hardest thing to learn to do well in paragliding, and probably the most critical, is to be able to fly completely automatically. In the beginning you have to learn all the basics. You have to be able to assess a forecast, assess if it's safe to launch, take off and be able to land anywhere, find thermals, cope with collapses, spins, stalls, use a speed system. Before you can get into the interesting stuff like choosing good lines, taking different routes, optimizing your speed, planning a big triangle and pulling it off, all the basics have to be done mostly subconsciously. They have to be something you don't really think about. In other words, you have to sort out the physical parts of flying so that you can get into the more mental parts. This is the same in every sport. Observation trounces the tool you're using every time. Race car drivers aren't thinking about how to switch gears – they're looking ahead. You can't observe very well if you're thinking too much about the tool.

Any particular takeaways or advice from your world championship win in 2007?
This comes back to the point I just made about changing something if it isn't working. The opposite is obviously true as well. If it's working, don't change it. In that race I was doing quite well every day, so I was in first place going into the last day. Everyone kept asking me what my strategy would be for that final day. Was I going to mark the pilot who was in second place so he wouldn't get ahead? Would I fly more conservatively? But I didn't change a thing. What had been working was working, so I just did the same thing I'd been doing.

How does a comp pilot go from being middle of the pack to one of the top-tier contenders?
Flying a lot of competitions is important. You have to do at least two years of comp flying and at least one year of full-time competitions, which is a huge time and money commitment, before you even stand a chance at the top level. Staying with the gaggle in top-level competitions is quite easy once you have the technical skills. But it's very difficult to win. It's very difficult to fly with the gaggle the entire task and find even one thing that can give you an advantage, because everyone else is looking for the same thing. But that's often the difference, just one little thing. You have to try to assess all the decisions that are happening in the lead gaggle the entire race, and find the one decision which isn't right. If you can then make the right decision where they go wrong, you win. I think people often think too much. They consider every decision at every stage of the day, in every stage of the flight. That takes too much energy. You only need to make your own unique decision once or twice during the whole day. If you can make that decision really count, you've got a good chance of doing well.

Gavin McClurg launches in Austria during an X-Alps prologue. Photo: Marcus King

patagonia
GARMIN
Red Bull

HOW TO THROW YOUR RESERVE

Nearly every serious accident I've witnessed was because a pilot didn't throw their reserve after a collapse, but tried unsuccessfully to solve the problem all the way to the ground. I've seen blown launches and blown landings that result in a sprained ankle and other minor injuries, and I've seen a tiny handful that end up worse, but by far the majority of the bad accidents, the ones that cause so much pain in our community, are from pilots at every level who don't throw. Throw it, throw it clean, and throw it hard – they work! Although, as we hear from Tom Payne in this section – not always.

"How low is too low to throw your reserve? There's no such thing. If you're 10 feet off the ground, THROW!"
Jocky Sanderson

"I've seen over 100 reserve tosses in the last 15 years and I haven't seen a single injury. At one comp I saw seven reserve throws in one day! They work."
Nick Greece

"I've tumbled my hang glider twice. The second time I was in the right spot in the wrong moment. I threw my first reserve, but I didn't feel the drag of the chute and the glider started to spin violently, so I immediately threw the second reserve. If the second hadn't opened correctly, I would not be here today. The glider was completely destroyed, and I had almost no time before hitting the ground."
Christian Ciech

"I would not recommend using a Beamer-style reserve as your main reserve. Get a round or a square and throw that a few times, and then decide if you want a steerable. I've seen steerable reserves

"When you train acro, you throw your reserve lots. What you learn when you train acro is how long it takes to recover from various situations and what kind of height buffer you need. What that translates to in cross country is how much time you have to try to solve a situation. Do I have to throw immediately, or can I take some time to work this out? What gets a lot of pilots, especially in competitions, is they wait way too long. They don't want to take a zero for the day and lose a good score, so they try to solve it all the way to the ground.

Fly with two reserves when you're flying cross country, and especially in comps. You could have a gear malfunction [bad throw] on the first reserve, and if something goes wrong, having that backup might save your life. Mid-airs are getting more and more common in competitions, and having a second reserve if you get in a collision is really important."
Cody Mittanck

"My first reserve toss scared the shit out of me [tumbling in the Owens]. The second one just pissed me off. I was at the Women's Hang Gliding Worlds in Austria in 2004, and I was in first place three or four days into the comp. It was a great flying day, nothing weird. I was in a climb, circling up near base, and suddenly something grabbed me. I got spun out of the thermal the opposite way, and then I'm just pointed straight at the ground. I'm basically doing a handstand, and my only thought was to not let go of the bar. Then my feet hit the sail and I realize I'm upside down, and suddenly I'm in a washing machine that's disintegrating. People who saw it said I tumbled six or seven times. The glider is just beating me to death. I had no reference to where I was, I was just in survival mode. I couldn't tell what was up or down. It was really violent.

And then suddenly something broke on the glider, and everything stopped and I could see the sky. I wasn't spinning or tumbling, I was just lying there. I could see all these broken bars protruding and nasty stuff sticking out, so that was all I was thinking about when I grabbed my handle – that I had one chance and really had to have a good clean throw.

I threw and came down in between some trees super softly, and I think the only injury I had was a bloody lip. I got really lucky. What pissed me off was not knowing what went wrong. As pilots we like to know what causes things, and that one just came out of nowhere. I still don't know how it happened."
Kari Castle

get pilots into more trouble than they already were, because they can track with the wind if you don't have time to actively steer them, or they can get riser twists, just like a normal wing."
Max Marien

"I should have died. I was practicing helis on my acro wing for the first time in a year, and screwed it up. I got twisted and started into a cascade and thought: "Well fine, time for my reserve," and I threw. It went straight into the wing. "No problem," I thought, "I have a second reserve." I threw it in a hurry… straight into the wing. My wing was still flying, I still had four riser twists, so the brakes were totally locked and both reserves were balled up underneath the wing, so all I could do was look at the rapidly approaching ground and wait for the world to go black. I tried like hell to pull on the lines of both reserves to get them free of the wing, but nothing worked. I hit the ground and thankfully it was a pretty steep slope, my harness had a lot of cushion, and somehow I walked away. If we look at pure probability, it's much more important to have a reliable first reserve than to have multiple reserves. In other words, the less reliable your reserve systems are, the more important it is to have more of them. Adding a reserve doesn't double your chances. For example, a first reserve has, let's say, a 95% chance of opening cleanly. If it doesn't, a second reserve will have below that probability because of the extra lines and material that are in the way. Adding a reserve does increase your chances, but you can't get to 100%, regardless of how many you add."
Tom Payne

THÉO DE BLIC'S CHECKLIST

Throwing the reserve is a lot more mental than most people realize. I've thrown my reserve more than ten times. In flying, doing anything well takes practice, and throwing your reserve is the same. You have to develop the right reflexes and run through the correct steps. I do all my acro training over the ground, and I feel I'm 100% safe because I know when and how to use my reserve and I don't hesitate to use it when it's necessary.

Personally, I don't fly with a cut-away system. I fly with a steerable Rogallo and a square as a backup. My honest opinion is that the safest setup right now is a cutaway for sure, but I have a normal setup, because I'm quite comfortable and confident with what I have.

Here's my checklist for throwing my reserve:

1. Before every flight, I make sure I'm mentally willing to throw my reserve. You have to think about this. You must set the intention by making sure that if something happens, you're mentally prepared to throw. Many pilots try to fix a problem all the way to the ground because they don't want to throw their reserve. So step one: always be ready to throw.

2. Check your altitude. It's the first thing I do. If I'm low, I don't hesitate, I throw. If I have height, I check the situation. Every configuration requires a different input and a different amount of time to fix. And some might require a different way to throw. For example, if I'm in an autorotation with a lot of twists, it's possible to throw the reserve into the wing, so I have to throw it in a different way than normal. Assessing all of this should take less than a couple of seconds. If you haven't heard of it before, autorotation is a configuration where the pendulum force moves from the pilot to a point between the pilot and the wing. You have the sensation of flying backwards. Autorotations can also describe a deep spiral which can get "locked in" and cause a pilot to black out from the increased G-force. Unintentional autorotations typically happen after an asymmetric cravat that isn't cleared. Getting out of an autorotation requires a strong disturbance to break up the wing's momentum, for example, heavy brake input and weight shift.

3. If I've decided to throw, I use my muscle memory to find the rescue handle. Sometimes you can't see it and normally you're not in your normal flying position, so you have to practice how it feels to find the handle. I run my hand down past my knee, then over to my butt so my hand goes directly to it.

4. I also strongly recommend keeping both brake toggles in one hand and held down deeply and throwing with the other hand so the wing doesn't "restart" or violently pitch forward just as you go to throw. By keeping your wing stalled, you greatly reduce the chance of throwing the reserve into the wing. The exception to this is if you're in an autorotation or locked-in spiral, in which case you might not be able to stall the wing and it's more important to focus on a clean throw away from the wing.

5. Throw as fast and as hard as possible away from your wing.

6. Check the deployment and make sure the reserve is fully open. Often it can be a bit fouled. If it's fouled and you have time, you can try to pull some of the lines to get it to fully open. But if you don't have time and you have two reserves, throw your other reserve.

7. Take care to disable your wing as soon as possible. A glider can quite easily downplane [fly against the force of the reserve] if it's still open, and your descent rate can be very fast, fast enough to get injured. You can disable your wing with the B lines or the brakes. If there's too much pressure, just try to pull whatever you can on one side asymmetrically, because that's still better than nothing.

8. Try to land on your feet and do a PLF. If you're coming in fast, it's better to break your legs than your back. A parachute landing fall is a safety technique that allows a parachutist (which is what we are when under reserve!) to land safely and without injury. The technique is performed by paratroopers and recreational parachutists alike. The technique is used to displace the energy of the body contacting the earth at high speeds.

All of this obviously happens quite fast, and you need to practice these steps in your mind repeatedly and frequently so it's second nature. Most pilots who get injured screw up step two and lose track of their altitude.

There's no shame in throwing your reserve. You must mentally train yourself to be prepared and willing to throw it. Before you take off, set the intention that if something happens you will throw. Every time you get into the air, practice reaching down to find your reserve handle. Make it instinctive. Every pilot is optimistic by nature. None of us would fly if we weren't. But too much optimism isn't good. We have to admit that there are times the glider will not recover.

Red Bull
YOU COUNT
DermaPlast®
BIONIC®
.DENTAN
BY SUTECH-ÉTANCHÉITÉ
SHV
FSVL
ADELBODEN
Frutigen

The All-Time Great

CHRIGEL MAURER

Chrigel Maurer is undeniably the most accomplished paraglider pilot the world's yet seen. With multiple wins in the X-Alps and the overall Paragliding World Cup tour, Chrigel's consistent success over the past 15 years has led many to call him the Roger Federer of the paragliding world.

But when I met him, Chrigel looked absolutely destroyed. Call it schadenfreude if you will, but it was some small comfort to see that he'd suffered as much as the rest of us. It was the end of the 2017 X-Alps, a race widely regarded as the most challenging yet, with unrelentingly atrocious rain and wind for nearly the entire 1,138km course. In fact, only two pilots made it to Monaco – the other being France's Benoît Outters.

Seven of the 32 athletes retired because of injury or exhaustion. Chrigel won, but won with a very noticeable limp after injuring his knee. The face that stared back at me was etched with the lines of suffering that he'd endured over the past 11 days. The comfort I drew was in seeing a human sat opposite me, nothing more, nothing less. And if you've ever been to see Chrigel give one of his wonderful talks, you'll know that the image that's been created about Chrigel in our community as an untouchable, supernaturally gifted demigod is not one that he's had much of a hand in. He flashes up a slide from 2009, showing his Advance prototype draped over a tree in the Swiss Alps, his harness dangling below. He talks about how his mum helped fish it out for him. The next slide shows a new wing – still Advance – gift-wrapped over the very same tree. "This was last summer – ten years later!" he jokes.

Chrigel messes up, just like the rest of us. But, my God, is he committed to his goals. He credits his success to meticulous preparation, and watching him sew together a mobile holster to fit on his flight deck before one X-Alps, or running through one of his many check-lists, his attention to detail is obvious. Chrigel's commitment means he flies more than 300 hours per year, and chucks a lot of endurance and strength training into the mix too.

The result? I don't believe there's a solo race that Chrigel has entered since his first X-Alps in 2009 that he hasn't won. You name it – the X-Pyr, Eigertour, Dolomiti Superfly, Iron Fly, Vercofly, the Gruyere, Bordairline – he's won them all (many of them multiple times). The thought of doing another hike and fly race so shortly after the X-Alps wasn't just preposterous to me – it was physically impossible. I could barely

> **"I love to dream. It's not training, just natural. I lie in bed thinking about infinity tumbling or how I can win a race or do crazy acrobatic maneuvers."**

walk, and it would be many weeks before I would go outside for a hike just for the fun of it. But Chrigel was already preparing for his next wins.

I was, of course, thrilled to talk to Chrigel about the X-Alps, but I also wanted to know what everyone wants to know – how does he do it? I'd heard all kinds of rumors about his training – flying in strong lee over the snow, kiting in 60km/h winds, and so on – and every one of them turns out true. I was also fascinated to hear how he applies what he's learned to the many pilots he teaches in his career as a professional coach.

These days, there's no debate. Chrigel is the best paragliding pilot in the world, and is hands down the most confident and perceptive flyer in the sport. No one picks out lines like the Eagle. There may be competition pilots who can outclimb Chrigel or beat him on a given day in a World Cup (he no longer flies many standard race-to-goal competitions), and there are acro pilots who are now doing tricks well beyond his current repertoire, but there's no pilot who can come close to Chrigel flying cross country in the mountains, especially when the weather is dicey. No one can touch him. But what can we learn from him?

Chrigel, your choice of wing in the X-Alps has been a subject of much debate. You fly two-liners most of the time, but in the X-Alps you have mostly chosen a three-liner. How come?
For me it's very important to have the right wing for this race. I choose the best compromise between performance, safety and fun. When I fly the two-liner I love the performance, but only when I'm in good shape. For one 10-hour flight it's fine, but in the X-Alps after some days I get so tired that I don't have the benefit of the two-liner. It's more important to feel comfortable on the wing than it is to have performance – and that goes across the board in paragliding.

In 2015 you told me something that really surprised me: you don't scout the course before the race, because you don't want to have preconceptions and you want to see it with fresh eyes. You said that if you scout it weeks in advance, the snow line, valley winds and so on will be different. Would you take that same approach if the race was somewhere you didn't know at all?
This is something I learned with my teammate Thomas Theurillat over time. In the first edition of the X-Alps we realized it wouldn't be possible to see all the places – we just

didn't have time. So instead we tried to just train hard at home, and learn as much as possible about the course with other tools like Google Earth. For example, with the X-Pyr races, I never had time to scout the course and it worked fine to just train at home. A great example from the 2017 X-Alps was the turnpoint in Slovenia. I'd never been there. I asked at least 12 teams about how to get into this turnpoint, but none of them really had any idea. The Garda turnpoint was the same – everyone said it wasn't possible to fly to it. They all said the valley wind was too strong and it was too stable. But on the day I arrived, the vallcy wind was very light and two of us flew right in. It's often better going in with an open mind. And it gives me more buzz to keep racing, because I feel like a child discovering all these new places.

Tell me about your training leading up to the X-Alps. I've heard some crazy stories about your preparation.

When I was a test pilot for Advance I was often flying right at the limits, because it was my job. So I've learned to really enjoy testing the limits of my equipment and also myself. As long as I feel good, I go forward. For the race I know I have to train really hard. If I train hard then I know it will be easier in the race. So for example I like to train in strong winds of around 50km/h, so if it's blowing 40km/h in the race it feels easy. Same for taking off. I practice high-wind take-offs in the snow so I only get a bit wet if it goes wrong. And then, in the race, if I have the same wind I know I can do it safely.

What about mental training? Is that part of your preparation as well?

I love to dream. It's not training, just natural. I lie in bed thinking about infinity tumbling or how I can win a race or do crazy acrobatic maneuvers. I just visualize doing these things. A week before the 2017 race I got really sick and I thought I really had no chance against the others. But then I just thought about my strengths and remembered the last editions of the race and the nice parts of the race that I really enjoy… the sunrises and sunsets, being with my team… and that really helped me a lot to feel prepared.

Are you influenced by what other pilots are doing in the race? You're always out in front, so probably not…

It's funny, because during the race a lot of people come out to see me and tell me what they think about where I should go. What trail I should take, what launch I should take… And I really listen to them, but you have to do what you feel is right. What is the best step for you, right now? If you do what someone else did, it can be helpful but if it doesn't feel right, you might not do it well.

Are you identifying your launches, or is that your team? And what resources do you use for weather, routing, launches, etc.?

I have two guys at home looking at Google Earth and the weather, so they can send me navigation routes, and my main supporter, Tobias Dimmler, checks them to make sure they make sense. But the goal is to get the information, and then the final decision is how it feels in my stomach. Ultimately, it's a gamble. In an adventure race it's never totally clear, so ultimately it's up to me and I have to decide.

Chrigel Maurer at Turnpoint 7, Titlis, Switzerland during the Red Bull X-Alps on 19 June 2019
Photo: Harald Tauderer/Red Bull Content Pool

In the 2013 race you had a really terrifying flight near your home. How do you manage your fear, and how do you justify flying when you have two young children?
It sounds strange, but when I do intense events like the X-Alps, I really focus on the moment. There is nothing else. As long as I can focus on the problem, I can compete. When I start thinking about other things or my family, I have to stop competing, because I'm not there, and it's dangerous. What I realize now is that when I was young I really took risk all the time, just to have fun. Now I only take risk when I can gain something, like winning a competition. So that means the rest of the year I don't have to take risk, I can just fly safely and have fun. And even in the competition I try to only take risk when I can really gain something from it. When there is risk, I try to be really aware of it and stay really focused: to be aware that what I'm doing isn't safe. That's definitely more safe than flying and thinking everything is going to be ok.

When you look at your wins, what are the things that stand out the most when it comes to your success that the rest of us maybe lack?
The first thing is just the experience I have. I learned to play with my father's wing when I was too young to fly. I ground handled so much that the wing became a part of my life. My father took me on so many tandems, and taught me how to fly in the mountains.

The second thing is: I like to gamble. This means making a decision and following it to the end, whether it's good or bad. It's important to follow your feeling. It's important to take risk. Most of the athletes want to go step by step to Monaco. They don't want to take risk. I don't mean safety risk, but sporting risk. I really like to take the risk to see if it's possible. I like to think about the best case scenario instead of the worst case. If you focus on the best case scenario, it gives you possibilities. For example, going to the Monte Baldo turnpoint everyone said it wasn't possible to fly there because of the valley wind. But when I launched that day I just thought about the best case scenario, which was to top land at the turnpoint. In the end it wasn't possible to land at the turnpoint, but I got really close. So I almost got the best case.

When I coach I teach how to think about the best case scenario. And I know that it's really difficult because many people are naturally negative and only think about problems. I'm very lucky to have a positive mindset. It's a big advantage.

I think when most of us fly XC, it's easier to gamble because the consequences of blowing it are no big deal. But in the X-Alps, leaving the course line by a big distance, or taking a big risk and blowing it can mean hours of extra walking, which is mentally really tough to overcome.

It's a math game. Let's say you're optimistic and you go for it ten times in one day, and it works out only nine times. That's still better than being conservative and only making three gambles which all pay off.

In your coaching, what comes up again and again? What is the thing you see that most pilots need?

Most pilots ask: "How do I fly more safely?", but I think this is the wrong question. You have to work out if you like to fly or not, if you like to take risk or not. People who fly usually like risk. They drive fast, they ski fast, they like adventure. Pilots who stay careful and focus a lot on living aren't a good fit in paragliding. It's very hard to teach how to fly more safely. It's the same with pilots that just like to fly and don't do any training. They don't do much ground handling or they only do one SIV each year, but they want to win competitions or they want to show how good they are. That isn't very safe. You have to visualize the life of being a pilot. You have to keep practicing.

I've seen you say when you're flying you're doing one of three things: climbing, gliding, or planning. How do you approach these concepts when you're coaching?

The idea is to focus on the moment. It starts at take-off. Pilots think about landing before they take off! You're not focusing if you're already thinking about the landing. Maybe it's good to have a general plan for the day, but it's more important to be in the moment and just take it step by step. Find a thermal. Climb. Glide. Find another thermal.

You can't fly well if your brain is too occupied. You have to be observing everything… the birds, the sound of your vario so you can get in the core. Then, when you get towards the top of the climb, you can think about the next glide. When you decide to glide you don't think about thermalling – you've switched the mode and the focus. The more efficiently you switch modes, the more efficiently you'll fly. And when you're gliding you should have several options in mind, so if the first one doesn't work you efficiently move to the next one.

Chrigel, how much of your flying do you attribute to intuition versus this kind of calculated decision making?
I just lead by my stomach. I'm not very good at calculation or the 'facts' like weather forecasts and that kind of thing. This other stuff takes me out of the moment and I need to stay in the moment. My decisions come from feel.

> **"People who fly usually like risk. Pilots who stay careful and focus a lot on living aren't a good fit in paragliding."**

You're famous for not turning. You seem to just know how to fly straight. How do you do it?
A friend of mine, Stefan Schmoker, once told me that when you're turning you're spending half your time flying in the wrong direction! With modern wings, even the new three-liners, you can just fly straight, straight, straight, and only turn when it's really important. It's a lot more efficient flying straight. When you are near terrain, there is always a little warm, lifty air to help you float along. When you climb you get into strong lift, but then you leave that lift and get into strong sink. So after you've spent all that time climbing up, you then just lose all that altitude, so it's much more efficient to just follow a ridge and stay low than it is to climb up and glide down.

And are you right on the terrain? Like right on the tree tops?
Often it's better to just follow the terrain and fly quite slow. So just trim speed or with just a little acceleration. This is much faster than climbing and then flying full speed. You can calculate this: when you turn, you fly 50% of the time in the wrong direction, as my friend used to say. It means instead of flying at 60km/h, you're actually flying at 30km/h. But when you fly trim speed without turning you're flying at 40km/h. And it's a lot more relaxed.

Before the last X-Alps you had an accident and broke an ankle. I understand this is your only accident?
It was a tandem flight with my wife in Zermatt after a big hike-and-fly, and I was really tired. I had a huge, heavy backpack and my idea was to land very close to the train station, which is a very small landing field, because I was tired.

So my mistake was choosing the wrong place to land. There was no wind, but it was turbulent. We hit big sink – it felt like around minus 6-7m/s, like going down under a reserve. And I was not thinking about the problem, which was our impending hard landing! We didn't have any back protection and I was trying to protect my wife so I broke my ankle when we hit. I've had much harder landings, but I just wasn't focused.

What can you pass along to us about gliding efficiently? I find it tricky to feel whether the glider is pulling towards more lift or more sink, and I find it can be very difficult to find lifty lines.
In the World Cup, there are 120 pilots flying almost the same wing, at the same weight, with the same harness. But there are maybe five who can climb better, and maybe ten who glide better. Everyone in a World Cup is very good, but very few are just executing better. For example, my strength is flying fast in turbulent conditions, but I'm not good at climbing in weak conditions; I'm not as good at finding the core and climbing fast. And I spoke to those guys who are really good at this because I wanted to get better, but they couldn't figure out how to change this about my flying.

There are two aspects to getting better: the first is to know what to change, and the second is to do it. Finally I just realized I'm not the best climber but I'm really fast in the final glide. So I have to focus on my strengths and accept my weaknesses and that keeps me motivated for flying competitions. I know that when the conditions are weak it's probably not going to be my day, but when it's strong I can do well. With students, it's much easier to teach them how to climb than it is to find good lines.

If you could go back to your 50-hour self, what would you change?
I wouldn't jump on a high-performance wing so early. The step for me was way too big. The second thing would be to not risk so much, or not to always risk so much. But that's hard, because that experience I got risking a lot also taught me a lot. So that risk I took was important.

You've ticked just about every box in the sport. What do you see yourself doing in five, ten years?
I really want to continue competing in hike-and-fly competitions, but my body will have to agree! I really want to spread my experience in coaching. But mostly I just want to continue flying as long as I can because I really love to fly.

What would you like to impart to other pilots? What's the most important thing you can pass on?
I think the most important thing is to think about your personal goals in paragliding. Why do you fly? After you think about your goals you can think about optimizing your efforts. If the goal is fly really far, then you need to identify all the small steps you have to take to get there. But first of all it's important to think about the personal goal, and why it matters to you. Everything starts there.

HOW TO PROGRESS SAFELY

How do we improve without taking risk and making mistakes? The easy answer is we can't, or at least not very efficiently. In every endeavor, improvement comes from leaving your comfort zone, from pushing a bit into the unknown. If every time we took to the skies we got the same magical feeling as our first time, we'd never need to do anything else – just easy, safe flights that last a few seconds. But we are humans, and humans get bored, and we inevitably want more. You can't get barreled until you surf hollow waves, and hollow waves means shallow and fast, where mistakes have higher consequences. You can't kayak class V water safely until you've spent enough time on lower-class rivers getting the technique and mindset dialed. Learning is one of the most addictive things we do. Learning something new is like falling in love. You can't get enough. The trick in flying is to make inexpensive mistakes, and to push at a level that aligns with your skills. Getting that equation wrong in aviation, where we're playing with the ground and gravity, doesn't usually pan out very well. Thankfully, we can get it right.

"A big, well-executed wingover is difficult to achieve for most pilots, but it's really important to be able to do it. You have to understand your glider and have perfect timing. It's one of the few maneuvers that takes you through every axis of the wing. Having a really confident full stall is more important than a perfect wingover, but after you get the full stall, progressing to a big wingover is a great objective."
Théo De Blic

"A great way to improve is to not let a single flight happen without trying to get better. Every single flight is an opportunity to improve your skills. You should be competitive every time you're in the air. Try to never let anyone climb up from below you, and always try to outclimb those above you. Try to outclimb the birds. Work on your pitch control, play with your speed bar, adjust your harness, fly without your vario. Make every flight a training flight.

"These things take time to learn. Paragliders are not easy machines to fly well. That's the problem. They're very easy to fly, but very difficult to fly well in turbulent air. The only way to really get good at that is by doing acro training and SIV training, and by flying in turbulent air. So in order to learn the skills you need, you have to put yourself at risk. In our sport we're always learning, always improving. There's always something that you're not doing as well as you could. That's the beautiful thing about our sport, and why there's so much longevity in it. But that's also what makes it dangerous."
Russ Ogden

"Working a progression in a thoughtful way is a beautiful art. It's a cornerstone of life. When your parents gave you the keys to the car, they put their money on the idea that they'd worked a good progression. We need to be thoughtful about progression with our flying as well. Make it look smart. It can't be rushed. You really need a community to help you out. Let's say you want to get into cross country. Before you take a thermal up and get blown down the road, it would be good to practice landing in different places first. Work on progressing to tighter and tighter fields, so when you start flying distance and don't know where you're going to end up, you have the landing skills.

No one gets to claim they're a good driver until they're too old to drive because they can't see, and they give it up, and have never had an accident. That's a good driver. Someone who stays off the accelerator, plays defense and keeps it between the lines. In a lot of sports, having a ton of ambition is great and you can push really hard. In throwing a javelin, or running a marathon, or racing a bicycle, you can charge hard and punish yourself and go for the win. But in flying, we should keep it between the lines. We shouldn't be ambitious. We shouldn't have an agenda to fly X distance. The odds are against you if you set a high bar and try to nail some expectation. If you're flying 10 or 15 years from now, you'll have some amazing flights under your belt without trying at all. Just keep it between the lines."
Chris Santacroce

Flying cross country well takes time. No matter how good you think you are, there are pilots who know how to get through a particular landscape better than you do. It takes a long while to tap into the flow that you need. I don't think any pilot can expect to get to a high level quickly. You have to spend a lot of time with really good pilots so their ability rubs off on you. You need mentors you can emulate. You can only get to a good level by putting in the hard yards."
Guy Anderson

"I have a concept that I call 'the body's tide.' We accelerate, we plateau, we regress, and sometimes we overreach. And we have to work with these natural and forced undulations in order to progress effectively. It's the nature of training that sometimes you feel you can rip a phone book in half, and other times you struggle to get out the door. We have to learn how our bodies react to stress. Sometimes we can push, but other times we need to pull back. When most of us learn to paraglide, or learn anything new, we often overreach. That can cause fear or doubt, and that can set you back. We have to go slow sometimes to go fast. You have to tune into your body's tide and know that these undulations happen, instead of falling prey to them."
Willi Canell

"This may seem obvious, but one of the best ways to improve as a pilot is to either live in a place that's conducive to flying, but also complicated and not obvious, or to travel as much

as you can. To be a complete pilot you have to know how to work weak conditions, strong conditions, flying in the lee, flying in wind. The more we can challenge ourselves to build skills, the better we become, and that happens automatically as you figure out flying a new place."
Michael Sigel

"I had an accident early in my career, and it was at least a year before I let myself fly again. I would go ground handle in very strong winds at my local launch. Until I could manage the glider perfectly, and repeatedly get to the launch point in control with everything looking smooth, I didn't let myself fly."
Antoine Laurens

"Be hard on yourself, but don't beat yourself up. Process the information and let it go. Take some time when you land to write down what you did right and what you did wrong."
Nick Greece

"For pilots who want to get into vol-biv and want to fly a lightweight wing, I highly, highly recommend stepping down a class. If you're flying an EN C normal wing, then get the light model of a high EN B. Lighter wings are more demanding to pilot, and bivvy flying demands more skill than we're normally used to."
Greg Hamerton

"Fly as much as you can with pilots who are better than you. Soak up everything you can and make yourself available. Offer to drive retrieve, be willing to help, contribute to your community, and good mentors will take you under their wing."
Dominic Rohner

"You have to have a level of self-confidence in this sport that matches the situation. Too much confidence can kill you, but if you're up in the air and it gets serious, you're up in the air! You and only you can get yourself down. Even as a student, you have to be comfortable with being alone and making decisions that have potentially massive consequences."
Phil Glutz

"Having big goals is great, but they aren't very actionable. About ten years ago I started thinking that I wanted to compete in the X-Alps. That's a big goal, but getting there requires first making a whole bunch of smaller, more achievable goals. It's these small, attainable goals that you can tackle step by step that will get you to the bigger goals. That might be improving your thermalling by being more observant of other pilots and being faster at moving to a better climb; or being more observant of the wind velocity and how it's affecting your glide, so you don't end up in a bad place. There's a sports performance term called "4% goals". We don't learn by shooting for pie in the sky, we learn by chipping away little by little."
Mitch Riley

"Fly as much as you can with pilots that are better than you. Soak up everything you can."
Michi Maurer, Frutigen, Switzerland. Photo: Martin Scheel

Walking the Line

CODY MITTANCK

The first time I met Cody was in the LZ in Valle De Bravo at the 2013 Paragliding World Cup. He was a wind dummy, and about as keen as anyone I'd ever met on figuring out how to fly fast and far. Two years later, Cody flew ten flights of over 150 miles in a single season in the very big air of Utah and Wyoming. He'd just broken the Canadian foot-launch record (unofficially, because he flew well past dark and had a little incident with the US/Canada border), and he was fast becoming one of the most consistent top 20 pilots on the World Cup tour. Cody is one of a handful of pilots in North America who can do the infinity tumble. He competed in the 2019 X-Alps, and was 11th at the 2019 world championships. Cody and I have spent a lot of time training acro together, towing over the dirt in the American Southwest, because we both believe that acro training makes us way safer when we're flying XC. It's been inspiring and instructive to see him methodically and purposefully figure out this game.

Cody, do you see a real distinction between XC and acro skills?
No, I don't. I think they blend together really well. I figured out really early on when I started flying XC that inevitably, even on the good days, you're going to hit some weird air, and having acro skills was going to keep me much safer. The two go hand in hand.

How did you approach your training in acro?
Unless you live in a place like Organyà or Ölüdeniz, the hard thing about acro training is just getting the time. If you live in Salt Lake City, where there's not much water and we haven't found a site like Organyà where you can soar high enough to safely practice acro, the only way to do it is by towing. That gets really expensive. In the beginning I watched a ton of videos and read as much as I could. That taught me that the first thing you really need to learn is full stalls, flyback, and then deep stall. Those maneuvers are fundamental. The deep stall is sort of the reset button in acro. Once I got those down a bit, I went to Ölüdeniz for five weeks and just did deep stalls from the top to the bottom over and over and over again. Once in a while I'd try some helis, but mostly I just deep stalled for five weeks! Once I felt comfortable with the deep stall, the heli came easy.

> **“Most people maybe do one SIV per year, and they might do three stalls on the last day. So the full stall remains really scary.”**

Is acro dangerous?
If you look at acro competitions, you don’t see people getting hurt. When you look at the good acro pilots, there are no configurations they haven’t seen, so they can pretty much get out of anything. You throw your reserve a lot training acro. You get really good at knowing what can and can’t be fixed and how long it takes, which is why acro training makes you so much safer when you fly XC. But there’s definitely a dangerous phase you go through with acro training. You can get through that phase safely by understanding what kind of person you are and how you deal with fear. Some people freeze up when they get scared, other people react really fast, other people overreact.

How can people identify how they react, and then how should they train to compensate?
Everyone is going to be freaked out before doing their first stalls. Regardless of the kind of person you are, it all comes down to training. The first ones are terrifying. But after a few, you realize they aren’t that bad. After 50 stalls you have a pretty good feel, you understand the mechanics of what’s going on, and they aren’t scary at all. After 300 it’s a non-event. Acro training is slow and step by step. You have to get each maneuver really, really down before you move on.

How should people tackle that initial trepidation?
The first thing is just developing trust in your gear. The gear doesn’t fail. So having trust in the gear removes that unreasonable fear from the equation. And then it’s back to understanding what kind of person you are. If you’re the kind who tends to freeze up, you need to practice initially over the water and do a really slow, thoughtful progression with a good coach. Most people maybe do one SIV per year, and they might do three or four stalls on the last day. So every year it’s really scary because you never get it sorted. It’s not enough training. You have to do this stuff repeatedly – you have to treat it as training.

Do you think all the acro training you’ve done directly correlates to being able to fly farther in XC?
What it does is make you more confident, and for sure that helps you fly far. I know for a fact that when I’m on full bar in turbulent air, I can recover anything, as long as I have

height. I've done it so many times in every possible way. I'm not going to get surprised. Having an acro background allows you to be aggressive when flying XC. You don't have to back off when conditions are strong. You have a lot more fun, and having fun also allows you to fly farther. When I first got started in XC, when it would get rowdy I wanted to be on the ground, but now when it gets rowdy, I enjoy it – it means the air is active and I can use it to cover distance. The caveat is how close to the ground you are. When you're low, your options go way down.

You and I witnessed two very serious accidents in the Owens, California, this year. Both were nearly identical where the pilots got into trouble low and didn't throw their reserves. Do you think acro training could have changed those outcomes?
It's hard to say absolutely, but what acro training does is teach you how long it takes to recover from whatever situation you're in. In both the accidents in the Owens, had those pilots instantly thrown their reserves, they most likely would have been unhurt. They both had the height and time to throw. My guess is had those pilots had acro training, it would have helped them recognize that they were too low to safely recover their wings, and they would have thrown their reserves.

Competitions complicate our thought processes and can definitely increase our risk. We don't want to take a zero for the day, and that can be in the back of our minds. "I need to recover this!" I'd like to think that because of all the acro training I've done, the training would take over, and I'd just throw. But that competitive racing instinct is another beast that we need to tame. Whenever I'm less than 50m from the ground, especially if I'm racing on full bar, I think "reserve". It's like planting the thought in the back of my mind. It's a reminder that if the wing completely goes to shit and is unrecoverable, my immediate reaction will be to throw. The skill here is immediately recognizing if the wing is recoverable or not, which can only be gained through experience and acro training. There shouldn't be a stigma about reserves. Nearly all the best pilots in the world have come down under them. They pack it back up and race the task again the very next day.

How do pilots know when they're ready to step up to a higher-level wing?
Every time I switched to a higher-level wing, I had a cascade incident that took me some height to get under control. That taught me that every time I step up, I must rise to the occasion of a new wing that requires new skills, and I also have to give myself a lot more margin in the form of height. You should never move up until you feel like the wing that you're on is really holding you back. That doesn't mean it's holding you back in comps because you can't glide as well as the comp gliders; it means you're comfortably using the full range of the bar, you have no fear whatsoever of the wing, you're not giving any of your mental bandwidth to keeping the wing open, you're getting a ton of hours, and you're ready and excited for the challenge of a more demanding wing.

How much are you flying in a typical year?
I fly a lot. I put close to 500 hours on my CCC wing last year, and then there's all the acro training.

Any problems with staying motivated when you're flying that much?
Sometimes, yes. What I try to stay focused on is the little, sometimes almost imperceptible, progressions. As long as you're learning something, it stays interesting. In acro it can be the tiniest things – just getting a transition from one move to another a little quicker, a little cleaner. Or in XC, figuring out how to thermal in really light conditions. The beauty of this sport is we can never totally figure it out.

Back to comps – you've done a bunch of comps this year. What are the big takeaways, and what will you try to take into your next comps?
The first thing I figured out is you need to be able to keep up with the gaggle and be able to gaggle fly. For pilots like us who typically fly XC either alone or with one or two other people, gaggle flying can be pretty uncomfortable. It's intense flying so close to so many other pilots. But you have to figure that out first. You have to get really good at climbing and gliding, just so you can keep up. Once you have that down, you have to figure out how to strike and do your own thing, otherwise you can't break the top 30. To do that you have to press out and be confident and make bold moves, but that's inevitably going to put you on the ground, which is frustrating, but it's important to learn. I think to do well consistently you have to blend it all together: solid gaggle flying and a little thoughtful pushing at the right time.

We're racing aircraft that are incredibly slow. Tiny differences over three or four hours really add up. If you can grab a little bit more of a core, or find a little tiny bit better line, that's all the difference sometimes. The subtle differences matter.

How much cross-over is there between competitions and flying big XC?
There's actually not a ton of cross-over when it comes to strategy. You get really good at climbing and gliding at comps just by paying attention to the people around you. If you're on the same wing and people are climbing better and gliding better, you're doing something wrong, and you just have to figure it out. Climbing and gliding well certainly helps for flying distance, but flying big XC days is more about mental and physical endurance and handling your wing than it is about racing. In competitions you're racing other people. For big distance, you're flying the conditions and adapting to the day and just staying in the air.

What's important in both is to fly as fast as you can, given the conditions. If it's 3pm and the day is really powered up, and the last two climbs were 4m/s climbs on the averager, and you stop for a 2m/s climb and take it all the way to base, you've just blown a lot of time.

We have to remind ourselves sometimes how simple it really is. We have to glide as fast as we can to the strongest climb of the day. That's it – wink, wink! And when it comes to comps, you have to think a lot about positioning. Always try to be in a better position. If you lead out low, you're not in a strong position. You're the marker.

If someone is climbing better than you nearby, move immediately. At the end of every flight, you should take some time to go back and review what you did well and what you could have done better.

What would you change in your progression if you could roll back the clock to your 50-hour self?
I wish I'd gotten a mentor early. Someone who'd have told me if I was doing something risky. Because when you're new you don't really know. And that applies to when I was learning the Infinite as well. I learned on my own, and one time I went into my wing. That kind of thing should be avoided.

We've been training over the dirt. Talk to me about when that's not appropriate for certain pilots.
In my opinion, acro training should never be done over the dirt until a pilot has a very solid command of deep stall and experience of throwing their reserve multiple times during real-life events. The two worst scenarios you can get into are going into the wing, and getting twisted up. Both of those can quickly get out of control. If you can be confident to avoid the first – going into your wing – and control the second – getting multiple twists – then by following some very strict rules like not doing any maneuvers below 1,000ft, I believe you can safely train over the ground. But to get to that point, you have to have deep stall totally dialed, and that takes a lot of training, especially on dynamic wings.

You have some advice for people when they throw their reserve that I want you to share.
When you throw your reserve, it's really important to lock both your brakes down with your non-throwing hand before you throw. Keep the wing in deep stall or, even better, tail slide. You want the wing stalled and in a stable configuration before you throw. Grab both brake toggles with one hand, keep the toggles down in your lap (too much brake isn't going to hurt anything – it'll just be a deeper tail slide). If you go to throw your reserve and let go of your brakes, there's a high chance of the wing suddenly shooting hard just as you throw, which is highly unstable. You could get wrapped up in the wing, or throw your reserve directly into the wing and get a poor deployment.

CODY'S TOP FIVE TIPS

1. Your first full stalls are terrifying. After 50 you have a pretty good feel: you understand the mechanics and they're not scary. Get started!
2. If someone's climbing better than you, move to them, immediately – unless you're too low to do so.
3. Before reaching for your reserve handle, lock both brakes down with your other hand. Keep it stalled and stable.
4. Positioning is everything. If you lead out low, you're not in a strong position. You're the marker.
5. If you're feeling burnt out, stay focused on the little, sometimes almost imperceptible, progressions that you want to make.

HOW TO RECOVER FROM FRIGHTENING EXPERIENCES

Coming back from injuries or a really scary flight that shakes you up is a recurring theme for pilots. It seems that the recovery to becoming confident again is different for everyone. The only absolute is that it takes time.

"I threw my reserve super low in Sun Valley on a really strong day right after launch on a really hot comp glider, and luckily it deployed right before I hit the ground. If it hadn't, I would have probably died. At the time I was ranked 39th in the world, I'd just gotten sponsored, I was doing really well in comps, and it was a big check on my ego. I had to swallow my pride and step back. I stepped down to a lower-end glider, and had to stay there for a couple years before I could get my mojo back. It took a while before it was fun again."
Nick Greece

"Fear comes from the unknown. If we can analyze what happened and understand the process that led to the accident or incident, the fear goes away and understanding takes its place. To reduce fear, we need to understand."
Veso Ovcharov

"After my tumbling incident on a hang glider in the Owens, everything changed for me. Until that point my attitude was: "Why would I be on the ground when I could be in the air?" I was totally addicted. But after the tumble,

"I think you have to be really honest with yourself and accept the fact that it will take time. Eight months after my crash in the Adriatic circle, Paul Guschlbauer and I returned to complete the expedition. When we arrived at the site of the crash and I realized there was still 1,000km to go, I didn't want to do it. My whole body was saying no way. But a part of me wanted to overcome this fear, a part of me wanted to go all the way. And Paul helped a lot. I think that's important, to have friends who understand and support you. He said we should take it slowly, and if I didn't feel good about anything, we should just land. A day or two later I was back at my best level. I wasn't even thinking about it anymore. I needed to get back on the horse. When I started flying again, I decided to start in Colombia because the thermals are smooth, it's not big mountains, you usually don't get strong wind. It's flyable every day and you get a lot of stress-free hours. I also went down to an EN C glider. It helped to fly something less demanding. We have to live with the fact that paragliding is dangerous. Sometimes you get unlucky. We have to either accept that risk or go home. I decided I have to accept it, because everything I love is out there."
Tom De Dorlodot

"Particularly related to paragliding, I think there are a number of layers of fear. Before we launch there's relevant fear. We have relevant fear when we look at the forecast and the conditions and we decide to launch or not to launch. "If I launch in these conditions I might die" – that's a good fear. Almost all the fear we experience after that point, once we get in the air, is pretty irrelevant. But it makes sense that we continue to have fear, because we're human beings and we're strapping ourselves into an ultralight climbing harness, tying it with 8mm lines to thin nylon and going to 18,000ft! It makes sense that we'd have fear.

We've all probably experienced some level of agoraphobia when we fly, a feeling of total helplessness at some point. It's hard-wired in us. It's tied to that basic fear of being out on the prairie with lions. We're totally exposed in the sky, and subjecting our nervous systems to hundreds of thousands of years of programming that says we're not supposed to be doing what we're doing. Our nervous system is screaming that the lion is going to eat us.

But most of this layer of fear is irrational, and if you understand this you can recognize it and set it aside. Flying can get intense. If you go to a little kid and start shaking them, they're going to get scared. That's basically what happens to us. We get rocked around by invisible air. It's something physical that comes into contact with our nervous system, and our nervous system wants to protect us. Fear is totally natural, it's built into us, but that kind of fear is irrelevant to the decision you're going to make at the top of the next thermal.

I also think we hold some unexplained fears inside our bodies. For example, I get tension in my lower back sometimes when I'm flying, and usually some deep breathing makes it go away. But I can't pinpoint what the source of the fear is. The point is: once you're aware of what you're experiencing, it's usually not a problem anymore. That's different from experiencing fear and trying to pretend it doesn't exist."

Willi Canell

the thing that I loved the most scared the absolute shit out of me. When I started flying again, as soon as I'd hit just the slightest bit of turbulence, I'd have to go land. I was a nervous wreck. Psychologically it was torture, because I felt like a gutless coward. I could remember how beautiful and amazing it used to be, and suddenly it scared me to death. Luckily my boyfriend kept pushing me and acted like it was no big deal, which I thought was really mean at the time, but if I hadn't had him pushing me, I'm not sure I would have been able to get back into it. In some ways he didn't allow me to be afraid; he kept insisting that it was no big deal and I had to just get over it. It took two or three years before every single little bump didn't totally freak me out. You have to acknowledge the fear and give it time. It takes a while to heal. A lot of people who have scary incidents just quit, so having people around you who encourage but don't push is important."

Kari Castle

"The day after I tumbled my hang glider in Elsinore, California, I flew and everything seemed fine. Then I flew all weekend and everything still felt fine. Then I went to Florida and flew in some comps, and those went really well and I figured I was totally ok. I'd had a pretty major accident, destroyed a brand new $12,000 glider and gotten really lucky, but I didn't seem very rattled. But then we went to Colorado, and as soon as we got back into the mountains and bumpy air, I was really, really scared. Every time I'd get in the air and feel a little bump, something that normally wouldn't even register, I'd get freaked out and land. This was when a group of us started filming a project called the Rhythm of Flight, so we were traveling constantly and flying as much as possible. I kept flying, but I remained really scared. I would have full-on black-outs in the air. I'd be flying in a comp and doing really well, I'd be out front leading, and I'd hit a little bit of bad air and then take a terrible sinky line all the way to the ground. I'd be on the ground and have no idea what had just happened. It was like I'd lost conscious thought for a chunk of the flight. I never stopped flying, even when I knew it was going to be a rowdy day. Sometimes I'd last ten minutes, sometime I'd last an hour. But I kept trying because I still loved flying. It took three years to get over it. I couldn't even watch the video of the tumble for two years. It was too traumatic and would bring it all back. Eventually what really helped was flying in competitions. When the air would get a bit bumpy but there were a lot of other pilots around me, it helped me realize my fears were irrational. Seeing other pilots flying happily along not bothered by something that was bothering me helped me set my fear to the side, and eventually the fear subsided."
Wolfi Siess

"Before the earthquake in Nepal in 2015, flying was the epicenter of my life. But after the earthquake, because the country was so broken and husband Jamie and I were so dedicated to the relief efforts, I didn't fly for almost a year. When I started flying again, I was really shocked – it was so scary. I just couldn't get comfortable. Any little bits of turbulence would make me really nervous, which was something I hadn't experienced before. It's been helpful to hear others say the same has happened to them after a long break. You get the currency back; it just takes time and patience."
Isabella Messenger

"When it comes to safety, what I've learned is that fear is often a good thing and often we need to listen to it more rather than less. It tells us when we're at the edge of our abilities. However, fear about irrational things can be debilitating, and we have to know how we react to fear. We're programmed to react to both the real and imagined danger with the same flight, fight or freeze response, so if we're the type who reacts to fear by freezing, that has to be addressed - SIV courses can really help. If you've had a seriously frightening experience, and are experiencing flashbacks, intrusive memories, or overwhelming feelings that are making

you avoid certain things you'd otherwise enjoy, then it might be worth considering seeing a psychologist with experience in treating PTSD. The best treatments currently are trauma-informed cognitive behavioral therapy, and EMDR."
Hugh Miller

"It's important to learn what kind of person you are and how you react to fear. Some people freeze up and need to learn how to react calmly through training. Other people get hit with adrenaline and react more quickly and make better decisions. If you're the kind of person who freezes, you have to move slowly, and it helps a lot to have a coach on the radio so they can talk you through the moves. Learning and practicing acro will help people learn how to deal with fear. Doing your first full stalls is scary for everyone, but after you do it and understand what's going on, and your mind starts to understand that they really are not a big deal, a trust in your gear develops and that removes a lot of the fear. After you stall several hundred times, it becomes a maneuver that doesn't cause any fear at all.

Acro training has removed fear from my cross-country training. I know exactly how much buffer I need everywhere I am in every kind of condition."
Cody Mittanck

"I've been fascinated with nature vs nurture for a long time. Unfortunately we nurture girls to be fearful. Parents push their little boys to take risks on the playground and to get outside their comfort zone, but little girls are urged to be careful and be safe. Parents think they're protecting their little girls, but really what they're doing is robbing them of all the lessons that we get when we take risk: decision-making, confidence, teamwork and so many of the great life-lessons that we acquire when we leave our comfort zone."
Caroline Paul

"Paragliders themselves are incredibly easy to fly. The problem is the red line can be crossed in a split second, and the red line is different for everyone. You're in the air, conditions change just a bit, and it's instantly terrifying. I

"If things get spicy and you start to get scared you've got two options. You can run and hide and go land. Or you can tackle it head on. You can say to yourself: "Holy shit, this is awful!" or you can say to yourself: "Right on! This is why I'm here!" The difference between these two perceptions is nothing more than a choice of what's going on between your ears. Attitude is everything. You can flip a switch and have a different experience. In our sport you can't not be where you are. Wishing for something isn't going to magically get you on the ground. You've got a choice – you can be miserable and scared, or you can choose to accept where you're at and accept the opportunity for the adventure you're in. If you're in danger that's one thing, but if it's just fear and discomfort, that's a choice. Fear is just an emotion, and you can control it."
Jeff Shapiro

think the most valuable thing to learn is when not to go. What all pilots need to establish is a healthy respect for what we're doing. Respect is different from fear. Mother Nature is stronger than we are, we can't fight her. First we have to become one with the wing, then we have to become one with our environment."
Max Fanderl

"I had a pretty scary incident at the end of last summer in the Wallis, near Zermatt, Switzerland, where I threw my reserve and had to get a helicopter to pluck me off the side of a cliff. I was unhurt and everything worked out fine, but when I came back to flying the next spring I had a lot more fear than I'd ever had, and it caught me by surprise. I viewed the collapse that led to throwing my rescue as the same thing as a crash; it bothered me that I'd let it happen, because it meant I really was missing important skills. Flying just isn't fun for me right now. Thermals scare me. I had a nine-hour 235km triangle in Bir, India, earlier this year, but I was scared the whole time. I'm still flying, but it's just not the same. I tell my students that if you have an accident in flying or you get really scared, there's a good chance you're not going to come back to it. Flying isn't skiing or bike-riding – it's much harder to wipe the dust off and keep going. If you approach flying step by step it doesn't have to be scary, but it's easy to get overconfident."
Bernhard Kalin

"I've been flying year round and getting over 500 hours a year for the last few years, but even now when I'm really current and flying confidently, I'll have a small blowout several thousand feet over the ground on a glider that I've done a ton of stalls on where there's really no danger whatsoever, and my heart will be racing and my breath will be short. It's just a fear response. It's natural, but it's irrational. I'm in no danger at all. Breathing slowly and deeply, whooping and hollering with your friends, or simply taking stock of the beauty of your surroundings can all help mitigate irrational fear."
Mitch Riley

"At the Superfinal in Colombia in 2013, I lost control and cascaded over 1,000m into the jungle below without being able to throw my reserve. Remarkably, I was unhurt physically.

Afterwards, every time I would fly I would get so scared I wished I could press a button to get on the ground. I was terrified. Gin knew I was really struggling and suggested I fly the Boomerang X-Alps, which was a lightweight glider and much easier to fly than the comp wings I was used to.

Flying a mellower glider really helped me heal. It made flying fun again. The fear still comes back; even after all these years the accident haunts me. I need a plan now when I fly. If I have a goal then the fear stays at bay, but when I have no plan and I start to get bored the fear comes back."
Joanna Di Grigoli

"Breathe slowly and deeply, and immerse your senses in your surroundings." Photo: Nick Greece

Rab

Obsession

DUSTIN MARTIN

In 2012, Dustin Martin beat out world number one Jonny Durand in Texas to go further than anyone ever has on a hang glider: 761km. The record still holds.

Dustin began his flying career in his early teens with radio-controlled airplanes, and his love and interest in the sky hasn't abated since. From RC he graduated to working in a sailplane club, saving up tow tokens that eventually allowed him to go solo. But his first flight in a hang glider at the age of 15 led to him being fired by his bosses. Hang gliding became an obsession that didn't allow for much on the side, and that continues to be the case to this day.

Having said that, Dustin has recently been bitten by the paragliding bug and, like his good friend Jeff Shapiro, has quickly become one to watch. Every time I interview a hang gliding Jedi, I realize how little I know.

Dustin, before we get to Texas and your history I've got to ask about your tear-drop shaped helmet, which I see a lot of hang glider pilots using. Are we paragliders missing a trick here?

I feel pretty confident in saying no. What makes a difference is having equipment that is relatively equal to those you are trying to keep up with, but small things like aerodynamic helmets add up to nothing. A bunch of us spent an awful lot of time tweaking tiny things like this and in all our testing it's never made a noticeable difference.

It all comes down to the line you fly. That's what makes a real difference – finding a good line. There's certainly a psychological advantage to being on 'the best' wing and 'the best' equipment. You have to feel confident with your gear, but the little stuff is imperceptible.

You started flying radio-controlled planes when you were a kid. Do you think that background helped you when you started flying hang gliders?

Absolutely. I quite often find myself imagining how I'm flying from the perspective of an RC pilot stood on the ground, if that makes sense? I think this ability to visualize

> **"I tried to go to a comp in Canada, but the border police actually didn't let me into the country because they said I didn't have enough money."**

in this way gives you a leg up on figuring it all out. I'm constantly relating in my mind what's happening to me and my glider – centering thermals, finding beneficial lines, from the perspective of being on the ground. It's definitely helped. My years of flying RC gliders has also translated directly into my flying hang gliders. I can't say exactly how, but it does something to your hand-eye coordination.

After RCs, you got into sailplanes?
Yes, when I was 14 years-old I got a job at a sailport in Arizona, making 50 cents a tow and $2 an hour. At the end of each day I'd try to get an instructional flight with one of the pilots. Then at the end of each month, I'd get handed a print-out of a negative check, because I never earned enough to pay for the flights!

I went solo when I was 15, but by then I'd already become fascinated by hang gliding. Back then you only found out about it through magazines and the yellow pages. Hang gliding in Arizona back then was a really big deal. It was 1996, and though hang gliding globally was on the decline, it was still a super-vibrant and active community.

I got fired from the sailport for just general jack-assery, and then met an instructor named Bill Holmes, who's still around instructing today. As soon as I got a little taste for hang gliding I just got completely obsessed. I borrowed a beginner glider in 1997, and between my school lessons I flew and got thrown off every sketchy no-wind cliff launch in this entire area. Luckily I got through all that mostly unscathed.

I didn't have any intention to step up to a more advanced glider, but then I saw a guy on a Moyes Xtralite and just thought it was the sexiest thing I'd ever laid eyes on. I just had to have that glider! Not just any Xtralite, but **that** Xtralite.

I stalked that guy around for an entire season trying to get him to sell it to me. Finally, after he'd put a ton of hours on it, he realized he had a sucker and let me take a test flight on it. By today's standards it's a pretty tame intermediate glider, but back then it was incredibly fast and scary. As soon as I'd launched, the speed and the sound of the air going past the wing was just terrifying. But I managed to do a couple of 180s without too much trouble and landed on my feet, and that was it, that was my glider.

How did you go from those early days to breaking the world record?
Shortly after getting that glider I started to have some success with cross-country flying and got a call from Ken Brown, who was the US distributor for Moyes. In 1998 Ken

offered to give me his used comp gliders, gliders that fully sponsored pilots would use for a season or two. This was about the time the first good topless gliders were starting to come out, which cost $8,000. I was getting really top-end equipment for free and I felt like the luckiest guy on Earth.

So Ken kept me in gliders, and I got a little funding to travel to my first comps from here in Arizona up north. I flew my first comp in Chelan, and then I tried to go to a comp in Canada, but the border police actually didn't let me into the country because they said I didn't have enough money. They said 200 bucks, or whatever I had, wasn't enough to live for two weeks. I kept saying: "Well, you don't know me!"

I got a hotel at the border and tried again the next day and luckily that time they let me through. I was driving an '84 Chevy Bonneville that was really clapped out. It was one of those cars where you hit a speed bump and it would bounce up and down for the next half-hour. It was pretty ridiculous.

But the flying and the competition up there was incredible. There were pilots from all over the world and it seemed like a pretty big deal. I learned a ton, and then incredibly ended up in second place. I tend to have my best days when I have the lowest expectations and the lowest confidence in my abilities, and back then I had no idea what I was doing - I was just hanging back and staying high, and it worked out.

After that Ken offered to fly me down to Australia to work at the Moyes factory, which was pretty much like winning the lottery. Working at Moyes and learning how to sew really helped me understand how our machines work. I'm sure that experience translates into better flying.

Was there an 'Aha!' moment in this period, something that clicked that allowed you to take a leap?

I don't think so. It was just pure obsession. Anybody can be pretty good at this sport. But to get really good at it requires total obsession. When you look at guys like Manfred Ruhmer, or Christian Ciech, or Alex Ploner, it's just total. I've never gotten to that level. I had that obsession for a long time, and I'm very thankful for that time, but there's some last plateau that those top guys reach that requires something that only a few pilots are willing to give.

When I got back from Australia in 2001, I got invited to join the Wills Wing team, even though I'd taken a break from competing. I was still a young guy and I hadn't grown up seeing accidents and people die, and seeing some of that had punctured some of my enthusiasm. But as soon as I joined Wills Wing, those guys were so incredibly stoked and energized by hang gliding, you just got pulled into it. Seeing their passion rekindled my own. I didn't consider myself a professional hang glider pilot until one year doing my taxes I realized I'd spent over $10,000 on plane tickets!

So you got back into comps?

I jumped back in pretty regularly in 2003. I competed in most of the Worlds that I was interested in doing until pretty recently. Now I'm not very interested in the big comps. I just don't find them very peaceful and fun. The gaggles are pretty intense, and it just doesn't fit the kind of flying I like to do.

Getting to base at 17,999ft above the massive expanse of the Utah desert, USA
Photo: Wolfgang Siess

How does chasing the world record start to come into the scene? I just got back from chasing big distance in the Sertão in Brazil and I wouldn't exactly call that 'peaceful' flying! It sounds a bit like Texas. There's a lot of waiting around for days and days with very little to do, all-night drives on sketchy roads, terrible food, crazy heat, and then when you do hook a good day even the best pilots can bomb out early.
It's an interesting contrast between chasing big distance and flying competitions for sure. I don't mind a bit of personal suffering. And when it comes to heat, I'm from Phoenix! When I showed up in Texas in 2012 it was 106 degrees Fahrenheit and that was a cool relief compared to Phoenix – I can hang out in 106 all day long! The suffering doesn't bother me, nor do the hours in the harness.

What I don't like is being scared. The day of the record there were a couple spikes of fear from being too low, but for the most part it was a completely safe day. It was the complete opposite of turning circles with 50 of your friends in every thermal all the way to goal. Flying gaggles is one thing on a paraglider when you just have to worry about not hitting somebody. In hang gliding we have another dimension: wake. And it can really throw you. So, you have to worry about not hitting anyone, but then also losing control from hitting wake, and then not being able to avoid the next pilot. It takes an incredible amount of strength and focus to fly in gaggles, especially in weak air when everyone is shallow-banked. That's a scary that I just don't enjoy.

You flew 761km in Texas when you broke the world record. How did you get Jonny in the end?

We were flying together for much of the day, but we were both on our own program. This wasn't an attempt to share a world record. We were very much trying to beat each other. Very late in the day we were wingtip to wingtip around Big Springs, over 400 miles out. Then I got lucky and slipped into a better climb at the beginning of a cloud street and just pulled the ladder up on him. And that turned into miles of separation.

Every cloud in front of me was dissipating and I just figured it was too late for him, there was no way he could catch me. But then about 7pm, just as I was passing the previous record of 438 miles and feeling pretty good about things, I looked back through the humidity and haze and there's a glider pointed at me! Jonny is a pretty imposing pilot when you're going head to head and the stakes are that high. He's a better climber and he's really good at flying lines, so at that point I'd kind of resigned myself that I was going to get beat.

But I was feeling really fresh. I was happy in my harness, I was hydrated and I'd been eating all day, and I was feeling good. All I really wanted at that point was a beer! And luckily at that time of the day the air is really easy, it's all going up and it's not very technical. You don't have to be a genius to get a good line. And Jonny was definitely showing a lot of signs of fatigue. He kept rocking up in his harness, stretching his neck, shaking his arms. And he was filming. He'll remind you, if you ask him, that he lost that flight because he was filming.

I'm convinced now, after chasing it in Texas and watching the seasons down there, that getting a day like we did comes around very, very rarely. I used to think there were probably a few days like that every year and you just had to be there and commit, but I think the reality is those perfect days happen maybe only once every few years. So being in the air on the right day also comes down to a lot of luck, and that's how I ended up getting Jonny in the end – I just got a little more luck.

Did getting the record do anything for you professionally?

Getting the record was cool, and getting the recognition feels good to a point, but I wasn't interested in using it for promotion. It certainly doesn't hurt to have the world record, but I went down there to fly 500 miles. I even had a declared goal right up the street from where we landed so it was a little disappointing to get so close, at 471 miles and not get it. But I wasn't doing it for the promotion. It's nice to have and it's nice to finally beat Jonny at something he's so good at.

Let's get into some technical stuff. Your good hang gliding friend Jeff Shapiro, who's also been getting into paragliding more recently, was flying in Brazil with me last week, and one thing we all noticed was how good Jeff is at flying in really light air. Do hang gliders have special knowledge that paragliders don't?

I'm guessing that ability comes from two main things. The first is two or more decades of thermal mapping that Jeff's learned flying a hang glider, which translates directly to flying a paraglider as you're basically doing the same thing. Being able to track and map in your head what the thermal is doing helps keep you off the ground. The second is

"Most people can get good at flying, but to get really good requires total obsession."
Photo: Wolfgang Seiss

that his home site is Missoula, Montana, where it can often be really tough to get up. There are always inversions and shears, and it's probably a very good place to train.

What about finding good lines and avoiding sink?

Hang gliders and paragliders have relatively terrible performance. We're all bad compared to sailplanes. What we all learn from the books is when you're in bad sink you turn 45 degrees and speed up. There are times when that works but other times it doesn't. Sometimes you have to be a lot more aggressive than that but zigzagging around all over the place is very inefficient, and maybe it's better to just keep flying straight and hope you get another climb.

When there's clouds it's pretty easy – the sky is showing you where to go – but when it's blue there's a lot more stumbling around, and I'm not convinced there's a hard rule that works.

In competitions there are a lot of pilots who only fly course line and do very little hunting around, and more often than not that works out. I'm the opposite – I do a lot of hunting around, and in my experience that has penalized me more often than the pilots who just fly straight.

When you definitely have to be aggressive about leaving sink is when you're flying in the flatlands in a lot of wind. If you hit strong sink in a strong tailwind, you have to leave it aggressively or you'll be on the deck.

Honestly, though, there's a level of magic when it comes to finding good lines that some pilots figure out that is pretty impossible to teach or describe.

I'm still very confused these days about how much bar to use when going downwind. You guys can fly MacCready, but what are we supposed to do?
Now we're getting into religion! When it comes to speed-to-fly with wind, nothing changes. It's exactly the same speed-to-fly whether it's nil wind, a headwind or a tailwind.

> **"Now we're getting into religion! When it comes to speed-to-fly with wind, nothing changes. It's exactly the same speed to fly whether it's nil wind, a headwind or a tailwind."**

If you're trying to maximize your average cross-country speed over the course of the day, your aircraft is only capable of a certain speed through a given parcel of air. I don't alter my speed whether there's a headwind or tailwind unless I'm on final glide and I have to arrive with a certain amount of height. So in other words, fly best speed-to-fly based on next thermal strength. If your destination is the next thermal, then you're flying the best speed-to-fly. If your destination is a point on the ground then that's the only time it changes.

So in other words, when things are working, fly as fast as you can.

If you look at the polars of your wing, the day might be saying to fly a little slower to get a better glide, but if you're with a gaggle and they are flying at top speed, they will hit a climb a little earlier than you, and you're going to lose them. Each climb and glide you'll fall a little farther back, and over the course of a day that adds up to a ton of distance. If you're racing, you have to stay with the gaggle, especially earlier in the race. If it's a 15-thermal course, you want to work together for the first 13.

Now that you are getting into flying paragliders a bit, is there something you've learned in all these years of hang gliding that paragliders don't know?
What I have to share is the same thing I'd share with new hang gliding pilots, and that's to check your ego. Every once in a while you have to step back and realize that, regardless of what we're flying, we're all flying super-ultralight aircraft that are pretty unforgiving. So check the passion every once in a while, and show a high level of respect for an activity that is a lot more unforgiving than other things we do.

If you could go back to your 50-hour self, would you change anything?
I wouldn't want to change a single thing for fear of changing everything! I wouldn't want to change a single breath.

HOW TO NAVIGATE INTERMEDIATE SYNDROME

I don't know any pilot who hasn't gone through intermediate syndrome: that period in our flying careers where we think we're better than we are. I don't have the statistics to back it up, but I'm sure most accidents in our sport happen to pilots in this phase. I've always loved the 'luck jar' analogy to describe intermediate syndrome. You have two jars: the experience jar, and the luck jar. When we take our first flight, the luck jar is full and the experience jar is empty. Every time we get lucky, a coin transfers from the luck jar to the experience jar. Every pilot has an unknown number of coins to begin, but inevitably the luck jar runs out, and we can only compensate for the lack of luck with experience. Many things contribute to intermediate syndrome, but ego seems to be the king sitting on the house of cards. When do we advance out of intermediate syndrome? Recent data suggests even pilots who have 2,000 hours are still well in the 'intermediate' phase, and of course all hours are not the same. Ridge soaring in laminar air by the ocean is not the same as flying in the Himalaya. My guess is very, very few pilots have advanced beyond the trappings of intermediate syndrome.

"I think there are trappings for a pilot at any level of progression. In your first years, intermediate syndrome is when you think you're a better pilot than you actually are. But the reality is you're in over your head and you're basically an under-qualified, overconfident pilot.

For more experienced pilots, it's called 'expert halo', where you feel invincible because you think you know it all, you're really proficient and you've proven to yourself that you're a solid pilot. So you continue to push into more and more dangerous situations because you think you can handle them.

Ideally you have some incidents when you're a beginner that don't have much consequence. These scary moments will force you to take a step back, develop more humility and respect for flying, and remind you to always be a student of the sport.

At times I've had a little bit of intermediate syndrome and gotten over my head. Pretty much everyone goes through this phase at some point, and it's a dangerous phase. But remember that flying remains dangerous at every phase."

Matt Beechinor

"Before you take off you have to remember that you're the pilot in command and you've got to make the right call every time. No one learning how to ski would follow an expert skier into a couloir between two cliffs. You could be watching a pilot make something look really easy on a really gnarly day, but that guy is Chrigel. To get to that kind of level takes a really long time, no matter how much talent a person has.

Just be careful when you start feeling too much like Superman. In my early days I definitely went through periods of irrational confidence and irrational fear. You have to be careful on both ends of that spectrum. If you're irrationally scared you have to back off and figure out what exactly is causing the fear. You can't be flying around thinking the glider is going to kill you. But you can't be flying around thinking you're invincible either, because sooner or later you'll get a potentially ugly reminder."
Honza Rejmanek

"In the accident curve, there's a noticeable blip at about 100 hours. This is the point we see pilots start to push and get overconfident."
Antoine Laurens

"Forget the numbers or competing with your friends. Become a whole pilot. Learn to enjoy the sport the way you want to enjoy it!"
Tom de Dorlodot

"Something I see a lot of are the people who are new to the sport and are really excited. We veterans of the sport can totally relate: we've all been there, we know how exciting it is when you first learn. But keen pilots get way ahead of themselves. They want to fly cross country, they want to do acrobatics, but they don't even know how to take off safely yet, and they don't know anything about the air. They need to slow down. Some people you can talk to and reason with, and some people are pretty bull-headed. They either get through it and figure it out... or they don't."
Kari Castle

INTERMEDIATE SYNDROME CHECKLIST

Do you agree with the following? If not, it's time to dig deeper....

1. I fly in thermic conditions, and regularly fly maneuvers and refresh my SIV skills regularly to keep current.
2. I always do a site and weather assessment, however late I am or whatever pressure I feel to launch soon.
3. I watch myself if I feel a tendency to critcise others' flying without recognising any tendency in myself to fly similarly.
4. I'm never over-confident in my wing's stability, even if it's very collapse-resistant (like a two-liner). My frequent SIV training reminds me of my ability level.
5. I never think, 'if they can fly in this, so can I'. And I never follow others in the air without making my own decisions.
6. I never ignore or override a gut feeling around a sense of danger.
7. I always appreciate the views of others - I think they're trying to be helpful, rather than criticising or belittling me.
8. I always recognize the potential to feel overconfident - an 'Icarus effect' that is common in flying.

GARMIN
RECCO
SALEWA
Red Bull
X-alps
SALZBURG TO MONACO 2015
SALEWA
GARMIN VIRB
USA1

The Meteorologist

HONZA REJMANEK

Czech-born pilot Honza Rejmanek competed in the Red Bull X-Alps between 2007 and 2015. He's the only US athlete to get on the podium, finishing third in his second race, and Honza then realized his dream of reaching Monaco in his fifth and last campaign in 2015.

Cross Country magazine readers know Honza through his long-running meteorology column, but I know him because of his ties to Sun Valley. When he moved here in 2000, flying cross country wasn't common. Even though some hugely talented pilots had lived there – Robbie Whittall, Nate Scales, Othar Lawrence, Chris Santacroce, Dave Bridges – they usually chose not to fly in the extreme midday conditions.

Then a long-haired, wild-eyed, twenty-something misfit turned up to fly tandems for the local commercial operation, and changed the way flying was done here. Honza flew every minute he could, and began flying really deep lines that had never been considered.

The stories of Honza's frugality are legend. He knew where to get free bread for himself and the tandem pilots that he camped out with in summer, and he'd help out in a local pizza joint, getting paid in pizza and beer. When Honza started flying far enough to need to pee in the air, and couldn't afford condom catheters, he built his own system with a scrap of garden hose and a turkey baster. It had mixed results. To maintain mental clarity for his six-hour Sun Valley bronco rides, he'd eat a ribeye steak just before take-off, grilled on top of Mt Baldy.

When Honza joined us for a few days on a vol-biv expedition across the Sierra range in California in 2012, I saw him do at least 50 backflips and ninja rolls over a raging campfire – after drinking a fifth of whiskey. The next morning his soot-covered face stuck out of his rolled-up wing as he snored happily.

These days Honza has toned things down a bit to become a responsible adult. He left Sun Valley to do an advanced degree in meteorology at the University of California, and he's now married with two children. The eldest, Martin, has done some long tandem vol-biv trips with his dad over the last few summers in the Alps. I've never met anyone more excited by flying, nor anyone as knowledgeable

> **"Ask yourself: 'If something happens in the next five minutes and I need to be on the ground, what's my plan?'"**

about weather. We sat down together to explore how to improve our flying by understanding the atmosphere.

Honza, in one X-Alps, we were both racing towards the Matterhorn turnpoint. We were dealing with a ton of headwind that day and I read somewhere you specked out by flying in wave. Let's start there: what is wave, and can paragliders fly in it?
In order to have wave you need stable air, you need wind, and you need something to perturb it. A good way of thinking about wave is if you have a smooth-bottomed river but there's one boulder, it'll form an undulation downstream that will rise much higher than the boulder itself. So yes, sometimes paragliders can use waves, but the wind is near the limit of what a paraglider would want to fly in. Of course, sailplanes and some high-performance hang gliders use wave regularly. The amazing thing about wave is that it reaches much higher than the terrain that induces it.

On day eight of the 2015 X-Alps I was just getting to the eastern edge of the Aletsch glacier, the longest in Europe. I climbed to about 4,000m because I wanted a lot of height before crossing to make sure I didn't land out, and I was pretty deep back towards the Eiger, which was to my north. As I went on glide across the glacier, I was punching into pretty strong wind, but there was widespread light and very smooth lift. Maybe 0.5m/s. After a while I was getting above most of the cumulus cloud tops, which weren't developing very deep. I realized I was flying in wave, and I really wished I had a little more time to see how high I could take it!

Eventually I continued to punch forward and ultimately dropped back out of it at about 4,400m, so I didn't take it very high. It was remarkably smooth. But it wasn't thermal lift – it was like ridge soaring on a really shallow hill where you just keep going up and up and up.

And how did you know you were in wave instead of widespread convergence?
My first thought was that it was just a big thermal tapering out. It took a while for it to dawn on me that it had to be wave. Convergence is typically pretty rowdy, and this air wasn't like that at all, so it definitely wasn't convergence. On a day with cumulus, an area of convergence would have had plenty of cumulus overhead. In this case I got above the tops of the shallow cumulus clouds. Thermals top out because they hit either an inversion or at least a very stable layer, and the top of lift itself doesn't have to be the same everywhere. I think

there was a bit of a dip over the large glacier area, and as I punched upwind I flew from the top of a thermal over the terrain into the stable layer above it over the glacier. Once I was in the stable layer, that airmass was all moving up. If it hadn't been the X-Alps, I would have kept going up to see how far I could go, but as I got higher the headwind kept getting stronger, and it wasn't efficient for the direction I needed to fly: west.

You've told me before that there's a really common misconception about how air moves over the terrain. Can you break that down for us?
Something that took me a while to figure out is what we see as the terrain is not exactly what the air sees. Terrain can be fairly complicated, and the air tries to smooth it out to a certain extent. On the upwind side of things it will create a stagnation zone, a little high-pressure area. This is almost like when you get a bunch of drops on a car windshield and you can see certain drops will go to the left, others go to the right, and some go right over the top if you don't have your windshield wipers on. And there's also a point where there's almost no movement at all. This is more evident on not very aerodynamic cars whose windshields aren't too slanted.

In this upwind side stagnation zone the air can be fairly still, even on something like a nicely shaped volcano. This can be deceiving if you happen to be a little below the summit on the upwind side. If you can't hike all the way to the top of the mountain to see how strong the wind is, and you plan on launching partway up, it's not a bad idea to walk to the crosswind side, to get a feel for the conditions and avoid a nasty surprise. The flip side of this scenario is that if you get to the top of the mountain and it's too windy to fly, it might be potentially safe to fly lower down. This would only be reasonable if there's a wind gradient and only the top is getting really strong wind. But if you're making your way down, check the crosswind side.

If you hike a thousand feet down on the upwind side, you might find almost non-existent wind and think it's reasonable to launch. But if you traverse at that same elevation to the crosswind side, and you find that it's blowing hard, you'll realize that you were being fooled by the upwind stagnation zone. All kinds of features can create this. In the 2015 X-Alps, after we got the Zugspitze turnpoint, I hiked up to a spot where I had almost no wind, almost nothing to even bring a glider up. And only 200m above me and off on a shoulder maybe 2km away, Tom de Dorlodot called me and said it was ridiculously strong, and he couldn't believe I was even thinking about launching.

I knew that once I launched I'd be flying into a river of wind, but it seemed like the transition wouldn't be that crazy, and it ended up being ok. Tom and a couple other pilots who were with him ended up hiking down to my spot to launch, and we all made some distance that day.

The takeaway is that even on the upwind side of terrain, you aren't necessarily feeling the true wind. A good example of this is when we look at the leading edge of a paraglider; we see something that's got a hole in it. But the wind sees a closed leading edge. This is the reason guys can stand up and pee out of their harness – because they're actually peeing out of the stagnation zone. Even though you're traveling into the wind, there's a small zone that's safe. But be careful, because if you screw it up you're going to piss on your face!

Let's talk about gust fronts. Ideally, we don't fly on days that have a chance of dangerous overdevelopment. But let's face it, if we only flew perfect days, that would take a lot of days off the table. And on a lot of days that do OD, you still can have a safe, workable window before it goes ballistic. How do you assess gust fronts, and how does your assessment change depending on where you are flying?
One thing to keep in mind is that a lot can change in 20 minutes because of the scale of convection. Fifteen to 20 minutes is generally the turnover time that a thermal takes to go from the ground to the top of lift. So that means a thunderstorm cloud parcel of air could have been near the ground, and only 15 minutes later it's up 10 to 12km above the ground. That's a radical movement in a very short period of time. If you watch a

> **"Every experience you have builds on your ability to create a better model."**

time-lapse video of a thunderstorm, it's amazing to see how much can change in just 15-20 minutes.

So I would certainly not advocate flying when it's really starting to blow up. During the growing phase of a thunderstorm, you have to be far enough away so you don't get sucked up. When it's a real storm that's starting to build, we can be confetti to a vacuum cleaner, and short of being able to free fall away, you might not be able to get out. Think about the force that's required to create proper, big hail. Hail starts out as rain that gets sucked back up into the storm and freezes, then it falls down under its own weight, only to be sucked up again, and recoated. This cycle can repeat many times, until in extreme cases you have hail that's bigger than a baseball. If you get stuck in a thunderstorm, you've made several mistakes along the way.

What kind of climb rate are we talking about in cloud suck[1]? Like the one that Eva[2] got caught in? Are we talking 20m/s?
Sometimes it can be 30m/s or even more. In the most extreme cells, the ones that you get in the US Midwest that cause tornadoes that make baseball-sized hail, ascent rates can top out at 60m/s. That's a 120mph vertical wind going straight up. That would suspend a sky diver if he was in the prone position. Those kinds of systems can almost

[1] Cloud suck is a phenomenon commonly known in paragliding, hang gliding, and sailplane flying where pilots experience significant lift due to a thermal under the base of cumulus clouds, especially towering cumulus and cumulonimbus. The vertical extent of a cumulus cloud is a good indicator of the strength of lift beneath it, and the potential for cloud suck. Cloud suck most commonly occurs in low pressure weather and in humid conditions

touch the stratosphere. 99% of weather is in the troposphere[3], and then above that there's the tropopause[4], which is a very stable layer, and then there's the stratosphere, which is like a massive inversion and is the reason no clouds go that high. But the really massive cells can shoot up another 5,000m into the stratosphere before they come to a true halt. That's the most extreme case, but it happens. Large volcanic eruptions like Krakatoa can inject fine dust into the stratosphere!

If you're flying around and you start seeing virga, there's the potential for a gust front. In drier locations, there's also the potential for a microburst. If cloudbase is quite high (cloudbase in desert regions can be 3,000m or more above the ground) and rain is falling but not reaching the ground, it means all the rain is evaporating as it falls. This evaporative cooling makes the air even more negatively buoyant, and it picks up speed as it falls. It becomes a bomb of air that might be a kilometer across; it can hit the ground and send 40mph-plus wind in every direction.

If you get caught in a situation like this and you're lucky enough to be flying over a dry desert so you can see the dust from the microburst, you might be better off staying high. Same goes if you're flying in the mountains; if you start seeing virga, or you're getting rain and the sky is changing fast, it's probably much safer to land as soon as you can up high, because getting to the valley could take 10 minutes or more, and that could be a problem. If it's not that extreme, you might be able to fly away from it. Especially if you're not downwind of it. If you're crosswind of it and the wind aloft isn't very strong, a modern paraglider can do 50 to 60km/h, and that can be enough to escape.

It really depends greatly on the terrain and the air you're in. Are the valleys wide so they can handle more air, or narrow so the air can get really accelerated? And visibility is very important for monitoring the sky. If you're in the desert and the air is dry, you can see 50-80km on most days, and you can watch what's happening from a safe distance. But in the Alps it's much more humid, and the air is laden with fine dust or aerosols, and visibility is reduced. And the valleys are complicated and narrow. There, taking on any kind of overdevelopment is much riskier. In the Alps you also typically have much lower cloudbase, so you could be in one valley and not even see a rain shaft or cumulonimbus in the next. In that kind of situation, you could have a cell drop out,

[2] On 14 February 2007 while practicing for a paragliding contest in Australia, Polish-born German team pilot Ewa Wisnierska-Cieslewicz was sucked into a cumulonimbus cloud, climbing at up to 20m/s (4,000ft per minute) to an altitude of 9,946m (32,600ft). She lost consciousness due to hypoxia, but regained consciousness after 30 minutes to an hour, and landed still covered in ice after a three-and-a-half hour flight. In the same storm, 42-year-old Chinese paraglider pilot He Zhongpin died after being sucked into the same storm system. He was struck by lightning at 5,900m (19,000ft). His body was found the next day 15km (about nine miles) from his last known position prior to entering the cloud.

[3] The troposphere is the lowest layer of Earth's atmosphere, and is also where nearly all weather conditions take place. It contains 75% of the atmosphere's mass and 99% of the total mass of water vapor and aerosols.The average height of the troposphere is 18km (11 miles or 59,000ft) in the tropics, 17km in the middle latitudes, and 6km (3.7 miles, 20,000ft) in the polar regions in winter. The total average height of the troposphere is 13km – about eight miles or 42,650ft.

[4] The tropopause is the boundary in the Earth's atmosphere between the troposphere and the stratosphere. It is an isothermal layer, marking the end of the troposphere. It lies, on average, at 17km (11 miles) above equatorial regions, and about 9km (5.6 miles) over the polar regions.

Honza and his son Martin on a multi-day self-supported tandem vol-biv in the Alps.
Photo: Martin Rejmanek

which sends a gust front down a valley, like a broken dam releasing water. That water has to go somewhere. Gust fronts are cold density currents. The strongest winds in a gust front run like water would. So usually the worst place to be is down low.

Are there visual cues to help you gauge the severity of overdevelopment?
Yes. Good clues are the size and darkness of the cloud, its vertical development, and whether the bottom is flat or concave. If it's a line of thunderstorms there might be no escape. But unless you're on a vol-biv or for some reason don't have access to the internet so you can look at weather, you should know about the chance of storms and how they'll track before you go flying. If you can check winds aloft at the 700mb level (about 3,000m) and the 500mb level (about 5,500-5,700m), then you know how a potential storm will be driven, and how fast. As the storm develops up through the troposphere, as it goes from ground up through 300 or 200mb (10-12km), you're not going to outrun it if it's moving towards you at 30km/h. Again it's important to realize things can change really fast. In a proper thunderstorm, you have cubic kilometers of air rising fast. A strong cell can switch normal valley winds, and when they really start to draw they can become monsters.

Thunderstorms aren't just fed by thermals. You've also got water vapor condensing into little droplets, which adds warmth, making the air ever more buoyant. A developing thunderstorm is like a self-stoking fire, except that humid air containing lots of water vapor is the fuel. The self-reinforcing cycle that occurs in a growing thunderstorm is like a runaway chain reaction. The warm air offsets the cooling as it rises, and the storm really starts to draw, even from shaded regions. I can't describe it, but just as thunderstorms start to build in your vicinity, there's a very strange feeling to the air. When you feel that, it's time to get on the ground fast.

There's a point when it's not a thunderstorm, but you're seeing big cumulus that are getting taller than they are wide. That's where everybody has to make their own call based on their skill level. As in any kind of flying, you have to have a series of escape plans at all times. You never venture into something without an escape. Ask yourself: "If something happens in the next five minutes and I need to be on the ground, what's my plan?"

I'm glad you brought up intuition there. I think especially when you're early and you're flying a site where there are a lot of other pilots, it gets pretty easy to be a lemming. "Well that guy is still in the air, so I'll stay in the air." When I was very new in Annecy, a big cell started developing to the north of the city. Most people went and landed, including us, but a lot of people didn't. And the cell just laid right back down. It was a non-event, and everyone that stayed in the air had the rest of the day to play with. We were bummed out, because we were new and didn't know that you should never kick yourself for making a decision like that. The next day we flew again and the sky seemed exactly the same to me. Same sized cell began to develop in the same location. So we and hundreds of other pilots decided to stay in the air. But it grew into a monster. Luckily my flying buddy and I were able to spiral to the ground before the meat of the gust front hit, but a lot of other pilots weren't and it got really ugly. People bouncing off roofs, landing in the trees – it was mayhem. I think it's really hard to gauge these things. It's better to play it on the safe side and listen to your gut. Honza, are there other tools we can use before we get in the air?

It's important not to be in a hurry when you get to launch. Take that 15-20 minutes while you're setting up to really observe what's going on. If there's a gust of any strength that you wouldn't want to launch into, or be in the air with, then you need to wait a reasonable period of time, at least 20 minutes, to make sure it's not repeating. You want to make sure conditions are calming and not strengthening. If it's questionable when you show up, don't even get your kit out. Go somewhere away from the group and sit down and watch everything and try to get a map in your head of what's going on. Is what you're feeling wind gusts or a thermal cycle? Gusts are typically shorter and abrupt. Thermals typically build and then back off over a much longer period.

What tools are you using for forecasting?

I use Windy.com a lot. Beyond the publicly available GFS model output, Windy purchases output from the ECMWF (the European Center for Medium-Range Weather Forecasts). The ECMWF uses a 9km global grid, which is more than double the resolution of GFS, so it can resolve smaller nuances in weather that's affected by

Honza Rejmanek and his support team during the Red Bull X-Alps in Chiavenna, Italy on 10 July 2015.
Photo: Kelvin Trautman / Red Bull Content Pool

large terrain. The advantage of GFS is that it updates four times a day, so you should use both and compare them. Windy also has finer-resolution regional model output. These regional models do a decent job of picking out potential thunderstorm development, large-scale convergence lines, surface gusts, and smaller-scale precipitation. It's a great tool. It doesn't have some things pilots like to know, like top of lift, but it's generally the tool I use the most.

A balloon sounding is more useful if the balloon goes up close to where you'll be flying at a time that's helpful. But even if that's not the case, they're still useful. They show you valuable things like the lapse rate and wind through the levels, and the temperature profile and the dew point profile. It's definitely good to know how to read a Skew-T diagram. That provides a good snapshot of the day. What's important isn't so much having the data that you get from a Skew-T, but what it means in your specific area. A professional forecaster in a certain area will get the model output and then apply statistical adjustments to a specific area. For example, a particular model could predict 5cm of rain, but that area never gets more than 2cm.

What we have to do as pilots is look at as many forecasts as we can, and compare them to what we see and feel in the air. It can take years to figure a place out. But after a while you can look at a forecast and a sounding and get a pretty good idea of the quality of the day.

Tell me about water and energy and how they relate.
Weather as we see it would be fairly boring if we didn't have water vapor in our atmosphere. Without water vapor you wouldn't get hurricanes. You wouldn't get thunderstorms or tornadoes. You'd have no rain. It takes a lot of energy to evaporate water. That's why a thin layer of sweat does a great job of keeping you cool as wind blows past you. When water condenses, it releases tremendous amounts of energy.

In a scientific sense, you don't see water vapor. It's a clear gas. If you're boiling tea, the water vapor is the clear part. Once you start seeing something, that's actually condensed tiny droplets. So a cloud is just countless tiny little droplets. Water vapor is basically the fuel for weather. Water vapor is the most common greenhouse gas, and creates the greenhouse effect just like adding CO_2, but it's the natural version. That's why in the tropics on a clear night it doesn't get cold, because the heat that was collected on the ground all day is radiated back down by the abundant water molecules in the humid skies above.

In other words, water vapor moderates temperature swings and that's why you see such large swings in dry areas. Lack of humidity is why dry areas have much higher cloudbase and much stronger climbs. This is because there's less water to evaporate from the surface. The surface gets hotter and heats the overlying air faster. To create buoyancy, you have to decrease density. In air you can do this either by heating it or by adding a lighter gas such as water vapor. However, it takes about twelve times as much energy to gain buoyancy by evaporating water into the air compared to simply heating the air directly.

Honza, can you explain blue holes from a meteorological standpoint?
If cumulus clouds are quite abundant and you see a blue hole, it means the thermals aren't reaching cloudbase. The same amount of air is going up as going down. It could be because of the underlying surface, or the way the convection is set up on that particular day. Unless you feel like you have the glide to make it across a blue hole, it might make sense to go around it. It can be tempting, because it might be getting a lot of sun and you think it will work, but to form a blue hole you have to have a lot of sinking air. The thermals are most likely lined up to feed the clouds on the periphery. Unless the blue hole is small, a deviation usually makes sense.

For those of us who aren't going to go as far as you have in meteorology, what are the important things we need to be using and understand when it comes to the weather?
Piloting has two complementary components: weather knowledge, and piloting skills. Up to a point, a deficiency in one can be compensated by the other, but a wise method of progression is to build the two together. Books like Understanding the Sky by Dennis Pagen and Thermal Flying by Burkhard Martens are fantastic, and there are many more. Will Gadd always talked about creating a model in your head for the weather and then refining that model each time you fly, and I think that's important. You need to understand the basics like pressure gradient, wind, stability, the big weather systems, the circulation around a high and a low. But a lot of the small-scale intricate behavior of weather, the stuff we mostly fly around in, we still don't really understand. That stuff isn't resolved in models. There's a lot of folklore about it and everyone

has a slightly different idea of what's going on. But even to this day, with all my meteorological background and schooling and real-world practice, I still show up to a site and am occasionally surprised and have to figure it out on the fly.

The most important thing is using your own observation and being able to develop a model of what's going on. That takes a lot of hours. Every experience you have builds on your ability to create a better model.

When I'm on launch and looking at the wind, I try to think of the three levels that are superimposed. There's the forecast wind – also known as the synoptic or meteo wind. That's what you see in the forecast that a model is going to show. Then there's the regional wind, which gets driven by things like the interface between the flatlands and the mountains. Those winds usually start developing at about 10 to 11am, depending on the day, as heat increases and elevated regions start to draw in the air. Lastly, there are the local wind effects created by things like thermals traveling up a slope. You could have as many distinct levels as you want; it's all really a continuum. If you think of it as three levels, you'll realize that any spot you're at, on a mountain or in a landing zone or in the sky, is being affected by every level.

For example, you could be on a west-facing slope in the afternoon and the forecast is calling for 10 knots of wind but you're feeling gusts to 25 knots. Regional wind and thermal cycles might both be superimposed on the seemingly light forecast wind, and the net result is wind that's too spicy. Or, you could be on a large east slope that's being heated and have nice morning thermals, but the plain-to-mountain circulation starts drawing in air from the west. Suddenly it's blowing over the back when you finally get set up to launch.

A lot of local effects depend on how strong the heating is on that particular day, which sides are facing into the sun, and the type of surface. All these levels come together to create the wind that you feel at any one particular spot. You can't be upset with a forecast if it's not panning out. These sub-grid scale features are not resolved in models, and you can't simply say the forecast was wrong. A global forecast just gives you wind at the largest of these three scales. A regional model with a finer grid size might resolve some wind down to the middle scale. Everything else plays a role and either adds or subtracts from the forecast. Then of course, there's a lot of channeling by the flow in certain areas. In some areas wind is reinforced and in some it's blocked. You can have 50% more wind and in some case 100% more wind on a ridge top just because of compression, especially early in the day before thermals start to mix things out. Air flows like a river. It separates, converges, it undulates. Most famous flying sites have their convergences sorted out, but if you're in a new place it's probably going to take a while to figure out. This intricate stuff is what meteorologists call sub-grid scale. The grid resolution of models is too coarse – it smoothens out the terrain way too much and doesn't pick up the nuances that really affect us as pilots.

It all comes back to building a personal mental model of what's going on. Is this the true wind that I'm feeling, or is it being accelerated because of compression or a venturi? If I hike lower and get out of the strong wind, is it safe to fly or will I be blown over the back? Every pilot has to assess and decide if the conditions suit their level, and I would recommend not just jumping into it. It's something that takes a long time to learn and it's better to build up this knowledge slowly.

You once told me an interesting observation on convergence.
I've learned that when it's really windy, sometimes the calmest wind on the ground is directly under the greatest lift overhead. If you aren't in dynamic lift, if it's too big to be a thermal and it's not wind hitting a mountain to cause the lift, then it's probably convergence. If it's really strong you've got two options. You can carry on with your flight and ride it up, or if it's just too strong and overwhelming and you don't want to land in strong wind, the calmest air is probably directly below you. It's a dicey proposition, because you have to go down directly through strong lift, but as you get near the ground the two winds will counteract one another. They'll create a calm zone, perhaps a kilometer wide, in the middle of two strong and opposing surface winds. These are not always the same strength, and the convergence line can tilt with height in the direction of the weaker wind. The slightly weaker wind creates an invisible ramp for the stronger wind.

Another "aha" moment I'd like to share: low saves are often the climbs that take you all the way to cloudbase. The reason these climbs are typically the strongest is that in order to have lift so close to the ground there has to be a lot of converging air near the surface. The lift is only going to get stronger as it goes up as the thermal accelerates. So when you get a low save, that thermal is likely to match or beat any climb of the day. You shouldn't need to leave it until you approach cloudbase. It's these low saves that are so memorable!

If you're fortunate enough to get to fly a lot of different places and you've built up knowledge and feel for the weather, you can usually go to a new place and have a pretty good idea of what's going to work. But there are always things that will surprise you. There might be terrain features that should work but don't, or vice versa. Sometimes it's just the way things cycle; sometimes the wind splits or meanders. Again, I use the river analogy. It's worth spending a lot of time looking at rivers to watch how they flow, because air behaves similarly, but in our case the river is boiling. A boiling river is very difficult to model, and can be infinitely complex.

Before you take off, you have to remember that you're the pilot in command and you've got to make the right call every time. No one learning how to ski would follow an expert skier into a couloir between two cliffs. Someone learning how to surf isn't going to follow Laird Hamilton into a triple overhead barreling wave. You could be watching a pilot make something look really easy on a really gnarly day, but that guy is Chrigel. To get to that kind of level takes a really long time, no matter how much talent a person has.

My final piece of advice to everyone is this: be careful when you start feeling too much like Superman. In my early days I definitely went through periods of irrational confidence and irrational fear. You have to be careful at both ends of that continuum. If you're irrationally scared, you have to back off and figure out what exactly is causing the fear. You can't be flying around thinking the glider is going to kill you. But you can't be flying around thinking you're invincible either, because sooner or later you'll get a potentially ugly reminder. Remember there are old pilots and bold pilots, but no old bold pilots. Stay safe, fly far, and don't forget to look around.

HOW TO MANAGE RISK

As Jeff Shapiro says: "Don't fly like the pilot you want to be, but like the pilot you are. It's just paragliding. No line is worth not coming home from." Maintain a margin that suits your skill level. Don't get in a situation where your reserve is your only way out. Lessons shouldn't come from serious accidents. Don't rely on luck.

"What we like to do with our paragliders is push it. But the risk is massive, and the reward is relatively inconsequential: your smile at the end of the day. Being at cloudbase and knowing that you're the only person in the sky for a hundred miles is amazing, but hardly beneficial to humanity."
Nate Scales

"Everyone who flies should have an answer to the question "why?" Why is it worth the risk? Everyone makes mistakes, everyone. And in flying those mistakes could certainly put you in the hospital or kill you. The answer is different for everyone, but asking that question helps me make better decisions. Not just in paragliding, but whenever I'm doing anything that has consequence."
Will Gadd

"Our sport has risk in it all the time. That's one thing we should all admit. In competitions, the decision becomes how much risk are you willing to take? I'll try

"If you expect very strong valley winds or if you get caught in a venturi, there are a few things to consider. 1) Can you land up high? It's almost always better to stay high. 2) Get your legs out of your harness and warm them up by moving them around well in advance. If you go in hard, you want your legs working. 3) Never worry about being inconvenienced. Laziness contributes to a ton of accidents. Land in the safest spot you can – don't try to land in a tiny spot to save yourself some walking. 4) Vegetation is your friend. It's better to land in a tree and destroy your glider than in power lines, or a hard field, or something that destroys you. 5) Constantly look for alternatives downwind. Don't get fixated on one place to land. When you're flying in strong wind, you can cover a lot of ground when you go with it. 6) When you land in high winds, as soon as you touch the ground grab one of your B risers, pull hard and run towards that side. This is the best way to depower your wing. DO NOT HIT YOUR BRAKES as that could propel you backwards. Many accidents happen after people hit the ground and then get swept into an object."
Antoine Laurens

"I stopped competing after seeing an accident at the Worlds in Valle de Bravo. We were all being lemmings, following a pilot who was shooting the gap between the Peñon, which is a notoriously rough place. So I was angry at myself to begin with. And then a really top Swiss pilot, Stefan Schmoker, took a collapse and got a small cravat. It was no big deal: he could have flown out over the valley to clear it or just landed if he couldn't, or he could have thrown his reserve. But he kept trying to fix it. Every time he went to fix it the wing would wind up into a spiral. The comp mentality overtook his judgement – he didn't want to take a low score. Finally he tried to clear the cravat too low to the ground, and he spiraled in and died. It was so unnecessary. We have to remember how frivolous comps are – they don't mean anything. You see a lot of accidents in this sport and it takes its toll."
Kari Castle

to win when I can do it by flying smart. If winning requires taking a chance, I'll let someone else take it."
Gurpreet Dhindsa

"I don't subscribe to the 'be safe' logic. What we need are tools. For example, the tool you use to not fly. I'll take a student to the hill on a good day to fly, and just have them stand down. Pilots must learn to listen to their intuition and be willing to walk away. Pilots who embrace the mellow side of the sport as viable and rewarding are headed in the right direction. That doesn't mean you can't go huge or go fly in edgy conditions or learn tricks, but when you go do those things you need to be honest with yourself about what you're doing: you're taking a chance. The biggest mistake people make is when they blur the simple, easy and predictable flights with the sketchy flights. They con themselves that the sketchy flights are safe. They aren't."
Chris Santacroce

"A risk that I wish newer pilots especially wouldn't take is committing to a place with fewer options and abandoning a good landing zone just because they're trying to extend their flight. Thermals close to the ground aren't usually very friendly and really increase your risk. Low saves are fun, but they aren't cool."
Mitch Riley

"Don't kid yourself by thinking it's not going to happen to you. You can't take all the risk out of this sport. We're flying around patches of sky looking for turbulence!"
Mark Watts

"Every 360 starts out as a figure 8. Whether it's on launch or on an XC flight when you're close to the terrain, do not turn towards the hill. If you get a bit of sink where you aren't expecting it and you turn a 360 too low, there's nothing you can do. Every time you think about circling near the terrain be religious about imagining you're going to hit really strong sink. Don't do it if there's any chance you don't have enough buffer."
Rob Sporrer

Crossing the Line

JEFF SHAPIRO

In August 2015, Jeff was going through a difficult and reflective time. He'd just lost two very dear friends of his – Dean Potter and Graham Hunt – to fatal wingsuit accidents. He was understandably cut up.

Jeff was no newcomer to risk. He'd been flying hang gliders for 25 years, had notched up major accomplishments in rock and ice climbing, and had been pioneering wingsuit exits for years. In 2015, the wingsuit Base jumping community had been decimated by more than forty fatal accidents culminating in the loss of Dean and Graham, which made headlines worldwide. I was intrigued by Jeff's personal take on risk and living a life on the edge.

Dean and Graham were considered elite: experts that Jeff and the rest of the Base community tried to emulate. If they could make a mistake, anyone could.

To the outside world, wingsuit Base jumpers are harebrained adrenaline junkies with a screw loose and a death wish. But anyone who knew Dean, Graham or many of the other wingsuiters and Base jumpers who've lost their lives would say they were the opposite of that. They all have a fierce love of life, and they exude passion. Most are introspective, thoughtful and highly intelligent. They aren't doing it for the fame, but for the reminder of the preciousness of life. There's probably no other endeavor that requires such calculated focus, and nearly all the jumpers I have met are highly analytical. Like paraglider and hang glider pilots, they like to solve problems.

I'm convinced the reason most of us love flying is the relief that it gives us from our monkey brains. When we're flying, that's all we're doing: flying. We aren't worried about bills, or what we're going to make for dinner, or the fight we just had with our spouse. We're in the moment. In the zone.

As Jeff points out, most aircraft are things you fly. When you wingsuit, you're the aircraft. No doubt there's a huge rush, and the thrill of the close calls can become a dangerous addiction, but you're basically Superman, flying in the purest form. But one recent study found that if you stick with the sport longer than six years, your mortality risk is close to 100%. Like us paraglider pilots, wingsuiters are not blind to these terrible odds. So why do it? Have you ever asked yourself the same question?

"Aviation in general isn't inherently dangerous. It's just absolutely unforgiving of human error."

Jeff, let's kick it off with your history. The madness for you started an awfully long time ago!
The theme that's driven me is the search for exploration and adventure. How rare is it these days to have an adventure where you really don't know what's going to happen next? Flying for me was always one of these magic things. You're raised to believe that humans can't do it, at least in the way that I dreamed about: flying like a bird, not in something like an aircraft, but actually flying.

I grew up in the Pacific Northwest of the USA, and my family and I spent a lot of time on the ferries that crisscross those waterways. I used to watch seagulls soar the ridge lift of those ferries, almost never flapping their wings. Those birds imprinted on me a sense of freedom that I wasn't sure existed. Later I got super drawn into the sport and art of climbing. I think it was always about finding the highest places and new perspectives – just like flying.

In my late teens I was heading to Yosemite to climb El Capitán, and a friend of mine was designing rock-climbing equipment. I went over to his house to pick up a portaledge, which you sleep on when you're doing multi-day wall climbing. This guy's shop had photos of him flying a hang glider, and suddenly it hit me. This was the answer to the question that I didn't really know how to ask! I knew that's what I had to do. But I was a stupid 17-year-old kid, and when I told this guy that I had to learn to fly, he didn't take me very seriously. He said: "I'll tell you what. If you read these books, and you call this number, and you buy this hang glider, and you buy this harness, maybe we can talk about it."

He probably thought I was just gonna go cross-eyed at having to do all of those things. But I picked up one of those books on the way down to Yosemite, and I read it cover to cover while climbing El Cap, and I got back and did everything he said. And to this day it was the best decision I've ever made. Walking that path has led to so many beautiful memories and experiences in my life that I certainly wouldn't change anything. I sold my car and bought a glider and a harness and my mom, as scared as she was, bought me my first reserve.

My first glider was this big beach trainer that was built in 1978. It was a Flight Design Saber 205 with fiberglass battens, and had duct tape all over it and the original side wires. It was horrifying, but I didn't know any better. I was on the training hill a day and a half, which consisted of stalling the glider and landing in a blackberry thicket, among other things. The second day my friend decided it was time to kick me out of the nest. So he takes me up to the top of a mountain near Bellingham, Washington, and off I go in a knee-hanger harness with no parachute and a bike helmet! I just thought that's how you did it.

I think most people who've experienced free flight would agree it's something that's just in you. It's either in you or it's not. And when it is, it's not something that goes away. Free flight has pretty much driven my life ever since. I get to pursue what I consider dreams and magic. When I was 18 or 19 years old, I'd find myself flying a glider two and a half miles out over the ocean on a jetty, just like I'd seen those birds do when I was a kid!

Who gets to do that? This was a serious eye-opener towards the rest of life. If you can do that, I guess you can probably do anything! I like feeling vulnerable. I like feeling small. I like seeing the world as being part of it, and not controlling it. With flying you're such a small boat in a huge ocean that you can't help but be humbled by it. Flying creates gratitude, and for me that's the key to happiness.

Tell me about your progression, and specifically competition flying.

Comps are not only an opportunity to learn, but an opportunity to be humbled, and to understand your weaknesses. You achieve a particular level of ability and expertise, and you may think you're getting pretty good, but then you go race against amazing pilots from all over the world and you'll inevitably recognize that there are still some big holes in your game.

How many times have I sat in a field after landing just a bit short by myself, scratching my head thinking: how many times do I have to learn this lesson? But that's the beauty of flying – no thermal is the same. Even if you fly the same course, it's going to be different the next day. The sky is so dynamic that we make decisions now that affect us three hours from now. And the cool thing about comps is you get to use your friends to benchmark your decisions. Your friends could be in a position that you can't even see, and they can't see you. And when you take a different line, because it's a race to goal you see who made the better choice, and you learn. The humility from all of that and from constantly getting beat ended up helping me in life in general, because you just have to accept what happens. You're going to make good moves and, even after a life of flying, you're going to make bad moves. You can stand in a field and kick your helmet, but you're still there!

Comps are great for our egos. We get the thrill of making goal, of flying fast, feeling the elation of winning a task, but also the crush of defeat. Comps force us to analyze logically, without emotion, what we did right and what we did wrong, so we can then apply it to the next day. Comps can be pretty intimidating to new pilots. There are the instruments and the big gaggles and all the pressure, but you can learn more in one comp than in an entire season of cross-country flying at home.

The reason is that you have to fly crosswind tasks and upwind tasks, and you have to dive into places that you normally wouldn't go, and they force you to fly the sky or the terrain in a way that you wouldn't if you were just trying to cover ground. In a comp you have all these clues: your friends, birds, dust devils, clouds and all the things that we pay attention to. And you can watch a pilot go a certain way and decide if it's a bad call or a good call. And then you get that immediate feedback loop that's so valuable. Were you right or wrong? Why?

Jeff during a 21-day vol-biv expedition in Alaska's Brooks Range in 2019. "Our goal was to cross the raw wilderness of the Arctic National Wildlife Refuge from west to east." Photo: Cody Tuttle

Everything we do perfectly prepares us for what's next. Whether you remember the lesson or make the mistake again doesn't really matter. It's made an impression on you, and you're still building a repertoire of experiences. When you're climbing in a thermal, you have that subconscious little voice that's going to tell you if the decision you're making is good or bad, based on your previous experience. You might not consciously tap into this, but it's there. These experiences we have in flying cross over into our lives. They apply to our relationships, and whatever you might be into. Learning a second language or ultra-running in the mountains – it doesn't matter. And I'm quite thankful for it.

You can probably put each one of us that enjoys flying into a single category of people: we're all curious. We all want to know what's possible. We want to know what we're made of and what we're capable of. And those are terms that change constantly. Our fear and limitations change along the way. And that's very cool! Our perspective as human beings is generally two-dimensional. We're stuck because of gravity. But when you're flying you're operating in an environment that's totally surreal and radically complex. Occasionally I'll find myself looking up at the glider, and I realize I'm actually surfing the sky. It's fascinating! And I've never lost that curiosity and fascination. I'm not necessarily attracted to being good at something. I'm attracted to getting good at something.

Live in the present, enjoy the moments that are now, because really that's all you have. The special part about flying is that a multitude of people and personalities can achieve really amazing things. You don't have to be a great comp pilot or great XC pilot or a great acro pilot, or be on the podium of the Superfinal, to succeed in this sport. If you just have curiosity and appreciate the magic, then you're winning!

What would you say to your 20-year-old self if you could go back and give that Jeff some advice?

When you're 20, you're stubborn. I think that when you're stubborn, that becomes open-mindedness, and that turns into drive. I think being stubborn is an important tool to drive you towards the unknown, or to drive you towards what you believe to be true and then you generally find out it isn't so true. But that's a journey you've got to have to figure it out; it's not one you can be told to have. So what I would want to say to my 20-year-old self and what I would want to hear are very different things!

Maybe the question should be, what would you like to hear at this age? I just turned 40, and I can tell you this for certain: I would listen very carefully to my 80-year-old self! I think I would want to tell my 20-year-old self to be patient. And that you can only be you. Here's what I believe: if you have two paths in front of you, the best choice is to take the more difficult one, because that's the one you're going to learn the most from. Follow your path, do what calls to you and everything's going to work out.

What I've learned recently through this wingsuit Base jump experience is that to do things for reasons of identity or achievement or ambition, especially when there's risk or consequence involved, is foolish. For me it's very important to listen to what calls to me in a way that speaks to my heart, fulfills my life as a human being and allows me to find the joy of being alive; not the joy of being good, but the joy that you remember from play as a child. Unhindered play.

Whenever I've had something go wrong or learned a pretty hard lesson, it's generally because I've forced it. When I let things happen, and it just feels right, then it goes well, and those are the times when the magic happens. But when you force it, that's when life can teach you some pretty hard lessons. Maybe that's something I'd like to pass on to my twenty-year-old self.

You've mentioned being in the moment quite a bit. Is that why we pursue these high-risk sports? To be in the moment?

The sky, the ocean, rivers... these are all things that make us feel pretty small. And yet we're trying to pilot our way through them in a way that maximizes our growth as people. Whether that's the intention or not, that's what happens. I think the reason we do it probably differs for each of us, but I think that's a universal result. When I land from a wingsuit Base jump, I've just seen the world for a few fleeting moments in a very different way, but it goes away pretty quickly. I recognize soon after a jump that life is going to be the same, and the world would remain unchanged whether I was in it or not. This feeling is fairly pronounced in a wingsuit Base jump, because you go through this experience where you have to pull the parachute to save your own life. Every jump essentially is kind of a near-death experience.

Wide open spaces during the 2019 Brooks Range traverse. Photo: Cody Tuttle

But it's not about cheating death, it's about the joy of flight – that's what we're all chasing. When you land and realize the world would be the same whether you're standing there or lying dead at the bottom of the cliff, what you're recognizing is your own mortality and place in the world. That's a very powerful moment. It makes us realize how lucky we are. That's what draws me to doing things that are consequential. It's not to cheat death or to get a rush. These experiences allow me to experience the joy of being alive, not living, but being alive. I don't want to do something and look back on it and reminisce. I think these states of consciousness that we get in after a big paragliding flight or a big hang gliding flight or a wingsuit Base jump or climb or whatever – these states of consciousness can be achieved with a quiet mind. It's just much more difficult to do. Hopefully we all learn how to do that as we continue on our path.

In all these high-risk sports that we love to pursue, to improve usually means you've got to push harder, which inevitably exposes us to more risk. How do we improve and stay alive?
Aviation in general isn't inherently dangerous. It's just absolutely unforgiving of human error. The problem with any of the arts that we do that demand the contemplation of consequence is that if you're attracted to getting better at something, you're going to have to accept that eventually you're going to step over an invisible line. In most sports

or activities there's a particular level of forgiveness. If you're skiing, for example, and you push hard and you step over the line and have a massive crash, you might get jacked up, but you're probably going to live. As long as you're making decisions that are based on your skill set and your level of experience, you're probably going to survive. In wingsuit Base jumping it's exactly the opposite. It's likely that you're not going to live. Life requires balance. Balance is everything.

Let's take something that's fairly benign in terms of safety. Like a relationship. In this balance beam the fulcrum is wide and it's rounded, and the weight on either side isn't that heavy. There's still risk involved with love when you walk to one side or the other. The

> **"Live in the present, enjoy the moments that are now, because really that's all you have."**

relationship can get out of balance, but you recognize it and you do whatever it takes; you communicate and you work your way back to a balanced situation. In a wingsuit Base jump, the fulcrum is a pinpoint. The balance beam is long and the weights are exceptionally heavy. If you step a toenail over that fulcrum one way or the other, you're on the ground.

That's the reason a lot of my friends who are exceptionally skilled, exceptionally experienced, very smart, and very, very risk-savvy mountain people have lost their lives doing it. We're not attracted to being good at something. We're attracted to getting good at something, or to the exploration involved with the progress or the process. When you've achieved a particular level in a sport and you continue to progress, you're progressing towards a line that you can't see. In wingsuiting, stepping over the smallest amount generally means you're dead. The fulcrum for paragliding and hang gliding is obviously much wider, and there's a margin, but we're still playing with gravity and the ground. If the answer then is to jump below your limits and to fly below your limits to create sustainability, are you learning?

Let's just throw out an arbitrary number. Say you've jumped a wingsuit 500-plus times all around the world, then you decide that because of the loss of a lot of your friends, you're going to jump below your limits. Is it worth it now? Are you learning enough to justify the risks? Because the risk is still VERY present. The problem is that 99.9% safe is not acceptable, because one accident in a thousand means losing your life. It only takes one time. So essentially every jump is the most important jump of your life, and every jump has to be perfect. It's not the next jump, it's not the last jump, it's not his jump or her jump, it's my jump.

This question of whether or not it's worth it is an individual thing that each of us has to ask ourselves every single time we do it. You have to be honest with yourself in a way that does not include ego or ambition or self-expectation.

Have you ever questioned whether the risk is worth it?
I had a tumbling incident at King Mountain, Idaho on a hang glider a few years ago. That was the first time in my flying-related life that I asked myself: "Why am I doing this? Is this worth it?" And then I realized, with as much honesty as it required, that I wasn't flying to be a hang glider pilot. I was flying because I loved hang gliding, and if I chose to stop because of fear and doubt, then I might as well stop everything. Flying is not what people think. People think that people who jump off cliffs are adrenaline junkies and reckless. There's a difference between risky and reckless. What we're doing is exceptionally serious, and we know it. Everyone who participates in free flight for a long period of time is going to witness carnage. Losing a friend or watching a fatality happen changes you. And when you see people die who are at the pinnacle of their sport, you realize that it can happen to anyone. It can happen to you.

Here's the problem with playing with a line that you can't see. We can go out and be positively reinforced for making terrible decisions, because we get away with it. And so you keep pushing. But eventually you're going to cross the line, and we're not mountain biking or skiing where a mistake might break a bone. A mistake could kill you. Crossing the line could be lethal. So we have a choice – we can certainly choose to live a life without consequence, but that's not very appealing to me. We all have to be honest about the potential consequences and each of us has to answer this deeply personal question for themselves.

THE FIVE HAZARDOUS ATTITUDES OF AVIATION

Commercial pilots are taught these at the beginning of their training, but the format is not as well-known in the free flying community. Jeff recommends we get familiar with them and learn to recognize them for what they are.

1. **Anti-authority**: "Don't tell me!" Pilots with an anti-authority attitude tend to believe that rules, regulations and safety procedures don't apply to them. An anti-authority pilot doesn't take instruction very well, may not be diligent about checklists and blows off what could be good advice.
2. **Impulsive**: "Do something quickly!" An attitude of impulsivity is found in pilots who "feel the need to do something, anything, immediately". Instead of taking a moment to think things through or select the best alternative, a pilot with an impulsive attitude does the first thing that comes to mind. Reacting too quickly can lead to irrational decisions, such as skipping a preflight or rushing to get home despite bad weather. Pilots are encouraged to take time to evaluate their options before choosing a course of action.
3. **Invulnerability**: "It won't happen to me!" Many people – not just pilots – fall into a pattern of thinking that accidents happen to others, but never to them.

This attitude of invulnerability can become a safety concern when pilots fail to consider the risks of their actions. This is also called 'survivor bias'.

4. **Macho**: "I can do it!" Pilots with a macho attitude are always trying to impress others and prove themselves by taking unnecessary risks. Both men and women are susceptible to a macho attitude, which leads to foolish and often dangerous behavior. While pilots must have a high level of confidence in their abilities, it's important to avoid becoming overconfident and adopting a macho attitude.
5. **Resignation**: "What's the use?" Pilots with an attitude of resignation lack the confidence and conviction to believe they can make a difference in what happens to them. These pilots tend to give up easily when faced with challenges and don't take criticism well. This attitude is particularly dangerous for pilots in an emergency situation because they may believe they are helpless and resign themselves to their fate instead of taking action.

The truth is, anyone can be guilty of one or more of the hazardous attitudes, which are a normal part of human nature. Understanding these attitudes and recognizing when they occur will help pilots make better decisions and avoid unnecessary danger.

HOW TO KILL COMPLACENCY

The first quote here should be one of your mantras. Say it before every single flight. Over and over and over again, the pilots that I've interviewed credit accidents that they've had or seen to complacency – forgetting for a brief moment that we're aviating and the ground is hard. I should have died or at least broken some stuff when I threw my reserve and discovered it wasn't attached to anything. How is it possible to make a mistake that stupid? Easy. I was complacent.

"This one flight, the one you're about to take, is the most important flight of your life"
Jeff Shapiro

"I have compressed vertebrae like most people in our line of work. Both of my accidents happened ridge soaring at my local site, one of the easiest places to fly in the world. I've never had an accident where the flying required my attention, so we can deduce that my accidents happened because I was too relaxed and too complacent."
Mads Syndergaard

"A lot of hang glider pilots have been hurt or killed because of simple pilot error, and one of the big ones is forgetting to hook in. An easy way to never make that mistake is to hook in your harness as part of your glider set-up. You don't get into your harness unless it's hooked into your hang glider. A lot of people will get in their harness before they hook in, because they don't want to be hooked in when they walk to launch. I love walking to launch being hooked in, it makes me feel connected. It's just being comfortable handling your wing on the ground, and if it's really rowdy, that's when you ask for help.

"I frequently see accidents happen when pilots break the really simple rules that we learn as beginners. I saw a terrible midair at a ridge-soaring site in Chile this year when one pilot just wasn't looking around. I see a lot of pilots have accidents practicing ground spirals or dynamic moves close to the ground in thermic air, which is asking for trouble. Accidents that happen on launch because pilots have weak ground handling skills are really frustrating, because they're so easily solved with a bit of practice. All of these and more can be bundled up into the complacency category. Don't be a lemming, especially when you're new to the sport. Don't assume you can do something that you witness. You might be witnessing one of the best in the world who you can't yet emulate, or you might be witnessing someone who doesn't know better."
Christina Kolb

"I went to work one day, and two weeks later left the hospital, and two months later came home. My whole life took an unimaginable turn in seconds. I was flying tandem in Zermatt in perfect autumn conditions. It was gently soarable on a big cliff face that we often fly. My business partner was also flying tandem just in front of me. We fly together all the time; we instinctively know what we're each going to do without even nodding to each other. But we were soaring an area that was pretty small, and when he turned back towards me we both turned away from the cliff in the same direction at the same time, and for a split second the right of way was unclear. We had eye contact, but two gliders closing at 70km/h doesn't give you much time to react. I had the right of way, but he knew he would hit me if he turned out, so he ducked in as close as he could to the cliff. I buried the left brake to turn away from the cliff and him, and spun the glider. At first I thought I could catch it and fly away from the hill, but we impacted the cliff almost immediately. Thankfully the glider got hung up, so we stopped nearly immediately. Inside 20 minutes we were in a helicopter and en route to the hospital, and that's what saved my life.

The question that lingers is how it happened. It's easy to say just stay further from the cliff and be more conservative, but I never had enough respect for how quickly it can go wrong. In some ways it's safer to be in a gaggle with 100 pilots than to be ridge soaring close to the terrain. In a big gaggle everyone knows how to behave. Even though we have right of way rules on a ridge, it just takes a split second of indecision. Because you're low the consequences of getting it wrong can be brutal. I can't actually teach anyone how to avoid an accident like the one I had. Just be hyper-aware of not being complacent."
Phil Glutz

Way too many people play too close to the hill. In the mountains you have to give yourself a margin. I've seen so many accidents because people are too low in a complicated environment. Your options go to nearly zero when you're low."
Kari Castle

"For many, many years, pretty much every time I landed I was doing a ground spiral and dragging my wing tip on the ground. That was just my style. I was doing a ground spiral on a paramotor and the field was wheat, which I didn't realize can grab your lines a little differently from grass. It was just thick enough to change my trajectory slightly and I hit my butt just a little wrong, which tweaked my T2. It didn't even look like a crash; it wasn't like I piled in – I just hit the ground a little weird. There was very little physical trauma, no broken bones. But there was a strange nerve thing that for a few weeks looked pretty grim, like my future was going to be in a wheelchair.

I think it's important to let yourself get philosophical about things like my accident. Until that moment I had no reason to believe anything bad would ever happen to me . It would happen to someone else. Blowing it, doing something wrong – that was something

other pilots did. I didn't blow it. I didn't get things wrong. Until that moment. When I got back in the air, I asked myself what I was supposed to learn. What I figured out was that for years my approach had been: "Look at me! Look what I can do!" And that was fine – that's what that period of my life was all about. The accident shifted my focus from me, to my community. My children, my wife, my students, veterans, people with chronic illness, old people; anyone I can lift up and inspire is my mission now. The accident saved my life."
Chris Santacroce

"One of the most common things I see pilots screw up that can lead to a pretty bad consequence is a poorly executed wingover. Wingovers are awesome, but they're really difficult to do well, and they need to be treated with respect. Pilots should practice any new maneuver with the thought that you're going to throw your reserve. If you're too low to throw your reserve, you're WAY too low to practice any maneuver."
Max Marien

"I'd been flying the Omega (an EN D wing) for a while and was very comfortable on it. Then one day I flew with my dad in Zermatt on a perfect day, so I decided to step down to my old Sigma so we were on better matched gliders. For me it was almost like a beginner wing. When I look back at the incident, it was purely a case of being complacent and overconfident because I was on the easier wing. On the Sigma I felt invincible. I came out of a thermal and had a big collapse because I wasn't paying attention. I leaned against it, which immediately twisted me up, and I was also still deep in the inside brake from thermalling, which put me in a twisted stall. I didn't have a lot of time, so I threw my reserve and landed on the side of a rock cliff with no way to walk down or escape. So we called the helicopter rescue and they long-lined me out. My dad was flying right next to me and watched the whole thing, so it was pretty scary for him, but luckily I had no real injuries."
Bernhard Kalin

Matt Beechinor soars the Mulanje massif, Malawi.
Photo: Jody MacDonald

The SIV Guru

JOCKY SANDERSON

Jocky Sanderson is probably the world's most renowned SIV instructor. He's been teaching pilots to deal with collapses and other 'incidents in flight' (SIV) since the early 1990s, and over time his courses have had to develop with glider technology. Jocky has a wealth of tips and knowledge to share, particularly on the psychology of fear and pilot development.

Jocky, you've been at this game over a quarter of a century. How did you go from flying comps back in the day with Pendry, Goldsmith, Silvester and co to instructing?
From 1989 to 1997, I really enjoyed competitions. Being paid to travel the world and fly with your friends was a tremendously fortunate thing to be able to do. But I never had the killer instinct to win. I realized that I actually enjoyed teaching and sharing and seeing people achieve things quite a bit more. I get to fly through the eyes of everyone we're coaching. I also stopped because I started a family, and I couldn't justify competitions when you've got young kids.

Because of the time, or the risk?
A little bit of both. I had to cut out a few things to keep me home more. I always look back at that time of my life with great fondness. It's incredibly bonding sharing those experiences with other pilots. Comps really teach you a lot about yourself. You learn so much about preparation and discipline, and these are skills that cross over into other areas of life. Comps are great to do, especially when you're young, but as in all things in life, you should only compete when you want to. They get a lot more dangerous when you're doing them for the wrong reasons.

How did you get into SIV instruction?
I used to be a test pilot for the testing bodies. We figured that the maneuvers we were doing in testing would be beneficial for pilots to learn. We started breaking down what we were doing in the test flights into a course structure. Things like deflations, searching for spins, searching for stalls, stalls and spirals, and various other maneuvers: all this

> **"Pilots need to build confidence in a nice progressive way. It can't be forced. It should be a buzz, not terrifying."**

evolved into 'Simulation d'Incidents en Vol' – SIV. We could see pretty quickly that people benefit from SIV practice. It gives pilots confidence, and an understanding of their gliders and their ability to control them.

Have modern gliders made paragliding safer?
In general, yes. Nowadays the curve of performance more closely matches the curve of safety. And because of better education, pilots are flying gliders that are well within their limits, rather than flying gliders way faster and more dynamic than what they're capable or trained to handle. It's still very interesting at the two-liner level – these are still very dynamic wings, but now, with the proper training, pilots can learn to manage them pretty safely.

How has SIV training changed as gliders have so radically advanced since the invention of the shark nose?
With more efficient profiles, the shark nose, raked-back lines and all the rigging changes we've seen, we've had to evolve the syllabus. We've had to develop just as the wings have developed. All SIV instructors have different styles of teaching, but the main aim is the same: to make pilots more confident and help them develop correct reactions.

How much SIV is enough?
People ask me all the time: "When should I do an SIV?" The answer is that you shouldn't have to do one. You should do one when you have the feeling that there's something holding you back. It's when you have a bit of doubt about using a little more bar or that feeling of "what would happen if…" That's when you know it's time to do a course, because that's the time when you want to free up more brain power to focus on good things – cloud formation, triggers, birds, other pilots – rather than looking up at your glider trying to control it.

You'll fly a lot better if 100% of your focus is dedicated to observation rather than worrying about your wing. But the key is you have to want to do it. If you're already a fearful pilot, an SIV course won't help you get over your fear. It will just make you more scared. You have to want to do it.

When should a pilot take their first SIV?
It depends on how you fly and where you fly, but normally it's between 50 and 100 hours. When pilots are getting into their first 20km flights, an SIV can really be

beneficial, because it gives you a better understanding and trust of the wing, and you also learn to trust in your handling. Pilots need to learn to be quick to react, but also quick to back off and not overreact. That's what SIV teaches. But again, it's important that the desire to do it is there. I've had 10-hour pilots who are so keen and excited I would never hold them back, because they're a blank canvas. They're just full of enthusiasm, they're like puppies. They're like Mr Magoo, they get away with anything with blind optimism, and they're generally flying very safe gliders. In three days they'll do maneuvers that they never thought were possible. Instructors have to be careful to make sure we only allow pilots to do maneuvers they're ready for – never to accelerate too fast.

Pilots need to build confidence up in a nice, progressive way. It can't be forced. Whether it's SIV, acro, pilotage or any form of training, you've got to always land and be excited to go back up and do it again. That's the key. If you land thinking: "Thank God that's over", then you're not ready for SIV. But if you land thinking, "wow, that's fantastic", then that's when SIV really works, and you'll get a lot out of it. It should be a buzz – it shouldn't be terrifying.

After your first course, how should you carry on with SIV training? Where do you want to leave a pilot after their first SIV, and what should they keep doing?
We always want pilots to go away armed with more confidence and a more positive attitude towards flying. If we see that a pilot's not responding or not really enjoying it, we have to slow down and focus on what they're doing well. What we want is a pilot hungry to learn more. The trend in the last decade is that, after the course, pilots have a lot more issues and stress about spirals than stalls. Pilots learn that stalls are actually quite easy. They start to get better with the finesse of the maneuver, whereas they become more nervous about getting locked into a spiral or blacking out, which is something that's a real risk on a lot of modern gliders that we have to address in the course.

SIV should not be about ticking boxes. It's not a binary 'on' and 'off' – there's a finesse and training to SIV, just like there is in all flying. At the end of the course, a pilot should feel more confident, and we hope that it's opened a door to obtaining more skills and being hungry to learn. But I don't think people have to come back to it all the time. Once you have the understanding of SIV it lasts for a quite a long time, and for some people it leads to acro training and things like Sats and loops and big wingovers that are really fun. Learning more makes you a more complete pilot, but I don't think it's necessary for everyone. Acro is like a different sport.

But I think acro training really correlates to XC, don't you? After my first X-Alps campaign I decided I really needed to do a lot more acro training, just so I could be safer and more confident in rough air. The sensitivity to your wing that you get from acro, and knowing what your wing is doing without looking at it and having the confidence to sort out any situation, has been really important for me.
Definitely. The great thing is the correlation is through play. That's the key. If you're up there playing and having fun and enjoying it, that's completely different from being terrified. Acro training gets you totally attuned to the glider. You get to where

Jocky Sanderson has coached several international squads, including the Turkish, Australian and British Worlds teams. He continues to teach SIV and XC to pilots across the globe. Photo: Marcus King

you're not even thinking about it. SIV sows that seed and gives you a little bit of confidence, but obviously a five-day SIV course will not make you a master. You have to practice and practice and get really into it. The X-Alps is a great example. When you look at the conditions you guys have to fly in, people who watch the race think you're lunatics. But it's not dangerous. It's not dangerous if you train. X-Alps pilots can pop up their glider in 40km/h of wind in a boulder field, no problem, because they've trained for that. So for instructors like myself who teach XC and SIV, all we're doing is showing pilots the door. It's up to them to go through it and practice to get to whatever level they want to achieve, so they can get 100% out of the sport they love.

Very few people can dedicate the kind of time necessary to get to a professional level in this sport, or the kind of time it takes to compete in something like the X-Alps. How should pilots who are limited with their time, those pilots who maybe only get to fly 50 hours a year, approach training?
Time is precious. If you're lucky enough to get a couple weeks of flying in each year, you need to join an enthusiastic group. It's important to surround yourself with people who are keen. The more people you have around you watching the weather, planning routes, organizing the transport and so on, the more you're going to get out of it. Positive peer

pressure really works. Stay away from the ground suck crowd. Surround yourself with people who focus on the positive. There are no shortcuts in flying, nothing replaces hours. The only way to get better is to go flying.

What are the common threads you've seen when it comes to accidents?
People flying in environments that they aren't 100% comfortable with, but they feel like they should be comfortable with. We all have performance peaks and troughs. Confidence and attention peak and trough, too. The beautiful thing about the sport we do is you have to be honest with yourself, because your judgments are final. If you make a mistake you have to quickly adapt and learn from it, or the consequences can be rough. If you've had a long break from flying, or are trying to fly in conditions that you used to find ok but aren't quite ready for this time round, listen to that nagging doubt you might have. Don't try and justify or rationalize things. Your head is probably screaming at you to back off. Listen.

When pilots fly outside their comfort zone but think they should be fine, that's when accidents happen. Pilots should push their boundaries gently when it feels right, but back off when it doesn't. A lot of people fly gliders because of external factors – for example because they're racing or because they're instructors and they feel they 'should be' flying a particular wing. This is wrong. Pilots should fly what they're comfortable with.

The great thing about aviation is the decision stops with you. The pilots who have long careers in this sport know when to step down if they aren't feeling happy at the time. They don't force it.

What three technical things do you see most pilots need to practice?
Launching. There's nothing worse than getting to launch doubting yourself. You've already started on a negative. You need to have all aspects of launching down. Nil wind, back wind, high wind, forwards, reverses, cobras… so you're not even thinking about it. Instead of worrying about launching, you're looking at the sky and planning your flight. You should be able to get to any launch and know you've got it. You cannot practice ground handling enough. To learn this skill, you don't just go to a flat field when it's honking and get dragged around. You need to practice in all kinds of variations and on all kinds of slopes and angles. We don't launch off flats, so you need to ground handle on slopes!

Know your kit. You need to be a machine when you get on launch. Unpack, set up, BOOM, you're in the air. If you don't have your kit sorted and dialed, it adds stress and wastes time. Everything needs to be prepared, and you have to be intimate with all your gear. Vario tones set correctly, instruments charged, radio on the right frequency, route planned, etc. All the research is done. All you want to be thinking about is the beauty of thermaling and doing the distance.

Practice with intent. If I'm just flying at my local site with no task or challenge, I get bored pretty quickly. But if one of my mates says: "I bet you can't get over to that hill over there," well then, game on! Set yourself challenges and make it fun. Every flight is an opportunity to learn.

Should people be flying with two reserves?
There aren't many scenarios where you would need two reserves. The likelihood of going into your wing and having to swim out of it is very small. Throwing your reserve into your wing does happen, and people think that's a good case for having two, but it isn't. You can just pull the lines on the reserve and it will open. You can pull it into your lap and re-throw it. But two reserves are highly recommended for acro and competition pilots.

> **"When you get wingovers, that's the maneuver that carries over the most into being a good pilot."**

How stressful is your job teaching SIV and XC?
Some people certainly keep you on your game! XC courses are more stressful because we don't have a lot of control when a pilot puts themselves in a position of risk. If we don't have radio communication, it can get really tense. In an SIV environment, when something goes sideways and a pilot is in a compromised position, you have to think fast. Your heart rate is going ballistic, but you can't let that excitement come through on the radio. The correct information has to go from your brain, out of your mouth, into their brain and down to their hands quickly. It's happening very fast for me and the pilot.

How do you deal with the dark side of our sport?
You've just got to focus on the good. You learn from the bad, but you focus on the good. If you're involved in adventure sports, you're exposed to the bad all the time, and sadly some of our friends don't make it through. What you have to do is focus on the love you have for it, and think to yourself: "Where would I be without it?"

Do you spend much time flying on your own, outside of the coaching? Are you still passionate about it after all these years?
I still love flying. The thing about guiding is I get to fly through the eyes of everyone we're coaching. And now my son is flying too, I get to see it from his perspective. As guides we have to fly for everybody else. When a client gets their first 50km flight, it feels like a 200km for me! Their stoke makes it rewarding. I would have lost interest in flying a long time ago if it was all about the numbers and trying constantly to beat what I'd already done. The key to enjoying this sport is appreciation.

What kind of pilots in your SIV courses are you the least worried about and the most worried about?
I'm the least worried about people who cross over from another sport where they understand risk. If they've come from a background where there's a similar

philosophy, where they've learned to take on information and act on it, then they're usually much more natural pilots and have the right approach to learning. I worry about the people who think they know what's going on, but they actually don't. Some people are not prepared to learn, and they are the ones we have to keep a close eye on. Typically, younger people are easier to teach. They tend to be more malleable and willing to learn.

A lot of people try to be something they aren't. A lot of people come to SIV clinics because they feel like they should, but they don't enjoy it. If you don't enjoy it, don't do it. You see this on launch all the time. People's bodies are going forward, but their feet are taking little tiny reluctant steps as if they're saying: "What are you doing?!"

What's the most important maneuver to learn in an SIV course, and what maneuver is the most important to keep practicing?
Wingovers, for sure. No pilot will have the wingover nailed in one course, because it's very hard, but when you get wingovers, that's the maneuver that carries over the most into being a good pilot. It can be applied to thermalling, switching direction in cores, getting up from dicey places, having the confidence that you can throw it around, controlling spins – the wingover is something all pilots should take away from an SIV course and practice.

Russell Ogden stalls a prototype wing above the village of Gourdon in southern France. Photo: Marcus King

HOW TO SIV: FABIEN BLANCO

Fabien Blanco coaches the French squad in SIV, and his pilotage courses attract pilots worldwide. These are his top tips for SIV pilots and instructors.

LEARN AT YOUR OWN PACE

At Flyeo, we're approaching SIV very differently from how it was done ten years ago. Our focus is on fundamentals, not on maneuvers. First we begin with the technical aspects of flying. For example, using and understanding the full brake range of your glider, adjusting your harness correctly, and keeping your vision wide instead of narrow. Then we work on the mental side. We believe it's more important to work on the pilot than the glider.

IT'S OK TO BE AFRAID

A lot of people have a lot of fear going into SIV. We push people progressively, but very slowly. You have to first create trust in their glider and their ability. In the old days it was all about just doing maneuvers, but if you're really scared, your brain can't comprehend what's going on. You can't recall what you've done, because it's all happening too fast. We believe you have to have basic technical and mental skills before an SIV can be valuable.

360 WITH RAPID EXITS TELLS YOU EVERYTHING

Regardless of the level of the pilot, we use a few tests to assess their skill level. One of these is the 360 with a rapid exit. With this one maneuver, I can see 90% of the skills of a pilot. Are they using weight shift and brake efficiently? Do they do it slowly or fast? Can they control the roll and pitch? How do they manage the energy of the glider? Even World Cup pilots can do it poorly, and then I know where we need to begin with the training.

SIV PREPARES YOU MENTALLY

Learning paragliding has three distinct aspects. The technical, the mental and the analytical. You can acquire the technical very quickly; it's maybe 25% of flying. The mental can be very volatile, and it's also maybe 25% of flying, and the mental side really hinges on your technical ability. The analysis side is 50% of flying well. Reading terrain, reading the weather, understanding where a thermal will be, etc, and getting this knowledge requires hours. So SIV really trains the technical and the mental side, and it can be very valuable. Climbers go to the gym to get strong in certain ways; it supplements their bigger climbing goals. SIV is the same thing. It's a great training tool, but no, it's not for everyone.

THE TOP THREE CAUSES OF ACCIDENTS

We've studied accidents in France quite thoroughly and have all the data on this.

The first is a rapid rotation after a collapse. When pilots don't react correctly when they have an asymmetric collapse and they are low, it can lead to a bad accident.

The second is initiating an unintentional spin. When you fly at low speed, say when you are setting up for a landing or trying to catch a thermal, and you use too much brake, the wing is very susceptible to spin[1]. Many pilots are not familiar enough with the spin point of their glider, and you see many accidents from pilots flying too slowly.

The third is the landing. Many pilots don't know how to properly approach or assess a landing. And a lot of people are lemmings, so they will follow other pilots into a known LZ that's a terrible landing to use in certain conditions.

We used to think most accidents happened because of flying in unsuitable conditions for your skill level, but the data shows it's these fundamentals. The aerodynamic behaviors of a glider, whether it's an EN A or a CCC glider, are exactly the same. If your skills are crap, the results will be the same! I don't care about the glider – I care about the people. We have to work on the self-knowledge and skills of the pilot. It's not about the car, it's about who's behind the wheel.

If you land thinking: "Thank God that's over", then you're not ready for SIV. But if you land thinking: "Wow, that's fantastic!" then that's when SIV really works.

[1] This doesn't just happen to lower-hour pilots. Pál Takáts, one of the most talented acro and XC competition pilots in the world, unintentionally spun his Enzo 3 playing above launch during the world championships in Kruševo, North Macedonia in 2019. He suffered minor injuries and later reported he had no idea he was so close to the spin point.

The Art of Progression

KELLY FARINA

Kelly Farina is a former British team pilot, but these days far more pilots know him as author of the best-selling book Mastering Paragliding. And hundreds have flown with him on his guided cross-country and thermalling courses in the Alps of northern Italy and Austria. Kelly grew up skateboarding and later snowboarding. That eventually took him to the Alps, where he saw paragliding for the first time. Since 2000, his profession – and his passion – has been to help pilots to enjoy the sport safely. Kelly's switched from racing snakes to guiding on intermediate wings; he coaches pilots using a systematic process. His approach to teaching what can be a gray and ephemeral subject is logical, and is informed by years of experience and by his deep study of meteorology. We sat down to discuss how he'd managed to distill his know-how into concepts that pilots of all levels can use.

Kelly, where did the idea for Mastering Paragliding come from?

I started flying in 1995, and flying was pretty much all I did until 2009. I competed, had a short stint on the British Team, and got into teaching in 2002, but by 2009 I was looking for a new challenge - I missed that feeling of being new at something. So I decided to get into Wing Chun kung fu. It's a martial art based on concepts that you learn through a rational, concise, step-by-step approach. As I got into it, I realized this was what was missing from how we taught paragliding. Pilots would sign up for a course and go through it in a week and then just get flung out into the world with their wings, but they really didn't have a clue. I wrote the book because I was frustrated with the lack of structure that we had in the sport. There was no road map to improvement.

What's immediately clear in your book is that you've given numbers and concrete ways to think about things that are pretty ethereal. Instead of telling a new pilot to "just map the thermal and find the core", you've come up with rules you can follow. Tell me about the four-for-90 rule when you're thermalling. I'd never heard of this.

In 2009 I'd been running cross-country and thermalling courses for a while. I could easily see the mistakes pilots were making, but I didn't have a reliable way to

> **"There's nothing basic about the basics."**

communicate how to fix them. Screaming at pilots to "turn tighter!" doesn't mean anything if they don't have any reference. How tight is "tighter"? One day I went out and had a long XC flight and just let my subconscious autopilot take over. But at the same time, I intently watched what I was doing, and made note of how every little thing I did impacted the wing and the flight. One thing I noticed was that all of my turns took roughly 16 seconds to complete, regardless of the strength of the climb. That's four seconds for every 90 degrees. The other thing I noticed was that as soon as I had the climb mapped, I'd release my inside hand and keep my weight shift on. These two things were something I hadn't consciously noticed about my flying in over 15 years! I'd never actually watched myself and thought about what I was doing or why. It was a complete eye-opener. As I started to write these kinds of observations down, I began to see a pattern.

I know you emphasize the importance of developing your personal toolbox rather than pushing the numbers.

Chasing numbers pushes people too hard. Pilots often skip some of the basic skills along the way, and start chasing distance or results before they have a really full toolkit with sharp, refined tools in the box. I very regularly run flying clinics that have pilots who are pretty good in the air, but can't get off the ground safely. If they're blowing launches, and then there's a sigh of relief both from the pilot and the spectators when they finally get in the air, that pilot has skipped some very important fundamentals. It's never wasted time to train at the lower levels. I call them basics, but there's nothing basic about the basics.

A pilot's toolbox needs hard skills and soft skills. Everyone climbs when it's strong and wide – that's when you need a hammer. But when it's weak and narrow, that's when you need a watchmaker's screwdriver. Turning in light and narrow lift requires extreme finesse. But if you're in a leeside climb and it's ratty and you have to keep the nose open, you want the hammer. Both of these tools need time to develop and maintain.

We have to spend time in training at every level of flying, and address our weaknesses. Route planning, flying in gaggles, taking good lines, using the speed bar and understanding the concepts that make us fly fast. As you progress, you put more and more tools in the toolbox. But you have to be honest with yourself and focus on the level that you're at – and return often to the level below, so you keep all the tools sharp.

Everyone can fly well on the booming days, but the really good pilots train the basics, so when the sun is a bit tricky and there's a bit of wind affecting the climbs – maybe there's a layer of stability – they can still get up and cover distance. Good carpenters take care of their tools. We should as well.

Something I've found over all these years is the flights that are technical and tricky and at times really slow, requiring a lot of patience and precision, can be a lot more rewarding than the huge days where everything makes sense and it's easy. Those tricky days make the beer at the end of the day taste really good! Let's get back to the basics. You mentioned that a lot of your students are pretty good in the air, but bad on the ground. I see this at World Cup level. Some pilots are Jedis in the air, but really sloppy on the ground.

You don't want to hope that the passive safety of your wing is going to deliver you into the air. I find that pilots who struggle with their launches and ground handling often perpetuate their weakness. They don't want to be embarrassed, so they don't work on it. If they just took action on the weakness and corrected it, they'd quickly turn it into a strength. It's a real shame, because it isn't something to get embarrassed about – we all have weaknesses in our flying. The good and great pilots don't ride on their strengths and ignore their weaknesses; they turn their weaknesses into strengths. That's just ego. And launch is an easy place to get hurt. I had an instructor tell me about 20 years ago: "A minute on the ground is worth an hour in the air." I still think that's true and it's still what I tell my students. Don't neglect your weaknesses.

Tell me about your thoughts on wing choice.

Obviously the more demanding the wing, the more it takes away your ability to run on autopilot. The more we run on autopilot, the more bandwidth we can apply to the game. So we can be thinking several moves ahead, like you do in chess when you start to get really good. The best pilots are several moves ahead of where they are now, just like the best race car drivers. They're thinking way down the course line. But if the glider is shouting at you and you're putting all your energy into keeping it open, then your bandwidth is pulled away from observation. Observation is really important, because it triggers our experience. It doesn't matter how much experience you have if you're flying a glider that's too hot, because your observation won't trigger it. The difference in sink rate between a performance B glider and a C glider is about 3-4%. That's not going to help a pilot much unless their skills are perfect.

Tell me about the "Golden Rule."

The Golden Rule states that no matter how the glider is moving above the pilot's head, the pilot beneath shall have no sharp increases or decreases in speed. What that means is that the pilot is acting as suspension to take out all the bumps, swings and surges that would convert height to speed. That increase of speed as the pilot goes through the air has to come from somewhere, and it comes from gravity. The pilot is turning height to speed, which is really inefficient – especially if you're trying to climb, but even if you're just trying to glide and you're allowing the glider to pitch forward, or allowing yourself to swing underneath it. All those little increases and decreases in speed end up costing you height. Every good pilot who can thermal well and glide well sticks to the Golden Rule, whether they know it or not. Any pilot who doesn't obey the Golden Rule suffers for it. Look at acro pilots: they break the Golden Rule all the time. That's why they go down so fast! Basically, it's a concept that pilots can use to make their flying consciously smooth and therefore efficient.

Nate Scales introduced me to the fact that in most sports that humans participate in, the pendulum is below us – skiing, mountain biking, surfing, skateboarding, etc. But in flying the pendulum is above us. When the arc is below us, carving a turn really makes sense, so I love this concept of carving a turn and being smooth, rather than just turning circles.
Because there's a large pendulum of instability, we have to act as the suspension. We're in constant motion under the glider, and we have to keep it as smooth as possible. Every pilot makes mistakes, but the better pilots make fewer of them, and this is one area you can really see a difference. If pilots have the Golden Rule in their heads when they fly, they'll instantly recognize when they have broken it, and in very little time they'll learn how to correct it so it becomes automatic.

Something I see low-hour pilots really struggle with is getting bumped out of a climb. How do you teach pilots to reduce this?
I think pilots put too much emphasis on turning the right way. Sometimes you get pulled into a climb and sometimes you get pushed out, and feeling the difference comes with experience. If your first instinct is wrong and you turn the wrong way, you can just turn 270 degrees and get back into it. Of course, if you're super low, going the right way is more critical, but usually if you go the wrong way it's not the end of the world. Better to relax, stay smooth and carve your turn rather than bang it around the other way and shatter the Golden Rule.

Kelly, you say there are two don'ts in thermalling. One is never change direction; the other is don't bury the brake. Cross Country did a great article a while back about how thermals tend to rotate in the northern vs the southern hemisphere, and we should turn against the rotation of a thermal to increase lift and reduce bank angle[1]. And it's rare, but when I'm flying especially in really strong conditions like we frequently get in the Rockies, I'll sometimes very quickly stall the inside of my wing when the thermals are sharp to help get me into the climb faster. Can you defend these rules, and are there exceptions?
Of course there are exceptions. There are no hard and fast rules. Everything in the book should be thought of as rules of thumb. Lower-hour pilots are not going to have enough finesse to bleed energy in and out like an expert pilot. An expert pilot can "bury the brake" and not break the Golden Rule. But by definition if you stall one side of your glider, which then creates a surge, that's going to break the Golden Rule, and that isn't efficient. But a really top pilot can absolutely manage that kind of energy efficiently.

[1] There is a fascinating thread on the Paragliding Forum for the science behind this. Search "In which direction do you prefer to turn in thermals?" to find it.

Winding the energy in and bleeding the energy out is a subtle and difficult thing to do that low airtime pilots won't accomplish.

The brake rule aims to stop a pilot from making a common mistake: using too much brake when they hit a core, and overreacting. A pilot might feel like it's efficient, but it's never efficient to break the Golden Rule. The turning rule is the same thing. Most of the time we can only feel the rotation of a thermal when it's very strong and it's near the ground. As a thermal climbs, it mixes out and it's nearly impossible to feel the direction it's turning. It's almost always more efficient to either turn tighter or open your turn to adjust to the core than it is to change direction. But if you're low and you can feel that you're turning with the direction of the thermal, or you're just in a ripper and can feel it, then it may be more efficient to change direction. If it's tiny, just bear in mind you might fall out of the core – weigh up the pros and cons.

Tell me how you came up with your 15km/h rule for flying in the lee?
I lived in the Zillertal valley on the north side of the Alps in Austria for twenty years. We fly up and down the Pinzgau, one of the most famous flying zones in the world. You fly in the lee regularly there, because in the afternoon the north winds blow in from the German flats but the sun is to the south, so you're flying the south-facing slopes to find climbs. Again this is a rule of thumb, but if the wind is above 15km/h, the lee presents too much risk and I've seen way too many incidents. The rule is simple – if the wind is less than 15km/h, the lee sides are safe enough to explore; if it's more than 15km/h you should avoid the lee and use the windward side and "bridges."

Bridges are terrain features that connect one valley system to another. Very rarely is there nothing between one range and another; there's nearly always an ancient moraine or smaller series of hills or some other feature that will provide triggers or a little convergence, or something that will give you a better line when there's a long transition.

But all lee isn't the same, of course. It depends on how large the obstruction is, the time of day, the strength of the valley winds or meteo winds, how close you are to the terrain, etc. In our area of the Alps, the problematic lee is almost always the south-west faces that are in the shadow of the valley wind. If you go into those spots you can be in trouble, but if you go in deeper it's fine. The top pilots probably don't even think about these things; for most of them they've learned the hard way and they just know where to go instinctively, but if lower-hour pilots can learn these concepts it can make them quite a bit safer.

A quote in your book about speed-to-fly is: "accelerate your wing to get your ground speed as close as you can to the trim speed of your wing." Tell me more about this.
This obviously holds only in a headwind or crosswind, not downwind. But over the years I've noticed that trying to fly MacCready and staring at my glide ratio calculator soaked up a lot of brain bandwidth, and wasn't getting me anything. But if I've got say 5km/h on the nose and I press enough bar to get up to trim speed, that's going to give me best glide. Obviously it depends on how much of a hurry you're in – this doesn't necessarily apply if you're racing – but if you want best glide, that's a pretty good cheat. It's not very scientific, but it works for me. Russ Ogden once told me that if the climb is strong in front of you, give it as much gas as you can while still holding the nose open.

But if I'm not in a big hurry I just accelerate until I see 36 or 37km/h, because I usually fly lower intermediate gliders.

Your book has some fantastic weather information that's beyond the scope of this interview, but I would like to hear about the "air mass spectrum." You lay out a range from volatile to stubborn: volatile, excitable, cooperative, lazy, stubborn. Or "fizzy to sticky."

Days are never carbon copies of each other. Every day is made up of a combination of wind, air pressure, humidity, lapse rate and sun strength. A day that's slightly more unstable will feel different and react differently from one that's more stable. The air mass will interact differently with the terrain, and the aerology is different. When you learn the nuances of how all these things interact on the spectrum of fizzy to sticky, you can plan your day around what you expect to find. On unstable days you'd expect an early start, but a short day because of overdevelopment, so you'd plan a shorter route. On stable days you'd expect a much slower start, slower climbs and very short glides before the inversion breaks – but these are also the days where pilots top land Mont Blanc, so they're still worth chasing!

Fizzy and sticky gives us a binary way of looking at the weather. Fizzy is really unstable, and sticky is really stable. But I wasn't happy with just using these two bookends to describe a day. If we make it less binary and more analog, we can begin to understand the character of the air mass. Each one of these characters has a slightly different feel. Volatile is obviously quite stormy. Strong climbs everywhere, early start and probably a very short day. Excitable is going to be quite fun to fly, but still quite a short day. Thermals aren't going very high because of the pressure, humidity and lapse rate and the amount of sun that's available. And then we've got the cooperative days, which are perfect in both the Alps and the flatlands. Nice cumulus clouds, reasonable wind, strong climbs with soft edges. Then we've got the lazy days that require a little bit more prepping, a little bit more encouragement. Climbs are slow and have sharp edges. And finally we've got the stubborn days when, whatever you do, not much works. It's still the fizzy to sticky spectrum, but it gives us a little more color between black and white.

You talk about being "natural".

Being a natural pilot is what most pilots should strive for. When we first learn, we fly by feeling without any instruments. Then we get more and more high-tech instruments, and we end up relying on them. I'm ashamed to say that I'm very reliant on my clumsy vario. I've tried flying without it, and I feel lost. I'm an instrument addict! But I'm persevering. I'm trying to become more natural. Obviously there are some things that you need technology for, like glide to goal and such, but as we've added more and more features and more and more complexity like thermal mapping, I think pilots are spending too much time staring at their screens instead of the sky. It's becoming virtual paragliding instead of using your brain to map climbs, as we've always done. And ironically thermal mappers work when the climbs are strong, when you don't need any help in climbing, but they don't work very well when it's light, when your intuition and observation are critical.

When students go through their initial course, the first thing they're sold is a GoPro, which makes me cringe. That's a recipe for having an accident. And then, because they don't yet know how to thermal, they get taught to use their thermal mappers on their instruments. But no thermal mapper on an instrument is a substitute for a strong natural mapping strategy. An instrument can't keep up with what you feel. What people do is up to them, but I believe to feel the true soul of flying you have to keep it as natural as possible.

Kelly, my last question is about foehn[3] winds. What do pilots who are new to the Alps need to be aware of, and what's a go vs a not go day?
A lot depends on where you're flying. Many places are more subject to foehn than others. You can fly in Passy in France, 20 minutes down the road from Chamonix, on a strong north foehn, but you'd be confetti on the same day in Chamonix. Generally the closer you are to the main ridge of the Alps and the closer you are to north/south oriented valleys, the more subjected you are to foehn wind. In places that are sensitive to foehn, when you have a pressure difference from north to south of the Alps of 4hPa, it's enough to trigger dangerous downslope winds. In other areas you can fly in up to an 8hPa gradient. But those spots are normally a very long way from the main ridge of the Alps, and have a lot of mountains between them that have east/west running valleys that break it up. Foehn is extremely unpredictable, because it builds and builds on the windward side and then suddenly dumps over to the lee side, but you can't know the timing. You could be flying with a north foehn on the south side of the Alps, doing just fine, and then come to a pass, and suddenly you're in a violent cascade of wind and you'll have very little control. Unless you really understand foehn and really know an area, flying in a pressure difference of 4hPa or more between the northern and southern Alpine ranges is a dicey proposition.

I think this is an appropriate place to remind everyone that we're always one flight away from either an accident or getting so scared that you'll never come back to the sport. And in my experience, playing with foehn is a pretty reliable way to at least get awfully scared. In training for the X-Alps and in the 2015 race, I subjected myself to pretty strong foehn several times. Every time I very luckily made it to the ground, it took a long time to shake it off. Flying in foehn is like flying in a class V river. It's not like dealing with strong but relatively laminar air. It's a vertical whirlpool.
I think of it as rotor within rotor within rotor. I call it fractal rotor. You have no idea when the dam will break with foehn.

[3] A föhn or foehn is a type of dry, warm, down-slope wind that occurs in the lee (downwind side) of a mountain range. Föhn can be initiated when deep low-pressure systems move into Europe, drawing moist Mediterranean air over the Alps.
It is a rain shadow wind that results from the subsequent adiabatic warming of air that has dropped most of its moisture on windward slopes. As a consequence of the different adiabatic lapse rates of moist and dry air, the air on the leeward slopes becomes warmer than equivalent elevations on the windward slopes. Föhn winds can raise temperatures by as much as 14°C (25°F) in just a matter of hours. Switzerland, southern Germany and Austria have a warmer climate due to the Föhn, as moist winds off the Mediterranean Sea blow over the Alps.

HOW TO TWEAK YOUR MENTAL GAME

Unless you're competing in hike-and-fly races or doing a lot of vol-biv, our sport isn't very physical. But flying is much more mentally straining than most sports or activities – and mental effort can be considerably more calorie-intensive than physical exercise. Being in the harness for eight or more hours can be exhausting, but our minds are doing most of the hard labor. How many times have we heard flying compared to chess? Chess masters try to dominate the middle of the board. It makes for better attack, and it's a more defensible position. It's all about finding the right balance.

"When I do well, I feel prepared in my mind. I don't mean just being organized with all my equipment and instruments, but having everything in order. I have to be physically ready; my body must be in order. I have to sleep well and not be stressed, so my personal and business life must be in order. If you're in a hurry to get to launch because you're not organized, you'll be in a hurry in the air and not be organized."
Christian Ciech

"In comps, it's so easy to get caught out. For example, when you're doing well, you keep pushing too much. You want to

"PRIMING: Negative priming is the tendency towards a negative reinforcement in your flying. "It probably won't work...They always out-thermal me anyway...I'm probably going to land." We need to work on the flip side of negative priming. Positive priming is a very slight change in attitude. "The good thing about my position is that I climb better than the pilots above me... I love being low because I'm skilled at scratching and finding broken lift."

PRESSURE: In most cases for most people, the more important it gets, the less likely you are to do well. When you have everything to gain, you sometimes have way too much to lose, and that can be very dangerous. If you're too stressed, you won't fly well. You must be sorted in your head before you launch a paraglider. Don't do things before you launch that add stress to your flight. For example, I don't like to be on task committees at competitions, because it adds stress before you fly. Don't talk about accidents on flying days. You have to be in a good mood to fly well. All we need to know before we fly is the weather – we don't need to talk about the gory details. Launch early and get into your own environment. Nervousness is contagious, and nervousness is abundant on launch. Don't sit around and get sucked into other people's stress."
Mads Syndergaard

"I've been working a lot on using Daniel Kahneman's concept of thinking fast and slow in my flying. Thinking fast is being in the Flow state, maybe when we're thermalling or launching and we don't have to analyze much. We're doing what's natural, we're happy and it's all good. Slow thinking is analytical, when we're planning ahead, looking at the clouds, trying to figure out a way through a tricky area, and we need more conscious thought. I've been playing with little tricks like furrowing my brow to create a trigger that snaps me out of Flow so I can get more analytical when I need it.

I often talk with my students about the three Ps. The first is preparation. There's the obvious stuff, like preparing your gear and having enough water – but I'm talking about preparing the small skill-based goals that we're working on for the day. Things like listening to a podcast or studying track logs or reading a book related to your goals. Then there's performance. The performance is the actual flight. In every flight, we're going to make mistakes and we're going to have successes. After the flight is the progression. This is sitting down and analyzing our performance by talking about it with mentors or journaling or studying our track logs and seeing what we're doing well and where we can improve.

Another important concept is fixed vs growth mindset. A fixed mindset is treating something as a genetic trait. For example, if you have a fixed mindset that you're good at thermalling and you get outclimbed, you'll likely blame the trim of your wing, or think the pilot is light on his glider, or some other excuse. A growth mindset would be "I can improve my climbing" or "I'm going to learn from this pilot who just outclimbed me." We need to be in a growth mindset to improve."

Mitch Riley

show your peers that you really are good, so you start taking too much tactical risk. Or you'll fall behind, and out comes your innner bully telling you just to give up. We need to learn how to identify and avoid these gremlins: recognize what they sound like and the situations they pop in, and then try to break the cycle. Learn to acknowledge them, but don't let them win you over!"

Hugh Miller

"I often worry too much. In the X-Alps, the line that I would most certainly fly if I was not in the race is often obvious. The clouds point the way. But if that line is taking me way off course-line that doubting voice gets really strong... "what if this doesn't work?" What I should be saying is: "this is going to work!" We have to learn to turn risks into opportunities. Ask yourself, "what is the best thing that can happen to me in the air, right now?" Then make that happen. If you feel yourself tense up, try to turn what you're doing into a game. Enjoy the scenery. Remind yourself that what you're doing is NUTS! If you're having fun, you'll do well."

Gavin McClurg

The Veteran

MAXIME BELLEMIN

Maxime Bellemin has won many national and international titles, and is known for his two-volume book, Performance Paragliding.

As an engineer, Maxime likes to break down the many invisible unknowns in our sport into numbers. Those of us less skilled in arithmetic can grasp and put into immediate use his methods and concepts. Again and again on the podcast we've heard that to get good, nothing replaces time and training. There are no shortcuts.

Maxime is proof that in fact there are ways to excel, even if you can't dedicate the hours that most top-level pilots have. He lives in Paris, far from the Alps, and has a serious job. He has very little time to dedicate to flying and insists he has no special talent for the sport, but he's one of the best in the world.

Maxime, in your book you write about how attention narrows as we get closer to goal and how often we miss stuff when flying. Can you say more?

I've been coaching competition pilots since 2010. Even at the very top level, I see pilots let their emotions and feelings completely cloud their thinking. They'll be flying to goal with their instruments 30cm from their eyes, and not look at them once. They have all the information needed to make informed decisions in their lap, and around them with other pilots, but they only stare straight ahead, and when they don't make goal, they've no recollection of what happened. It gets chalked up to bad luck. I noticed in my own flying that I would get very distracted at times. I call it going to sleep in the air. So now I set an alarm on my watch every hour – something external that reminds me to stay focused.

At the 2019 world championships in North Macedonia, I noticed day after day that many of the top pilots were making the End of Speed Section barely above the ground, and then having to find a climb to make goal. This is a pretty risky move! Historically you only leave for goal when you feel pretty sure you can get the glide ratio needed to make it, but it's gotten so fast at the higher-level comps that, to score well, pilots have to push for ESS much sooner than we used to.

The tactical risk is very high when you fly this way. Pilots in high-level comps are now

> **In the beginning you have to get solid technically. You have to learn to climb well, to glide well and to stick with the gaggle.**

mostly on the same wing, so we fly very homogeneously. If you're in a gaggle near the end of the race with 50 other pilots, and 49 of them leave for ESS and you don't go with them, there's a chance they all bomb out and you're the hero. But it's more likely that you'll come in with more height and make goal more easily, but you'll be three minutes behind. You can't win at this game being too conservative.

In your book you describe the arc that comp pilots have to go through to become good. In the beginning you have to get solid technically. You have to learn to climb well, to glide well and to stick with the gaggle. When you have that down, you have to spend some time racing too fast, but that inevitably puts you on the ground frequently. The final step is learning to rein in your emotions so you can strike at the right time.
It's fun to practice being the rabbit, and some pilots will always be rabbits, and that's ok. But if you want to climb the ladder, each step is more difficult than the previous. Everyone can make progress, but the marginal gains require more and more effort, because at the top level they're tiny. At the very top level we can only improve in the mental area – there are no more technical or tactical advantages to exploit.

If you want to reach the very top, you have to have extreme control of how you behave and make decisions. And that might be counterproductive to having fun. You have to find the balance. For a long time my goal was to win and be at the very top, but in recent years I've shifted my priorities more towards having fun. It was very difficult for me to accept that there were external factors that I had no power to change. For example, I've had a lot of success over the years in competitions, which I'm very proud of, but I've never been selected by the French coach for the world championships. This was bothering me so much that I had to rethink what the sport meant to me. It became clear that what makes me happy is traveling and flying with my friends, and when I reset my goals to just enjoy the sport, my flying improved because I was more relaxed. Your goals must be clear.

You spend a lot of time in both books on identifying weaknesses in order to improve your flying.
My opinion is that, maybe with the exception of Chrigel, pilots can't be good at everything. We all have weaknesses, and failure is part of the game. We must identify where we can improve, but there might be things that can't be improved, and you'll have

to rely on your other strengths to overcome a given weakness. Maybe you're not good at following, which can be very important in competitions; but you're good at analysis and climbing fast, so you can use these assets to compensate. No one can fly a week-long competition perfectly. We have to minimize the volume and consequence of our mistakes. When we make a mistake, we have to be self-aware enough so they can be corrected. Keeping a journal can be a very effective tool. As soon as you land, make a note of what you did well and where you can improve.

Let's talk about the physical. You mention in your book that a five-hour flight can burn 4,000-5,000 calories, because the brain burns a ton of energy. This is right up there with a moderate day in the X-Alps, and more than double what a typical adult needs per day. And there's another side of the physical that I think isn't often considered, and that's resilience. A fit person who's done a lot of strength training can walk away from a hard landing uninjured, whereas a lifelong smoker who doesn't spend much time in the gym – not so much.

Fitness is important for performance, not just for flying a task, but for recovering quickly before the next one. Your brain requires a ton of fuel when you're flying. We have to monitor and regulate our food and hydration. And the quality of the food and what you drink is very important. Once you're dehydrated, it's very difficult to recover. You can't just drink a glass of water – it can take days to get your body back in balance.

Being fit is also a matter of safety. It makes you more resilient and durable, but also if you have an accident you'll recover more quickly.

Maxime, something I'm really struggling with lately is: "What's next?" The biggest problem I have with doing big projects like the X-Alps or crossing Alaska is that they end. There's so much planning and preparation and anticipation and training, and then suddenly this magnificent, all-consuming experience is over.

Our brains are not just rational; they're very emotional. What you describe is human. When you live through something so vivid and rewarding as the X-Alps and it ends, you feel lost. What's important is: were you present when it happened? Was your mind open? Were you taking every opportunity to execute a task? Were you letting yourself enjoy your surroundings? Or were you just struggling to achieve a certain result or trying to prove something? You must remove any potential pollution from the endeavor, so you can be present. If you're filling yourself up during the event, you won't be empty when it's over.

I interviewed Chrigel about this phenomenon. He said he went to a pretty dark place after his first one in 2009. He says he's cured this problem now by having goals. So as soon as he's done with one event, he's thinking about the next one. But is that just distraction? Shouldn't I want to get comfortable with my own discomfort?

Goal setting is very important. A goal that's too easy won't be very fulfilling when you reach it. But if your goal is too hard to reach, you might give up, and this can be hard on your self-esteem. Having several goals with intermediate steps is the right approach. This can help your self-esteem and motivation because it can be measured and it's tangible.

Tactics matter. "When you've got a side-wind and you're flying with another pilot, I recommend flying on the windward side of them." Racing in Roldanillo, Colombia. Photo: Nick Greece

There are all the reasons that Chrigel is Chrigel, but I think what defines his success the most is his confidence. Maxime, one of the things I've thought about a lot is the headspace that a lot of the athletes get into during the race. You get into an extended flow state that allows you to fly in conditions that normally wouldn't be acceptable. I've flown entire days in super windy conditions in the X-Alps without being even slightly concerned, absolutely knowing I've got the moves required. A day after the race, if I was flying in the same conditions, I'd be terrified and I'd go land! I'm sure that's part of the addiction.
The way I think of flow is that you don't need cognition. You don't need to make a decision. Your body will react according to your feelings, your intuition. In flying the process goes from information directly to action, overstepping the decision phase. You're simply doing things. You have the impression that time passes very slowly. And yes, it's been proven that this state of mind is very addictive, maybe even more than the most powerful drugs.

I'd like to get into some of the specific tips in your books. The first is your advice on using speed bar. You say that in a competition you should fly full bar permanently if climbs are greater than 2m/s. Is that true even at the beginning of a race?
Everyone has to be aware that to fly fast you have to climb fast. If you can't climb fast, you can't use the full extent of your speed system. It's different from flying cross country,

because in a comp there are so many other pilots you can watch, and you should be able to find cores very quickly. Once you're a good climber, flying full bar depends on the MacCready theory (speed-to-fly). MacCready tells us two things: what strength of thermal we can anticipate, and the probability of finding it. If the expected thermal is strong and the probability is high, we should fly faster.

So in theory, if it's early in the day and conditions are not that strong, MacCready will tell us to not fly full speed. But in practice the leading points bell-curve incentivizes pilots to push harder early in a task to stay out front, so they might race faster than they should. Conversely, the closer you get to the end of the task, the more we get ruled by emotion with the smell of goal so close, and the more we want to give up completely on MacCready and just race fast and ignore climbs that we should take.

You say: "The right question is not whether conditions will improve, but are conditions good enough?"

This touches on the purpose of my books. I want these books to apply to every pilot, and it's important to point out that "performance" relates to comparing yourself to others, but "performance" also relates to your own personal development and reaching your own best possible level. This quote is meant for the former in a competitive environment, and what I mean is that when it comes to weather conditions, who cares? Everyone will be flying in the same conditions. You can't wait for something hypothetical. You can't bet so much on the future. If you're on launch and there are 15 minutes until the start and it's good enough, you can't wait for it to get better. Of course, you have to be aware of the evolution of the conditions and anticipate changes, but there's no point in too much analysis.

Talk about optimized waypoints with wind.

If you're flying in a headwind going to a turnpoint, then every time you circle, you're drifting away from your destination. For example, if you're in 15km/h of headwind and climbing at .5m/s, you're gaining nothing – you're drifting away as fast as you're climbing. But if you're going downwind to a turnpoint with 10km/h of tailwind a 1m/s climb is equivalent to a 2m/s climb in nil-wind. What you read on your vario is not the real rate of climb when you're in wind and flying towards a turnpoint, because it ignores how you're drifting, either towards or away from your goal.

When you've got a side-wind and you're flying with another pilot, I recommend flying on the windward side of them. If you're downwind and the pilot finds a climb, you'll have to push into the wind to get it. And in the flatlands, when in doubt, straighten out towards the wind or towards the sun to better connect with the core.

In flatlands you talk about dividing the sky up into thirds, which I think most of us are taught. If you're low you're flying the terrain. When you're in the middle, you're flying the terrain as well as the sky. When you're in the top third, you fly the sky. But what I hadn't heard was that when you're in the mountains you drop the middle and just divide the sky into two halves.

Yes, in the mountains you have only the terrain and the sky, so you can drop the middle.

Talk about improving your position. You say: "When you're solo, you try to limit collateral damage."

Leading points are currently weighted more towards the beginning of the race, and they're absolutely allocated towards the optimized route. So if you decide to fly a really creative line and get ahead of the lead gaggle, but it's on a line away from the optimized route, you could foreseeably come into goal in great position but get no leading points, and your result will be drastically worse. Right now leading points, in my opinion, don't reward what they're meant to. They were designed to encourage pilots to push out and not pimp, which they are doing, but they should also reward making good tactical decisions and they should reward pilots for being bold.

You say we should pay more attention to altitude above goal. I've always just watched glide to goal, I've never paid much attention to goal altitude?

Let's make things simple and say we're flying a wing that has a glide ratio of 10:1. Now let's imagine that a headwind cuts this to 7:1. But what if the headwind picks up just slightly and suddenly your glide goes to 5.5:1? You may not assess that the difference is very important if you're just looking at your glide ratio. But if you look at your altitude above goal you can see that it's very important, and you see how much risk you're taking. In this example maybe at 6:1 you'll arrive with 200m, but when you drop to 5.5:1 you'll arrive with no height above the ground. Watching altitude above goal gives you a valuable data point.

Talk about optimal activation points and the difference between mind and body activation?

Activation can be thought of as the optimal amount of energy that you need for the activity you're doing. A boxer entering the ring has a very high activation point. A chess player has a very low activation point. When we fly, we're boxing and playing chess. When we take off, we should already be warmed up and activated, because it will require effort. During the flight there'll be phases when we have to be sensitive and active, for example when thermalling, and other phases like gliding when we require more from our minds. Optimal activation means matching the energy requirement with what's needed at a specific time.

Tell me about the "funnel" concept?

Before we take off, we get the task briefing, the weather briefing, we spend time looking at the sky, thinking about the route – we're accumulating information, but we're not making many decisions. Our vision is very wide. The closer you get to the flight, the more you want to limit distractions. You have to start focusing on your own flight. You don't want people interrupting you as you clip in. You want to only think about what's relevant and what resources you need for launch. Do I take off or not, do I turn right or left after launch? That's all I want to be thinking about.

The funnel concept is a way to process and organize your day from the moment you wake up until you launch.

You say in your book: "Learning to lose is not learning from failures; learning to lose requires psychological work on oneself to be able to choose the right mindset. To learn from failures is to look for causes, correct them and then not repeat them."
We're living experiences. I don't say that there's always something positive to be taken out of every experience, but there's something to be learned. Maybe it's something you don't want to reproduce because you're not proud of it. It's about building an attitude of resilience. Failures can help us improve.

Maxime, when we look at the high-level comps you see the same names in the top ten over and over again. Is there something not obvious that these pilots are doing?
I think consistency is the true mark of a really good pilot. We fly like who we are. Pilots who produce good results are not nervous people. They're calm, they're cool. The pressure has very little influence on them. They're smooth in their lives and in the air. This attitude then becomes self-fulfilling. You get more self-confidence when you win and become sure of your own abilities.

"We fly like who we are. Consistent pilots are not nervous people."
Racing in Chelan, Washington. Photo: Nick Greece

HOW TO GO BIG

There are many components to putting together big flights. And big doesn't just mean big distance. It could be a technical flight that's less than 100k but takes six hours to pull off. It could be flying an aesthetic line that's personally inspiring. "Big" is putting together the preparation, technical skills, route plan, head space, weather knowledge and confidence to do more than you have before. For some people "big" is chasing a world record, for some it's a particularly interesting triangle, for others it's upping their personal best. But big doesn't just happen. It takes training, thought, motivation, action and a whole lot of hours.

"The distance between a 50k flight and a 100k flight is planning"
Jon Chambers

"Mindset is really important. To do big things you have to be in the right head space. I'm really lucky. My wife is super supportive, so I try to be a good husband all year, but I try especially hard in the spring! I need to have a good home, and that makes it really easy for me to be all in on the good days. I love the fact that when I go to the hill and somebody asks me where I'm going, I can honestly say I have no idea. There's nothing else that we do where you just GO and end up somewhere! You get to go a little bit crazy and you're all by yourself and nobody thinks you're weird. Or maybe they do!"
Nate Scales

"Going big is like surfing huge swells. You gotta wait for the swell. You have to wait and be patient and be really prepared, ready to go on the big days."
Nick Greece

"You'll stay in the air much longer and have more fun if you make flying more mission-driven. By that I mean take time

"Big days are the realization of years of planning and waiting. You have some ideas as to what you want to do with a particular day based on its conditions. And if you can schedule the day for flying and have a plan in mind, you're much more likely to execute that plan instead of randomly coming up with something while airborne. A plan is always subject to change, but having a plan means you're more likely to pull it off. There have been plenty of days where I haven't thought big enough. I've only thought about a flight up to a certain point, and arrived there with a bit of day left with no idea what to do next. Now I try to look ahead as far as possible, knowing the day can go better than expected. It can also go worse, and you should be mentally prepared for both. Have a plan."
Bill Belcourt

"Having confidence in putting yourself in the right place at the right time is the key to big flights. That comes back to good forecasting and weather knowledge so you can make a plan and be confident in executing it. The other thing I've learned is if you're thinking about how far you might have to walk when you're looking ahead, you're probably going to land. One thing training for the X-Alps and X-Pyr races has done for me is I no longer think a six-hour walk is a big deal. When I fly I've got walking sticks and extra food and water, and I know I can walk a long way. That's really helped me make better moves in the air.
I have a saying: "Never exclude continuations that were wrong before a condition changed." In other words, things are going to change in every cross-country flight; don't make the mistake of using only what's worked so far. We have to remain nimble. Often I'll collect data and observations in the first hour or two of a flight and velcro to that information as the answer for the future. Doing that will often put you on the ground. Adapt to the day as it changes."
Willi Canell

to study the forecasts; study your track logs after your flights and learn what you've done well and where you can improve; have your gear super-organized; get involved with a group of hungry pilots who'll get up early and drive long distances to achieve a great flight. Preparation is really important. If you just sit in the back of the car checking social media while your friends look out the window and plan their flight, before you even launch they'll have an edge on you."
Hugh Miller

"Ted Boyce had the right attitude for breaking world records. He flew every day, and he'd take off before anyone else and try to make it work. He wouldn't try to predict the weather or pick the days – he'd just try no matter what. If you want to go big, you have to keep hammering and hammering, and eventually you'll plug into the right day."
Larry Tudor

"With people like Berni Pessl, who's constantly doing massive triangles in the Alps on an EN B wing, you'll see from his track logs that he's almost always the first to launch, but he's never too early. Getting really big flights is finding that magic balance between flying fast without bombing out, and using every single usable minute of the day. Climbing in only the best climbs, climbing fast, gliding efficiently by choosing good lines. Basically, to go big you've got to be a really good pilot!"
Till Gottbrath

"There's a real added risk to chasing numbers. Not just a safety risk, but a risk of bursting your passion for the sport. When it's nothing but numbers, you stop flying the shorter window days, you don't go out for the 50km flights that often have more magic than a 200km flight. The flight databases are a great resource, but there's a troll lurking under that bridge. We can really take advantage of the marginal days by experimenting with different techniques and turning them into a challenge and a training opportunity."
Greg Hamerton

Red Bull

Get Your Kicks For Free

NICK NEYNENS

Nick Neynens is my favorite Red Bull X-Alps pilot. His mom and brother have been his supporters in the last two races, and while the rest of us all have big flash camper vans with stoves, showers, refrigerators and comfortable beds, they do it with a standard rental car, a single burner camp stove, and tents.

Nick is one of those guys in the race you can never count out. On a perfect flying day in the 2015 race he had to top land to fix a knot in his lines, and ended up dead last at the end of the day. But 11 days later he got to Monaco in 10th place by taking creative, deep lines and simply outthinking and outmaneuvering a lot of the other pilots.

I first met Nick a couple of weeks before the 2015 X-Alps while training in the Bavarian Alps. We were both rookies going into the race and had approached our training in profoundly opposite ways. He was planning on doing a good bit of the course in jandals (that's Kiwi for sandals) and his physical training had consisted of some "tramping" back home, whereas my own training had been exceedingly deliberate and strict. In other words, Nick didn't appear to me to be taking it all that seriously. But when the gun went off in Salzburg, it was clear that his care-free attitude and many hours of pursuing vol-biv all over the planet pays huge dividends in a long event like the X-Alps.

Before we get into the X-Alps, how did this all start for you?
I'd seen paragliding in the Alps back when I was a kid tramping around with my dad in Switzerland, but it didn't really click until I was back in New Zealand much later. The bush can be pretty brutal there. I remember one hike took me about half an hour to walk around 30 meters. I was basically swimming in the stuff. To be able to fly over that mess and cut out a day of hard labor was really the idea that got me into it. In 2006 I learned on the internet that a paraglider only weighed 5-6kg, and I couldn't believe it. As soon as I saw that, I didn't even need to try it out. I just signed up to learn and jumped in with both feet.

> **"When it's too rough or too strong my mantra is: don't go land, go fly somewhere else!"**

I gather your real passion is vol-biv, not really competitions?
I'd probably like competitions more if I did well in them! But the great thing about vol-biv is being able to get the most out of the day. When you're in a competition you miss a ton of potential flying, and there's a lot of waiting around. Most of the time you're only flying in the middle of the day. Some of my best and most memorable flights are really late in the evening or just early morning glides. Some bivvy days are not flyable generally, but there are periods where you can fly here and there, and I enjoy the challenge of hitting those windows. What's great about vol-biv is that you get to operate from sunrise to sunset. I'd much rather be hiking through the mountains with my wing not being able to fly than sitting on a hill talking to depressed paraglider pilots about when the weather is going to change!

That's a good point, and you live in a part of the world where the weather changes really fast and you have to grab it when you can.
Often with cross country we reduce flying to a number. It becomes about the kilometers. If you're doing the same route and you fall a bit short, instead of being a great flight you get bummed out. But when you're flying vol-biv and just have a short flight off a mountain, it's really special – it's not something you forget. Sometimes those five-minute flights are all you need to get your head straight.

I have a question for you about how pilots new to vol-biv should get into it. My first big one was an 18-day expedition across the Sierras in 2012 with Nick Greece, Antoine Laurens, Eric Reed and a couple others. Near the end of it I was totally ecstatic with the whole experience. I'd never done anything so incredible. I was interviewing Nick a few days before we finished and I asked him: "Don't you think everyone should be doing this?" And he was like: "Dude, are you crazy? No!" He reminded me that the kind of flying we were doing was really at the top end of what should be done on a paraglider. Top landing in strong conditions, flying through a ton of rough air, not having access to weather forecasts, and all the things that are pretty standard with vol-biv. In the X-Alps you have to fly day after day in conditions that are a long way from recreational, so I know what you're willing to fly in. So where should someone start who doesn't have those kind of skills? What progression do you recommend?
I don't think it's much different from what you should learn normally. In the beginning you need to learn how to launch and land safely, do a ton of ground handling, and you

should learn meteorology. You need to look at as much weather information as you can, and then go outside and fly, and see how and if it matches up to what you thought it would be. You need to learn how to read the sky on the fly and understand what hazards might be developing. In my early days I wish I'd spent more time doing coastal flights just ridge-soaring, because you can get so much more time in the air, which is really valuable. It's hard getting that kind of time when you're new because you don't yet know how to fly XC. When you're learning, there's a lot of different things you need to think about, and you eventually want to make as much of those things as automatic as possible.

When I first started I flew my school wing, an old Gin Bolero Plus, for two years, which is a pretty long time. In those two years I was doing vol-biv in New Zealand and the Alps. For sure I wasn't going very far, but I was learning all those skills. I was a lot more focused on traveling and learning than I was on buying new gear.

Why did you decide to get into adventure races, and when did you feel like you had enough skill to take on the X-Alps?
The first was the X-Berg, which is an X-Alps style hike-and-fly race in South Africa. I signed up only because I happened to be in Cape Town and it sounded like fun. I don't think I had a flight longer than 10km in the race, but I loved having the defined purpose. Sometimes I feel when I'm doing vol-biv for fun that I'm not exactly sure what to do. Making decisions can be quite tricky – should I take off, should I keep my height, should I have a meal, or should I just keep walking? But when you're in a race with a set goal, decision-making gets a little easier. You just keep going!

Immediately after the X-Berg I signed up for the X-Pyr in Spain, and that was totally amazing as well. I never thought walking down a road at night would be much fun, but when you're in an event like that I really enjoy it. So after the X-Pyr I thought maybe it was possible to have fun in the X-Alps. I mean, when you watch the X-Alps you see a lot of people suffering. Chrigel seems to be having fun, but a lot of the guys seem to be going through hell!

In the lead-up to the race your approach seemed pretty untraditional. Care to share thoughts on that?
When I got accepted to the race in November, seven months before the race, I thought I would sign up for a bunch of endurance events and that kind of thing. Then a few months later I hadn't done any of that and figured I'd just keep doing what I was doing, which was just flying a bunch and doing a bit of tramping around. I spoke to Ferdinand van Schelven, who's done the race a few times and done quite well, and he told me that if I was an average Kiwi I'd be fit enough, and he suggested I try and fly 200km in NZ, but otherwise keep as I am. I never really changed anything. I've been really fortunate in my life to have spent a lot of time outdoors and spent a lot of time tramping, so it's not like I went into the race cold – I just didn't have any kind of structured training program. When you tramp around New Zealand, you can't just follow the signs. There's a lot of thinking about the big picture and reading maps and making decisions, which is what you do a lot of in the race. My attitude is: me and my body are on the same team. I try to listen to my body, and my body is pretty patient with me as well. I don't have this attitude like I want to break through pain barriers or that kind of thing – I do the race to have fun.

You had two years off work before going into the 2015 race. What was your motivation?
In the 2015 race my main goal was to have fun. But I thought that might be my only chance to do the race, so my supporter, Louis Tapper, and I took the technical preparation quite seriously. We had lists and maps and all that kind of thing all planned out. But what I love about paragliding is that you can really get a lot out of it for nothing. You can invest very little and get a huge payoff. If you're a tight-ass, like I am, it's a terrific sport. You can use nature's energy for free, and you can have everything you need on your back. You're not reliant on anyone. For my 2017 race, I hadn't flown so much, as I'd got into a full-time job as a meteorologist. But paragliding is mostly in your head. I don't think it matters that you haven't flown much unless you think it matters.

> **“If you're a tight-ass, like I am, it's a terrific sport. You can use nature's energy for free, and you can have everything you need on your back.”**

So just trick yourself?
Exactly.

You mentioned in your blog the importance of ground handling. Is that still a big part of your training?
I love ground handling. It's one of those things that can be a lot more value than flying. How many times do you spend a couple hours driving to a launch, then it's blown out and you don't fly and then you drive home? You could have just gone to a park and ground handled for a couple hours, which is super fun, and gotten a lot more out of your day.

Give us a list of places to pursue some vol-biv if you were new to that style of flying.
The Alps are a great place to start. It's very convenient with logistics, and if you're not really sure about things, it's a good place because you've got a lot of exit options. The Pyrenees are also quite good, there are loads of grassy landings everywhere as long as you're in the deep part and not out in the Spanish side, where it gets a bit thorny and dry.

Kyrgyzstan is an amazing place, but you really have to be pretty confident by the time you get there, because conditions are pretty strong and rough. But there are landings everywhere, and it's amazing culturally.

New Zealand is super-remote and you'll have problems with the weather, but if you know where you're going, you can have some great trips here. The great thing about New Zealand is the big, wide, open valleys. So even if there's a bit of wind around, there are often plenty of landing options.

The Himalaya can be pretty tricky in terms of landings, depending on where you go. We went in the spring and were stuck pretty low most of the time because of the moisture, and there were a lot of storms.

South America is wild. The air is crazy in the Andes because it's so dry and thin, and the sun is so strong and tropical. I landed there once before midday because it was just too much for me. It was too hardcore. I actually had my brake line chafe through because the air was so active.

Have you had any accidents?
I have. I racked up more hours in two weeks than I had in the previous six months when I went to India, and I was trying to push myself pretty hard with cross country back then. Looking back, I think it was a lack of confidence. I basically freaked out about landing down below in town because I'd heard so much about all the power lines, so I tried to slope land in this little slot between the trees, and hit the ground pretty hard. I came out of that one with a pretty bruised heel, but I was still able to fly the next day. I think by now I would have broken my back four times if I hadn't followed my instructor's advice of keeping your landing gear out whenever you're close to the ground. My biggest fear in the Alps is the invisible cables that seem to be everywhere[1].

I went over there this summer right after the Alaska expedition to do some training with my supporters, Bruce and Ben. I don't think I realized it until I got there, but Alaska took a lot more out of me than I realized. I got in the air and I just wasn't feeling it. I was just kind of out of it. And the conditions were not that terrible. It was windy and it was demanding, but nothing like some of the days in the X-Alps. I ended up in a place at the end of one day in kind of bad light where I literally flew within inches of huge high-tension lines three or four times. One after another. I went over a cable that I didn't see with only a few inches of clearance, and then went right under a cable that I didn't even see until I'd passed it. These were really high, big cables where the outcome would have been horrible, and I never even saw them. You train yourself to look for those cables, and in the Alps I'm always on guard for them, so I don't know if it was just because I was tired or what, but cables can be really scary and some of them are impossible to see[1]. The night I got into Monaco in the 2015 race, a bunch of the guys who'd already gotten in – Durogati, Guschlbauer, Petiot, and van Schelven and I were all sharing some pretty scary stories of situations we'd gotten into during the race. How do you justify the risks that something like the X-Alps usually gets us into?
When we're learning how to fly, we're taught that if it's too rough or too strong you should go land. I've had to adapt that flying in places like the Alps because of the sometimes really strong valley winds, or just weird situations you can find yourself in. Now when it's too rough or too strong my mantra is: don't go land, go fly somewhere else! There were a few times in the race when we were flying in a lot of wind, and I'm sure like everyone I got into some places I shouldn't have been, but when that happened I flew somewhere else and then it was ok. That's one of my strong points: trying to

[1] Hint from the author: when flying around cables don't fly with polarized sunglasses. Polarized sunglasses remove the glare, which is often all that marks a cable.

"Fear is pretty subjective. It's all about decision-making and confidence." Nick flies past the 2,830m summit of Mt Earnslaw (Maori name Pikirakatahi) on an epic flight from Wanaka to the west coast, New Zealand
Photo: Nick Neynens

figure out those non-classic conditions and figuring out how to get through tricky places. I really enjoy that kind of flying.

Do you find the X-Alps makes you do things you wouldn't normally do?
I had the impression from a lot of the pilots that they were pushing themselves to do things they wouldn't normally do. I think that wasn't really the case for me, because in vol-biv you come across a lot of those situations, and in the X-Alps you've got a lot of people watching you. You couldn't be much safer in terms of support at least, and in the Alps you've got first-world infrastructure and everyone is going to know something happened, so I actually felt pretty safe.

That's not to say I don't get scared. When I get scared, I try to do a couple of things to calm down. One thing is to turn my vario sound off. A screaming vario can be pretty stressful. But when you turn it off you instantly relax. The other thing I do is imagine what I look like from the ground. Even if the wing is all over the place and it's really hard to control, from the perspective of someone on the ground it looks pretty mellow. I like to objectify things to help mitigate fear. Fear is pretty subjective. Your feelings make a big difference to the actual risk, because it's all about decision-making and confidence. If you aren't in the right headspace, actual risk can increase considerably. When you're a pilot you have to try to remove emotion as much as you can, and just deal with the problem logically the best you can.

Often in the race or in vol-biv I think a lot of my fear comes from the fear of bombing out, rather than the fear of being hurt. It's hard to separate those kinds of fears. They feel very similar, and probably have similar repercussions. When you're really heavy in vol-biv, or you're in the race and bombing out means another monster hike and losing several hours, there's a lot of anxiety before you take off, and it makes it much harder to take decisions in the air that would be natural and easy if you didn't care about walking. A good example is Chrigel. Do you think Chrigel takes the most risk of anyone in the X-Alps?

No, I think he takes the least. He seems the least stressed of anyone.
Exactly. So if you take more risks in the race than you're used to taking then you'll probably get into bad situations, and then those mistakes compound and it becomes a vicious circle. I think you should do what you're comfortable with in the race, and you'll perform a lot better.

Nick, what do you think separates pilots that operate at a very high end of this sport in competitions like the X-Alps or the World Cup and the rest?
I don't think it's anything special. I think it's just practice. Some of us just have the luxury of spending more time at it than others.

You've just gone through an intensive course to become a meteorologist. Is that affecting your flying in a positive way?
It's hard to say. I've definitely picked up a few things that I hadn't thought of before, and the course has certainly given me some more tools, so that has to help, but most of what we've learned is on a huge scale – stuff that's going on in the upper atmosphere. We're concerned with more micro scale when we're flying.

You mentioned in your blog that you flew for a long time without a vario. Is that something you recommend?
Flying without a vario helped me fly faster, because you don't fart around in little dribbles of lift. If it's not obviously going up, you don't stop. But I've always flown without much instrumentation. I fly with my phone, which has XCSoar, but I have the screen turned off 99% of the time. I only flip it on to check airspace or check my ground speed or something important. The most important thing to do is look out the window. You can miss a lot of important information if you're looking at your instruments.

NICK'S FEAR TIPS

When I get scared, I try to do a couple things to calm down. One thing is to turn my vario sound off. A screaming vario can be pretty stressful. But when you turn it off you instantly relax.

The other thing I do is imagine what I look like from the ground. Even if the wing is all over the place and it's really hard to control, from the perspective of someone on the ground it looks pretty mellow. I like to objectify things to help mitigate fear.

HOW TO GLIDE BETTER

How do we describe something that's nearly 100% feel? Sure – we can follow cloud streets or obvious signs in the air, but being an efficient glider and finding the magic lines that maximize glides is a dark and important art.

"Something I learned recently is to think about micro changes in the use of your speed bar. So instead of just doing one, two, or three steps on your bar, divide it down into tiny little micro steps that align with changes in your sink rate. Keep the changes smooth, but feather it back and forth rather than locking it in."
Mitch Riley

"Gliding seems to be mostly intuitive, but you can only build intuition through experience. Try and get in tune with how clouds develop and cycle through the day, and you will learn to start reading the energy of the sky. You can practice this when stuck indoors staring out at a great sky or even better when you've bombed out! Over time, you'll learn to see lines as they develop. You'll couple this with an understanding of how the wind will affect things. Competitions really help because with so many other pilots you can see instantly what's working and what isn't. Take some time after every flight to visualize what just happened. Try to figure out if you got in the same position again what you'd do differently."
Cody Mittanck

"If it's late in the day, tuck your arms in and glide at trim. Going from trim to full speed effectively halves your glide ratio, so if it's glassed off and there's no heavy

"Every single time you touch your brakes when you're on glide, you lose performance. You MUST stay off your brakes. It doesn't matter if you're flying a CCC wing or an EN B: if you're on glide, stay off the brakes. It's always better to back off the bar than to hit the brakes. When you're on glide, keep your hands up. It can make up to a 10% difference, considerably more than the difference between an EN B and an EN C. Almost all gliders these days have the ability to control the glider from the back lines (the B lines on a two-liner, the C lines on a three-liner, or a hybrid system that connects the B and C lines). A competent pilot should be able to stop any frontal collapse with input on the back lines, but every time you pull on them you're still distorting the wing's profile and it's hurting performance, so the less input you give, the better glide you'll get."
Marko Hrgetic Hrga

"Gliding well is probably one of the hardest things to describe. Chrigel is, of course, the master of not turning: he always talks about his mentor, Stefan Schmoker, who said: "When you're thermalling, you're going backwards half the time."

First, you need to read all the books by the old school hang glider pilots AND all the current stuff. Sailplane and hang glider pilots know how to glide. As our paragliders become more efficient, we can use more of their techniques.

In competitions, if you're in a pack on glide, all the people spread out in front of you are showing you the air mass. Once a gaggle of 30 or 40 pilots leaves a thermal, they all spread out and look for lift, so a trick is to scoot around behind the ones getting the best lines. Any bump that any pilot gets in front of me, I'm going to Pac-Man and gobble up. Pounce on all those good bits of air and try to put yourself in the most positive air by moving laterally.

Often if we're on a big long glide and the whole group is getting a bad line, I'll go off to the side. There's often good air really close. You just have to scoot over and get it. I'm not afraid to move quite far outside the pack to look for a better line. Often if you do that, you can catch people in front of you because they'll be lower than you at the next climb. I've applied this same idea to my cross-country flying. If I'm in bad air I move around and look for better air. It's a simple concept, but it takes a lot of training. Pay a lot of attention to your L/D (glide ratio). You need to master the speed bar. In fact, think of it as your glide bar. Your glider is no more susceptible to collapse on bar than at trim – in fact the higher aspect gliders and especially two-liners are more collapse resistant on bar – so we need to use it a lot more than most pilots do. Speed bar is a tool that beginner and intermediate pilots need to work on constantly, because using the speed bar well leads to more efficient gliding.

Your average glider gets about a 9:1 glide ratio. If I'm getting 5 or 6 to 1, I'm going to look for better air and try to do something about it immediately. If I'm getting 12 or 14 to 1, I'm going to stay in it for as long as I can, and even ride the rear risers a little bit to get some advantage from the lifting air."

Matt Beechinor

sink to cut through, don't burn through the tank!"

Hugh Miller

"A little trick I learned from someone smart along the way was to always be upwind of other pilots on glides if there's a cross wind. That way if a thermal pops to windward you're in a better position, and if someone downwind of you gets a better glide you can jump to them much more easily. When flying in a cross wind from one waypoint to the next, always orient to windward. Go upwind whenever possible because it's easier to fall off as you near the waypoint than trying to push into wind. In other words, when in doubt on glide slant upwind."

Gavin McClurg

Back to Life

PAL TAKATS

Pál Takáts has a dizzying flight resume that began at the age of 16. He's a crossover kid, starting his career in acro and then moving into XC competitions. Pál invented many of the modern acro maneuvers like the Esfera, Joker, Booster, and Cowboy. He holds the tandem Infinity world record (140 loops), is a three-time Acro World Cup champion. Pál has finished in the top three in World Cups, and also flies paramotors at the Red Bull Air Races. He's created several successful SIV and acro instructional videos and definitely sports the coolest hair in free flying!

But it hasn't all been a smooth ride for Pál. A speed flying accident in 2012 put him in a coma and nearly ended his life. After he'd recovered, a Base-jumping accident later the same year resulted in an even longer recovery time. Then at the 2019 world championships, Pál mistakenly stalled his Enzo 3 while playing on launch, proving that even the best in the world make mistakes. Pál has devoted more than half his life to flying, and his passion for the sport is unwavering, even in the face of terrible setbacks and pain. His story is instructive, humbling and inspiring.

I'm not very intimate with your beginnings so I may have this wrong, but it seems to me that your focus has changed quite considerably in the last few years from acro to cross country and other pursuits? What drove this transition?
My first Acro World Cup championship win was in 2007. In 2011 I set out to become Acro World Cup champion again, just to prove to myself that I could repeat it, that it wasn't just a one-off. I knew that if I won, I would change my focus and leave it there, so after I did win that was basically my retirement from competitive acro. I never announced this in advance, but it was always my plan. Most people thought it was the accident in 2012 that ended my acro career, but I had already decided before I got hurt that I was going to leave it behind.

Being an Acro World Cup pilot requires a ton of dedication and training, and to get enough hours there are really only a very few places in the world that work, so the lifestyle becomes quite redundant. The other thing that became quite discouraging over the years, and definitely played into my decision to leave competitive acro, is that

> **“I’m convinced we would see a 90% reduction in accidents if pilots were proficient in ground handling and full stalls.”**

it’s a judged sport. Often the scoring would be subjective and prone to human error or emotion, and not necessarily reward the best pilot.

Judging acro is a very difficult job. It all happens very fast, and I’m not criticizing the judges at all – their errors often go both ways. But I became frustrated with this side of the sport. In cross-country competition it’s totally objective. You have a track log and a time, and you can’t cheat the system. You win or you lose depending on how fast you fly, period, and the best pilot always wins.

What happened in Zermatt in 2012?

I was speed riding on a 6m^2 wing, which we know now is really too small for speed riding. It’s just too fast. It was only my fourth run on the glider, so I didn’t have a very good feel for how it behaved. When I really needed more lift, I didn’t get it, and I hit a rock ledge before the edge of a cliff. That disturbed the glider so much that it totally collapsed, and I basically did a Base jump over the cliff and free-fell about 20m. I don’t believe I was hurt from hitting the ledge – that wasn’t a major impact, it was just enough to foul the glider. The damage was done when I hit the ground at the base of the cliff. Luckily there was snow, but I compressed several vertebrae, had an open fracture in my leg, and was badly bruised all over my body. But the thing the doctors were worried about was my head. I had a massive concussion and bleeding in my brain, so they put me in an induced coma for two weeks. During the coma I got a lung infection, and this was a dangerous combination that I understand the doctors were very worried about. It was very scary for my family. For a while during the coma, the doctors really didn’t know if I would wake up and have lifelong mental disabilities. I came out of the coma on my birthday. And it changed my perspective on life quite radically.

Did getting injured on a wing you normally didn’t fly affect how you processed the accident? Did it make it any easier coming back to flying knowing the reason for the crash?

I don’t know. I wasn’t a very good speed riding pilot and I’m not a good skier, so maybe it helps not having to wonder how I screwed up. Alejandro Rodriguez, the younger brother of Raul and Felix, died when he screwed up a misty flip low over the ground and didn’t have enough time to sort it out. He had done thousands of misty flips – that wasn’t a maneuver that he normally screwed up. But when we investigated his accident, we found that he broke rules that even the best pilots should never break. He was flying a new glider that he didn't know very well, and he was doing a complicated maneuver low where you don't have time to fix a mistake. Sometimes we all screw up.

Was flying different for you after the accident?

I was very motivated to get back to flying after the accident. It felt like the right thing to do. But then in October of that same year, only a few months after the Zermatt crash, I had another flying accident. I smashed my kneecap and broke my knee into pieces when I screwed up a landing after a wingsuit Base jump. Emotionally, this second accident was really traumatic. It made me feel so stupid. I didn't even want to tell anyone because I was so embarrassed. After all the rehab of the first accident, and the hell I put my family through while I was in the coma, then I go out and do something really stupid and get hurt again? It was impossible not to think about what everyone was thinking about me. "Is Pál stupid? Is he doing all of this just for sponsors?" That kind of thing. And what made it even worse was knowing how easily it could have been avoided. There was no bad luck or mitigating circumstances, I just blew it.

Coming back from the first accident, which was life-threatening, was much easier than coming back from the second. Physically the second was worse – I was on crutches for a long time, the physical rehab was much more painful, to learn how to walk and run again was excruciating, but none of the physical part compared to the mental part. The real struggle was to get my confidence back.

Did filming or providing content for your sponsors contribute in any way to your accidents?

Having a camera on you makes what we do more dangerous. People these days are filming everything and putting it up on Facebook and YouTube. There's so much of it that professional athletes always have to figure out a way to stand out and do something unique for the companies we represent. I had cameras running in both of the accidents, but I don't think they contributed to either. For sure, if a professional athlete is injured, it's never the fault of the sponsor. I've never, ever been pushed to do anything by any of my sponsors; the responsibility is on me and me alone.

The only situations where I do feel a lot of pressure are when I'm involved in a show, like for the Red Bull Air Races. When there are thousands and thousands of people watching, it makes it a lot harder to back down. A lot of accidents happen in these situations. It's why we see so many accidents in competitions – the ego gets in the way of making good decisions. I'm seeing a lot of professional photographers and videographers getting into flying lately, which is great for the sport, but I really worry about these people. When you're flying you have to be focused, no matter what level you are, but especially when you're learning. I see the same risk with newer pilots trying to get sponsored because they're setting out to do a cool project or adventure. Getting good content is difficult – it's a full-time job. Not many people can operate at the level that's needed if they're also engaged in getting footage.

What would you change if you could rewind the clock on your career?

I don't think I would change anything. I also had two other accidents before these two in 2012. I broke my ankle doing a ground spiral, and I broke my arm making a stupid

Pál Takáts has flown over 500km, won international competitions, and is an acro expert. Having recovered from a coma after suffering a serious flying accident, Pál understands the importance of training better than most. Photo: Marcus King

mistake when I was learning, trying to land in a small spot. Just normal injuries, the kind that happen to a lot of people. But of course, without these mistakes I wouldn't have learned, so I wouldn't change them. The beautiful thing about flying is it can be enjoyed in so many different ways. Someone who takes evening sledders can enjoy it just as much as someone who flies 200km. There are so many different disciplines that we can pursue – acro, XC, ridge-soaring, vol-biv, instruction, etc – but one thing that is important for everyone to understand is that it can be dangerous at any level. The pilot who only flies in very calm air and only takes sledders can be at more risk than a pilot who flies 300 hours a year and really trains hard and is much more current. The sport requires skills and training and good judgement, regardless of how you participate.

I'm glad you brought that up. I think it's often the pilots who have limited time who are under a lot more pressure. As Will Gadd says, they'll try to "see the world as they want it to be instead of how it is."

That's when the shit hits the fan. Not everyone has the privilege of making a living from flying or the time to fly as much as they want. People with less time should take every advantage to improve their skills when it isn't flyable. Most people have time after work to do a bit of ground handling. Ground handling is really foundational. People really underestimate it. It isn't pushed at all in the basic courses, and it's now being sold as almost a different course and skill, and this is bullshit. It's the most important thing you can learn, and should be one of the main things taught and signed off in the schools. And it should be practiced diligently and regularly – by everyone.

How should a pilot approach learning acro?

The most important thing is to learn the basics on a regular B wing. You don't want to learn on a freestyle or acro wing. These wings are way, way too fast and dynamic to learn deep stall or any of the finesse maneuvers. This is the biggest mistake I see pilots make. You can learn pretty much everything except rhythmic Sat and tumbling on a regular wing. A regular wing is slower and safer, has longer brake travel, and doesn't shoot violently like the freestyle and acro wings.

When you're learning your brain can't process things fast enough to manage an acro or freestyle wing. Once you can easily control deep stall, tail slide, wingovers and full stalls, and you have your helicopters absolutely stable in both directions, you can move up to a wing built for acrobatic maneuvers. You will have to go step by step again through all the basics when you do, because of the much higher speed that things happen, but moving up too quickly is the main reason we see problems. In the Master Acro[1] videos for 95% of the maneuvers I fly the Ozone Rush, a standard EN B glider.

Is acro more dangerous than XC?

No! Acro is much, much safer than cross country. This is a big misunderstanding in the sport. If you can control your wing in the full gamut of the three-dimensional space, the full gamut of the polar curve of your wing, you'll be a very safe pilot. 99% of cross-country pilots can only fly their glider in the positive range of the polar curve – from minimum speed to full speed. But you can fly backwards or full stall or spiral dive or spin. Full stalls and wingovers are two elementary and the most important maneuvers that all pilots should have to master to get an intermediate license. The tail slide is your only full reset option. It's your only chance to avoid throwing your reserve, getting into an autorotation or suffering a big collapse or cravated wing. The wingover is your tool to maneuver at the limits of the three-dimensional space that we operate in. If you fly a wingover correctly, you understand all of the important dynamics of controlling a wing: weight shift, brake use, and timing.

Most accidents happen because pilots don't have the minimum skills of glider control. It makes me really upset to keep seeing this. If a pilot gets into a stressful situation and doesn't have the training and skill to deal with it, they either seize up and do nothing, or they do the wrong thing. If doing a full stall isn't totally natural and easy, then how can a pilot possibly use it when they need it? There's no way. Some pilots in that situation might even try it and get into bigger trouble than they already were. The full stall should be a standard, basic maneuver for all pilots. I'm convinced we would reduce accidents in this sport by 90% if ground handling and full stalls were part of basic and mandatory training. We would turn the accident statistics upside down.

[1] Pál Takáts released the Master Acro video series in 2019, available for purchase on justacro.com. This three-part series, "Safety First", "Basic Skills", and "Full On", are four hours of comprehensive instruction dedicated to every level of acrobatics in paragliding.

HOW TO FLY COMPETITIONS

You'll learn more in a week of comp flying than in a year of recreational flying. Competitions give you instant feedback on what you're doing well and what you're doing wrong. They're a great opportunity to share the sky with your friends and enjoy our remarkable community. Some pilots have early but typically infrequent success, but the consistent masters of the comp game have all put in a lot of hours. They aren't for everyone, and every comp pilot will be frustrated by the inevitable down days or short tasks that don't use the whole day. But flying cross country with a hundred or more gliders in the sky all trying to achieve the same goal is special.

"Competitions are the best place to become a really proficient cross-country pilot. If you keep your eyes open at a contest, and decide that you're not there to prove anything or to win but you're there to learn, you can gain vast knowledge flying competitions."
Matt Beechinor

"In those beginning contests I did well, but originally before GPS we had to shoot the turnpoints with a camera. I took more bad pictures than anybody. I could have won several contests if I hadn't taken pictures of my thumb, or my knee, or pulled out the camera and watched all the batteries rain to the ground, or take the picture, let go of the camera, and then watch it fall away because it wasn't tied to me. It was soul-crushing."
Nate Scales

"If you walk through the woods blindfolded, eventually you'll run into a tree."
John Pendry

"When you fly competition tasks – which aren't just about blowing downwind or trying to go as big as you can, but trying to complete a course with pilots who are a lot better than you – lo and behold, you learn a ton.

When I first started competing, a light went on. Getting to travel the world competing on a hang glider has been one of the most beautiful vehicles to discover new people, cultures and places, and it opened my mind to a world that I didn't know existed.

Comps are an opportunity not only to learn, but to be humbled, and to understand the weaknesses that you should be working on. You get to see where the holes in your game are."
Jeff Shapiro

"It took me a long time to go from a gaggle pilot to going out alone and pushing to goal and beginning to win tasks and comps. The best pilots are great at staying with the gaggle but also able to push out and win, and that's a difficult skill. It was frustrating to make the switch to pushing hard, because I bombed out a lot and blew my overall position at a lot of comps, but I viewed it as necessary training. The other thing you have to get really good at is using a lot of bar. A lot of pilots don't use enough bar and don't understand appropriate speed to fly."
Aaron Durogati

"My first competition was a World Cup in Abtenau, but I wasn't in the actual competition. I didn't have any money and I hadn't qualified, so I just showed up and pretended I was supposed to be there. I would sneak on to the bus to get to launch and sneak into the food tents so I could eat. Then I would take off before everyone and get out beyond the start cylinder on my EN B wing, and then get smoked. I don't think I made goal once in my first four comps. But the knowledge you gain from comps adds up quickly, and pretty soon I started figuring it out."
Nick Greece

"Most pilots at a high-level competition are pretty solid at thermalling and gliding, so the main edge you can get is the psychology. I started putting a lot of energy into reading sports psychology books, and that really changed my approach. Rather than go to a comp and get upset after a bad result, I started working on getting better and letting the results come. What you can really influence is your preparation. Make sure your gear is really set up well. Don't get too tired or dehydrated or hungover. And don't get discouraged if you get behind. That's often the best place to be, so stay positive and be patient."
Josh Cohn

"My breakthrough in competition results came by changing my attitude, from one of thinking that Indian pilots were never going to be able to compete with the Europeans, to believing that we were good and we had the skill to win. As soon as I believed I was good, I started winning."
Gurpreet Dhindsa

"At World Cup level, if you just gaggle fly, you're not going to break the top 60 except when you get really lucky. You need to get good enough to stay with the gaggle, which means climbing and gliding really well, but to get into the top 30 you also have to be bold and confident enough to make your own moves at the right times. Your strategy in comps is completely different from regular cross country. You're flying cross country, but more importantly you're flying the course and using the other people in the comp to make better decisions."
Cody Mittanck

"If you approach competitions to learn something, as you did when you first started flying competitions, you'll get the best results. Don't focus on the results; focus on the learning and progression.

Don't have many expectations about the weather and conditions before you launch in a comp. You have to fly the conditions that present themselves, not the conditions that you planned for."
Christian Ciech

"I think it's important to think about task relevance. What data is relevant to the task at hand? At one end of the spectrum you have direct observation and past experience, and at the other you have intuition. Intuition is a tricky thing because it's often attached to emotion, and emotion is not a task-relevant piece of data. For instance fear, or ambition, or eagerness, or attainment in particular. These are emotions that can get attached to intuition, but in a bad way. We have to be aware of when these kinds of task-irrelevant pieces of data are too prominent in our decision-making, compared to things like observing the day or pattern recall from earlier in the flight or previous flights."
Willi Canell

"Don't screw up the first day. On day one just get to goal and get a score on the board. That'll give you a mental advantage going forward, one that all those pilots who didn't make goal won't have. Then you can just step it up every day.
Don't worry about getting behind. When you're behind you have a lot of gliders in front of you showing you what's working and what isn't. Being behind can often be a great advantage."
Marko Hrgetic Hrga

"There's definitely an element of luck in competitions. You can improve your luck by putting in more practice, but it's still a lottery at times. I've seen some of the most consistent and reliable pilots in the World Cup, who are typically out in front leading, end up on the ground before the start. The best pilots in the world bomb out. This aspect of our sport is lovely, because it keeps things interesting. You'll notice the real veterans in the sport

"Rule number 1: You have to really like what you're doing. If you're the one smiling all the time and flying because it's fun and not for the results, the results will come. You've got to feel well to fly well.
Rule number 2: Set up a scene with your mates where you're mutually supporting one another. You need mentors, and you need a supportive environment.
Rule number 3: You have to fly the best wing. A tiny advantage gives you a huge advantage in the head, and the head is everything. Forgo sponsorship deals because you have to fly the right wing, and no company will consistently make the best wing – it changes every year.
The first thing you need to learn in competitions is how to lose. Doing well early happens because of luck. To really become a good competition pilot, you have to lose a lot and learn from the mistakes.
It's never the local hero that wins the comp. Not knowing an area allows you to go with the flow and fly what you see rather than what you know."
Mads Syndergaard

"Since I've been doing fewer competitions, I've been getting much better results. I don't really understand that, but it might be because I'm not too fussed about them. I don't feel pressure like I used to. I like winning by going for the win, not by holding back and letting others make mistakes. I realize being disciplined and not charging out front is the way to win comps, but that's never been my style. I like winning by winning. A lot of pilots think about tactics and strategy and all that, but I try not to think about much. It's not that complicated: you go round and round in the strong bits and straight in the sinky bits. When you're high you've got options, you can crack on. When you're in the middle, rein it in a bit. When you're low, take anything you can. If you can stay off the ground for 10 minutes, something will present itself. When you're low you can't be impetuous. Don't freak out, try to let your subconscious take over and stay in the air."
Mark Watts

don't get very upset when they bomb out or blow a comp, because they know it's just a part of the game we're playing."
Guy Anderson

"Nothing replaces hours. There's no big secret to being good. Every good competition pilot has dedicated an awful lot of time to flying."
Michael Sigel

"Stay calm and enjoy the process. Paragliding smacks down the best of us; it's the people who can get back up the next day with a smile and a good attitude who'll inevitably win. Take it day by day. Don't get ahead of yourself. Don't think about the win, don't think about the end or 'what ifs'. Find a routine that works and stick with it. Eat and drink regularly; you need to tap into your parasympathetic system, and taking little breaks gives your brain a necessary rest. Flow comes and goes. When it comes, go with it and enjoy it, but when you fall out of it, don't stress about it. Just fly the best you can. The results will come."
Nick Greece

Adel Honti's pre-comp checklist:

1. Create a five-hour music playlist for pre-launch - a motivating background sound, not something that distracts you.
2. Be prepared physically - it's a long haul.
3. Arrive several days early, fly one or two practice tasks, make sure you warm up properly.
4. Your equipment should be familiar. Do not change anything at the last minute. Remember to drink regularly and eat during a task. Put protein bars, gels, and isotonic water in accessible pockets.
5. Make sure all your instruments have all the cables and chargers you need. Never fly with a new instrument.
6. Get a local SIM for your phone and save all the competition numbers. Bring a power bank and a cable, and keep them accessible.
7. Weigh your take-off weight two to three weeks before the event, make sure you are not over the top. You can always ballast up with water on strong days.
8. Remember the best performance will come when you're relaxed and focused. Enjoy every minute.

FAI PARAGLIDING
WORLD CHAMPIONSHIP
MONTE AVENA - ITALY
BRAZIL

Team Work

RAFAEL SALADINI

In what's fundamentally a solo sport, the Brazilians have become a true paragliding peloton. Their teamwork has seen them smash the world record time and again. It's clear we could all learn from their tactics. Whether we're trying to fly 20 or 200km, our chances of success are greater together.

Rafael Saladini first set the straight-line distance world record in 2007. He's done it twice since – most recently flying 582km in 2019 with Marcelo Prieto and Rafael de Moraes Barros. He's one of the core crew of Brazilians that's pushed the potential of the Sertão in Brazil's far north-east, defying others' doubts around the relatively short days by launching right after dawn and staying airborne till dusk.

I met Rafael in 2016. The crew had pushed the record to 514km the year before, launching from Tacima, a relatively unknown hang gliding site. Unfortunately Rafael bombed out early that day. Frank Brown, Donizete Lemos and Marcelo Prieto went on to take the record from South Africa's Nevil Hulett (502km). It was during this trip that the team's discipline paid off; they flew as a gaggle throughout, working as a team, not trying to outdo each other in the final moments.

Two months after our interview, Rafael, Donizete and Samuel Nascimento smashed the record again with a 564km whopper, again from Tacima, again flying and landing as a team. To pull that off, the crew based itself at Tacima for 36 days, but only managed to fly three times! The launch is extremely windy and dangerous. Conditions are nearly impossible to forecast, and the first section requires clearing a 25km wind-blown plateau filled with power lines where cloudbase is rarely more than a couple hundred feet over the dirt. It's committing, to say the least.

Rafael and the guys established the Sertão as the place to fly big, and XC pilots from all over the world now travel to the area between October and December. Most pilots are now towing rather than foot-launching – it's vastly safer, and easier to get established. And the wind and conditions mellow through December for those who 'only' want to do 300km.

But it's not all distance-chasing for Rafael. He's won several Brazilian Championships, the Pan-American Championship, several tasks in the World Cup, and

> **Many people in this sport think they're better than they are. Stay grounded. If you feel like you're Superman, it's an illusion.**

won PWC Brazil outright in 2017. All this excellence didn't happen overnight. Rafael had several accidents in his early days, and quit the sport for two long periods. How do you go from that to flying farther than anyone ever has – several times? Rafael teaches us how to avoid the Superman illusion, how to recover from accidents and fear, and where he thinks 600km is possible.

Rafael, I understand you started paragliding in Brazil before it was legal?
When I was 14 years old, my father took a hang gliding course here in Rio, but he quit the first day because he thought it was too dangerous. But I was fascinated – I thought it was just amazing. This was back in 1997. A couple of years later, when I was 16, I found an instructor who was willing to teach me, but as a minor I needed my parents' permission – it's not legal in Brazil until you're 18. I had to go up to launch hiding in the trunk of the car. That's why everyone calls me Sardinia. It means sardine, I guess I looked like a sardine in a can every time I was in the trunk of the car!

I tried back then to follow my cousin and first great mentor, Rodrigo Montero. He was a PWC pilot and he was already chasing distance, but I was really irresponsible back then. Rodrigo tried to teach me to respect the dangers. But then I had a serious accident that changed my life. I broke my hip, my left foot and my right arm. I just exploded like a tomato on launch, and it really traumatized me. I'd only been flying for six months, and I just stopped flying after that. I couldn't do it. I became totally insecure and quit for nearly four years.

How did you get back into it?
In 2003, my cousin and a friend put pressure on me to start again. But my low self-esteem and lack of confidence in my decisions made me as dangerous as my over-confidence had before. I began making the same mistakes, and started having small accidents again. Then, after a couple of years, something just happened. I can't explain it. It was like divine intervention; suddenly everything just clicked and I stopped making stupid mistakes and started being able to manage any situation. Since then I've never had an accident. I've thrown my reserve once, but I've never been hurt.

I was lucky to have so many great mentors. When Will Gadd broke the straight distance record in Texas in 2002, Marcelo Prieto was also there. Marcelo[1] has now broken several world records. He is the Jedi knight of northern Brazil. Guys like Frank

Brown and Donizete Lemos[2] have also taught me so much. Having pilots like them around means you take shortcuts and make big jumps in your progression.

After only a few years back in the game, I broke the world record in 2007[3], which is pretty crazy, but I'd started competing the year before, and had been surrounded by some of the best pilots in the world. Seeing and watching the best pilots, you learn how they behave and what's important and what isn't. You learn what you should do to keep safe and how to keep your head grounded, and not to fall into the illusion that you're Superman, believing you're better than you actually are.

How did you recover from those accidents and get over the fear? And how did you get those mentors?

Those accidents are still really fresh in my mind even now. It was really, really scary for me to get back into flying in 2003. I had some people encouraging me, but there weren't many people who wanted to teach me because I'd been in so many accidents and they didn't want to have a student who got killed!

I decided I just had to train really hard and earn the trust of the pilots I looked up to, so they would allow me into their circle. I started going to every competition I could. I followed Frank Brown pretty much everywhere. I did all the Brazilian league events, and I traveled as much as I could. In those earlier comps I was flying the Sigma 6, and I started doing pretty well in the Serial class. Those results maybe gave me the credentials to go to those guys and ask for help. They could see I really wanted to learn, and it's also really the Brazilian way, to help each other. Brazilians really want to share.

We have amazing flying all year round, all over our country. There are whole communities of pilots here that no one knows anything about. They don't want to compete, they don't care about results or records, they just want to have fun. Here it's a lifestyle. If you want hours you can get them. And luckily one of the places I used to spend three months every spring was in Araxá, where Marcelo also flew. He was putting together a world record team, and knew we had to team fly to do it.

How did you guys approach chasing the world record? Was there a moment where it all clicked?

To fly huge distances in the north-east of Brazil, you have to stay in the air for 11 hours. We just don't have the same amount of daylight you get in South Africa or Texas, but we can launch super-early. We knew we had to figure out how to fly as long as possible. Before we tried team flying, as solitary pilots the best we ever did was eight or nine hours. The jump happened when we started flying together. Teamwork triggered the whole thing. Marcelo had already taught me about all the basics – flying convergence lines, reading the clouds, how to use cloud streets – but we started going much bigger when we flew together.

We don't talk on the radio. When we train together it becomes like a flying organism. We don't say anything to each other. We just fly together, it's automatic. It comes from training and training and training together. It's completely different from flying a

[1] Marcelo Prieto, Rafael Saladini and Rafael de Moraes Barros hold the current world record of 582km
[2] Frank Brown, Donizete Lemos and Marcelo Prieto broke the world record in 2015, flying 514km.
[3] Rafael flew 461km from Quixadá in 2007, beating Will Gadd's record of 423km in Texas in 2002.

gaggle in a competition. In a gaggle you are trying to be higher and faster, but this is flying as a team. In a team you have to fly at the same pace as your friends. If you're in a better position you have to use your position to help them. If you're higher, you fly out to the side of the climb and map as much air as possible. At the end of the day, if you do that as a team, it's going to make a hell of a difference.

With all of you guys having so much comp experience, is it hard to switch gears from race mode to team mode?

It's all about what you do with all the tiny advantages each of us get handed. Since we begin flying, we're kind of programmed to compare and compete. In the beginning we compete against ourselves, and then against others, using our tiny advantages to get ahead. When we team fly, we keep that same mindset of fighting for the small gains, but then instead of using them against each other, we use them to help our friends, maintain the integrity of the team, and help the whole group fly farther. Building this concept of team flying sounds easy – "Let's just fly together!" But it's actually really hard. It's taken us a lot of work. I still catch myself all the time slipping into competition mode. It's more natural and instinctual for most pilots to want to win and to race. Frank Brown is the best at it. He has more experience than any of us. Frank and Marcelo used to compete against each other a lot. But they got sick of it, the one-upmanship, and we've learned that working together is a lot more rewarding. We've all done a lot of flying alone. We all tried to break the world record on our own. But flying in that immense space, all alone, with no friends around, it's not the same atmosphere that you get when you reach an objective together. Sharing that experience as a team creates much more powerful memories. To share these experiences was the best decision we've ever made.

Where's the best place to get the world record?

Texas is the place. On a good day there, 650km is possible for sure. The problem with Texas is you have so many hazards – the border with Mexico, airspace, huge fences, no roads, lots of private property, incredible heat, and lots of really sketchy terrain where landing would be very difficult. But Texas has very long days and a lot of wind, so I think the potential is better there than anywhere else. I don't think anybody has fully explored its potential, and until that work is done, we will continue to explore the Brazilian Sertão to its full potential and fly even farther than the longest flights in Texas.

Tell me about what it was like to bomb out on the day Donizete, Marcelo and Frank broke the world record of 514km in 2015?

We started a one-month attempt to break the world record on 5 October. The record happened on 9 October. On 5 October Frank bombed out. On 7 October Marcelo bombed out. On 8 October Donizete bombed out. So on 9 October it was my turn. But for me it was the best thing that could have happened. I'd stopped paragliding between 2008 and 2014, but these guys had been struggling up there in north-east Brazil every year. But throughout those years there hadn't been good enough weather. They stayed really focused on getting the record, and they deserved it. I didn't, I hadn't struggled

enough. I would have been really spoiled if I'd been with them and shared the record. Back in 2007, we were all really connected, flying as one. We were flying fast, not talking on the radio, moving as one. But in 2015 I wasn't really connected to the team. They invited me because I had the world record and I'd been a member of the team, but I wasn't yet ready to be a part of the 'organism'.

Marcelo and Donizete flew 513km again on 3 November, equaling the record. But that whole month I was always trying to catch up. I was using those guys; I wasn't helping. I was like a parasite. If you aren't working with them, you'll be left behind. Not because they want to, that's just the way the organism behaves. I wasn't ready to join them, I wasn't organized, I hadn't been struggling enough. To get a world record you have to struggle. It shouldn't be easy. You need to deserve it.

What happened between 2008 and 2014?

Two things. The first was that I was really bored. I broke the world record in 2007 and I was flying really nicely, but I was flying so many hours I became really jaded. If the thermal wasn't 5m/s, I'd complain. I had really bad humor about everything, and all of my happiness was tied to paragliding. If I did well in a competition, I'd be happy, if I did poorly, I'd be depressed. It was like being bipolar, and it wasn't healthy. The second thing was my family. We had businesses that needed my attention, and they needed me to come back from this other universe that I was living in. So I just quit.

Now I've come back to the sport with a totally different approach. I am more mature about all of it, and I've put paragliding where it should be. It's no longer my entire life, it's just a part of it. It's like they teach you in finance: you have to diversify. Right now, I'm diversifying my happiness. I have a family, I have kids, I have my work, and I have paragliding.

How do you maintain the passion for chasing a world record given all that? When we're learning, the absurdity of it all keeps us pretty excited, but the hours required for the retrieves and waiting around – it requires so much time and energy!

Back in 2007, before we broke Will Gadd's record, people were really skeptical that it could happen in Brazil. People didn't see the potential. That changed in 2007. But these days what keeps me interested is the journey, it's not just reaching the mark. Being with my friends, struggling together, learning together, learning to be happy with simple things, being around the humble people who live in the Sertão – it's the whole atmosphere that enchants me. Competitions are nice, but I really just go to those to learn to fly faster and see my friends. What drives me is chasing these world records. That's where I feel alive. Chasing the world record and expanding our sport's limits is much more interesting for me than going to a PWC.

How do you see your career moving forward? Have you thought about any kind of transition as age becomes more of a factor?

I'm the youngest member of the team right now and I've still got lots of time left. I see myself doing tandems with my wife, my kids, and just having fun with it, because I love to fly. I love the knowledge that it's given me, the friends I've

Texas - where hang glider pilots have flown over 700km. Photo: Nick Greece

made, and how it's made me look at the world in a different way. Other sports like swimming and cycling are great, but they don't give you such a different perspective, they don't teach you the chemistry and physics and leave you with the awe that you get from flying.

You just won the last task at the PWC in Portugal.
When I broke the record back in 2007, I was a good cross-country pilot, but I was never a good competition pilot. I was never consistent. I would go well one day but terrible the next. So when I came back to flying in 2014 I really focused on being more consistent. And for me, winning competitions was really good for my self-esteem and confidence. I think you need that confidence to do well.

Tell me more about being consistent. A lot of pilots can take risk and lead out and win a day with some luck, but being consistent and winning a competition is a different game.
What I've realized observing the pilots that I really admire is the pilots who are really consistent have nothing to prove. For a long time, I would lead out and push because I wanted to prove I was good. But the consistent pilots just breathe and relax. They're patient. They take much more calculated risks – they don't take risks that are ego-

driven. It's arrogant to think you can lead out when you're flying with the best pilots in the world. They will catch you. There's no perfect pilot, so you have to share the responsibility of getting to goal. You have to fly together. The key is to fly to win, not to fly to prove anything.

It actually sounds like there's quite a bit of cross-over between World Cup flying and the team flying that you're doing chasing records. Obviously World Cup tasks are faster and much shorter, but the concept of staying together sounds similar?
That's actually what I'm trying to learn to do better now. I'm trying to use the gaggle more, and take less risk. When we're team flying, we're like a band of birds, we share the leadership. Whoever has the most energy and is feeling the best will lead for a while, and the rest of us spread out behind. And that keeps changing all day, depending on who feels the best. And that way we share the energy, and no one gets too tired. That's actually similar to what the best competition pilots do. Because of the leading points formula, you can never win if you don't lead out a bit. So at times you have to be aggressive, but then you also have to fly with the gaggle.

RAFAEL'S ESSENTIAL HOW-TOS

HOW TO FLY CONVERGENCE LINES

1. Don't lose time trying to understand all the hows and whys. Just surf the line as fast as you can and leave working it out for later. Convergences last much less time than we think.
2. Even if the convergence is not pointing straight to where we want to get to, it's often the fastest way to get there.
3. Convergence lines offer abundant climbs. You might be tempted to keep going straight, but if you're less than two-thirds of the way to base, if you hit a strong core don't leave it till you're above that altitude. You never know how long it will last.

HOW TO READ CLOUDS

1. Beautiful clouds are born from perfect triggers. Try to spot and understand what the trigger is every time. The better you do this, the better you'll fly in different conditions.
2. In my experience, almost 100% of the time, the climb is on the windward side of the cloud. Only if there's a very light breeze or no wind at all should you try the sunny side of the cloud.
3. When starting a long transition from one cloud to the next, you may have to choose between two clouds in different life stages. Always choose the baby cloud or the most established looking cloud – never the perfect one. By the time you reach it, the baby will be perfect, the oldest will be reborn as a baby, and the perfect will be dead.

Rafael and the author getting ready to fly from Tacima, Brazil, 2018

HOW TO USE CLOUD STREETS

1. Never climb right up to cloudbase at the start of a strong-looking street. Glide straight below it testing out its intensity. If it's strong, just go straight below the street until you work out if you'll reach cloudbase by the end of the lift. If not, find a strong core and climb two-thirds of the way to cloudbase, then go through the rest of it. Gliding in too low below a perfect cloud street can be a really frustrating experience as all the lift is in the top 1,000ft (300m) or so.
2. Keep in mind that flying cloud streets is often an aggressive act. Keep yourself focused and act fast – the window is short and ruthless. If you time it well, it can be the best experience of your life.
3. In a cloud street we always have a lifting zone and a sinking zone. To avoid getting sucked inside, use both of them wisely! Keep gliding across at 45-degree angles to find the sweet spot between the two.

HOW TO CATCH LOW SAVES

In warmer locales like Brazil and Colombia, when we're extremely low, every bubble – it doesn't matter the strength – will end up drifting to a stronger lifting area, so just keep drifting until you hit the main flow.

If you're extremely low and manage to reach a potential trigger point that you can soar, don't be anxious about searching on. Keep soaring the trigger until the next cycle comes.

As a last chance to find a thermal in the flats, try to fly along the border of two areas with differing energy absorption. Rocks and grass, crop fields opposite open fields – anything that has a clear difference between the two sides. Color contrasts are also good.

SEVEN TIPS ON HOW TO FLY AS A TEAM GAGGLE

1. First, learn the difference between gaggles and teams. The word gaggle means 'flock of geese' or 'noisy or disorderly group of people'. In competitions we form gaggles exclusively for our temporary personal interest. It's a constant, selfish, competitive mode. If someone stays behind, we just don't care, and at the end we want to beat them all – it's all about winning. Team flying is the opposite. Our mantra is: *Unus pro omnibus, omnes pro uno*. We stick together, no matter what, for the common good. We train to be totally synchronized and altruistic. We wait for one another. It's a constant fight against our selfish competitive mode. If someone stays behind, we do whatever we can to help, because at the end of the day, we want to land together to share the whole experience.
2. Acknowledge your strengths and weaknesses. Then acknowledge your partners' strengths and weaknesses. This knowledge will guide you to choose the right partners. Sometimes your style will just not match to someone else's style. Matching styles requires lots of training. If you're willing to do it, focus first on matching your instincts to lead out – you need to know your partner well to predict his or her decisions.
3. Train to take off as close as you can, to wait for your partners above launch, to start the flight together and land together. Use any temporary advantage you get to your friends' advantage, not your own. It doesn't matter how far you go – in the beginning the most important thing is to learn how to become a true team.
4. Train your brain to ignore any temporary minor advantage you have and instead learn to stay side by side with your partners. If all of you can learn to do this, you'll be unbeatable.
5. When you get too low, never leave your partner. Together you are always stronger. To become a team, you should commit lots of mistakes and face early bomb-outs. If not, your team is flying too conservatively.
6. In a transition, try to fly side by side, around 50m apart. It's the best way to find the next thermal.
7. If you're higher than your team, use your extra altitude to push in front. Tell them you're leaving, go full bar, and radio them to tell them to use you as a reference to choose their lines. Use your speed bar to equalize out any differences in height during a long glide.

WHY SIV AND GROUND HANDLING MATTER

If you fly a paraglider, you must practice SIV and ground handling regularly. You can't possibly understand how long it will take to fix your wing after a collapse if you don't practice SIV. You can radically decrease the risk that you take every time you fly cross country by learning to backfly and doing at least 300 stalls – yes, 300! Even if you only fly recreationally, diligent training must be done regularly to develop potentially life-saving skills.

"I've been teaching SIV for a very long time, and I've come full circle in how I approach SIV. Nowadays I don't have a specific maneuvers agenda. It all has to fit the pilot and where they are. There are certain maneuvers that EVERY pilot needs to learn, maneuvers that I would teach a brand new pilot. Things like controlling pitch, stabilo pulls, hammering the brake to get out a cravat, turning circles to experience the glider's energy, dealing with riser twists, tweaking the As, etc. All that stuff I teach over the dirt with a clear conscience. The next level is done strictly over the water. Things like working up a nice progression to accelerated asymmetrics without the brake in hand, asymmetric accelerated frontals, spins and finding heading, and stalls. I think the outcomes are great if we approach SIV in this progressive way.

In my experience pilots need to take some time to mentally prep themselves and do some research before they take a maneuvers course. Pilots have to do it with a high level of intent. They have to want to do it without hesitation. I want to come back from the lake with no stories. Everything should be calculated and done with thoughtful precision. Pilots should have thought it all through and visualized the maneuver in their minds over and over before they actually do it."
Chris Santacroce

"SIV will very likely save your life. You need reflexes and muscle memory for when things go wrong. If you get into a situation and have to use your conscious brain, it will take too much time to solve. Solving problems needs to be instinct, and good instinct comes only with training."
Veso Ovcharov

"People will try things in an SIV course, for example stalls and spins, but for most people that's all they do. They don't master them and they never do them

"Normal pilots only think about flying. They don't spend enough time on training and working on the foundational skills. Ground handling needs to be done regularly, in conditions that aren't dangerous but challenging."
Chrigel Maurer

"Acrobatics requires a lot of repetition to get the maneuvers perfect and second-nature, so I prefer to train in a place like Organya in Spain, or where I train near Chambéry in France. These places have micro-weather systems that allow us to thermal or ridge soar back up after maneuvers, and the weather is usually good. At my local spot I can often spend seven hours in the air in a day. You never land. You just fly your tricks and go up again, and you end up getting a lot of momentum and muscle memory doing it over and over again. To really progress fast in acro, find a place where you can reload and stay in the air. "
Théo de Blic

outside of a course. A single SIV course can actually make them have more fear of doing those moves. To master a stall you have to do at least 300. You need repetition. Resetting your glider needs to be something you can do automatically, perfectly and without hesitation."
Ondrej Prochazka

"Pilots who struggle with their launches and ground handling often perpetuate their weakness because they don't want to be embarrassed, so they don't work on it. If they took action on the weakness and corrected it, they'd quickly turn it into a strength. It's a real shame because it isn't something to get embarrassed about – we all have weaknesses in our flying. The good and great pilots don't ride on their strengths and ignore their weaknesses – they turn their weaknesses into strengths."
Kelly Farina

"Even if you're on a coastal ridge site, practice sidehill landing constantly. Keep those skills sharp. You need to be able to put it down where you want to precisely and without stress."
Honza Rejmanek

"Pilots need to stay current with current SIV. SIV has changed a lot in just the last couple of years as modern gliders have changed. Gliders behave very differently than they used to. A lot of the things we used to teach and do are outdated and shouldn't be done anymore. Pilots who haven't done an SIV in a few years but are flying a modern wing need to get current with their SIV training. Something we're seeing more and more of with modern wings are pilots going into autorotation after a collapse and pilots then throw their reserve into their canopy. An autorotation is very easy to get out of with proper weight shift and brake application, and can easily be practiced in an SIV course."
Marko Hrgetic Hrga

"Every glider behaves a little differently when it stalls. EVERY time you change your wing you need to stall it and get used to its particular characteristics. Everything you fly you need to be able to stall and spin and then recover."
Christina Kolb

"It's much better to practice ground handling on a slope than on a flat field. It allows you to be a lot more playful, do a bunch of touch and gos, and it emulates the real thing, so it's a lot more valuable."
Greg Hamerton

Apply Yourself

RUSS OGDEN

Discipline, discipline, discipline. It's not a word that we're used to hearing as we fling our wings out on the slopes with our friends, desperate for freedom after a hard week at work. But the concept of discipline within paragliding is central to Russ Ogden's approach. Given that, as I write, he's ranked number one in the world, it's perhaps a concept worthy of further investigation.

For more than 20 years, Russ has been at the core of our sport, as a professional development pilot for Ozone, a pilot and coach for the British Team, and one of the most consistent podium pilots on the world tour. We recorded a talk that Russ gave in Sun Valley, right after the 2012 World Cup – it remains one of the most-watched instructional videos on technique. His concept of discipline is something that I still think of nearly every time I fly. It doesn't come easy, but it should apply to us all, whether we're doing pre-flight checks before our first solo launches, checking for traffic in a busy climb, or keeping our egos in check in a fast race, as Russ explains.

Russ, I'm keen first to hear your advice for a low-hour pilot flying in a wet, unflyable country – something you can probably remember from your early days of flying in the UK. What's the best way to improve during the winter and prepare for the first competition of next season?

The best thing you can do in winter is fly and ground handle every possible day. Get really good at kiting your wing, whatever the wind. Then, when you fly, learn how to get yourself to the top of the stack. Then once you get good at that, push out from the hill as far as you can and come back in as low as you can, and then get yourself back to the top of the stack. Repeat as much as you can. And when you're ridge-soaring, practice using your speed bar. Nothing crazy, but get used to using it. Most intermediate pilots don't use their speed bar very effectively or enough, and with the performance of today's EN B and C gliders, using the speed bar well means the difference between a 50k flight and your first 100k flight.

> **"The pilots who've been flying three or four years know just as much as Chrigel. Chrigel is just better at applying what he knows."**

What about speed-to-fly and best glide?
I like to keep things really simple when it comes to speed-to-fly. I don't use my instruments to tell me MacCready, or put my polars into my instruments, or anything like that, I personally don't think it makes a bit of difference. Speed-to-fly is simple:

- If the day is good, you should be at least half bar on glide.
- When you know there's a thermal in front of you and you're certain you're going to reach it, you need to be on at least 3/4 bar.
- If you're on a high-end glider you should be on full bar.
- If you're flying into wind, apply as much bar as you need to keep your GPS ground speed at around 38-40 km/h, which is a similar speed to your glider's normal hands-up trim speed in still air.

Sniffing out good, lifty lines through the air is much more important than what's on your instruments. That attitude might inhibit me a very small percentage of the time, but most of the time it allows me to free my mind and open my eyes. The key to racing well and flying cross country well is sniffing out great lines, and that is all feel.

OK… so how do you sniff out good lines?
Again, I keep it quite simple. If you get a good line, then sometimes it's relatively easy to stay on it because the lines often align themselves up or downwind. The trick is getting on to a good line when you're on a bad one. Sometimes you're in heavy sink because you're just about to hit a thermal, rather than being on a bad line. And the key is to be able to recognize the difference between the two. That comes with experience and hours in the air. In a competition you've usually got a bunch of pilots around you, so it's quite easy to see the good and bad lines if there are pilots in front of you. You can see it visually. If I'm on a bad line and I can see other people a hundred meters or so to my right or left on a better line, then I'll shift over quite quickly. There's a lot of sneaking around. Often to find the maximum efficiency you have to be inefficient by sawing back and forth going off course line.

Climbing is the same. To climb really well is not easy; it requires you to sometimes be inefficient to keep searching for a better core, as there's almost always something a bit stronger than what you are in. So you've got to go have a little sniff and change your circle slightly. But changing your circle often makes you lose height as well. You have to accept the inefficiencies to gain on efficiencies. You have to take that risk. You have to take that gamble – and gliding is very similar. If you're on a good line, try and stay on it. If you know you're on a bad line, then you have to assess whether you're about to go into a thermal or you're just on a bad line, in which case the best idea is normally to fly on a 45-degree line from your existing track. And that way you're still covering the ground in roughly the direction you want to go, but you're just changing your position in the air mass.

I know you're a disciple of discipline. Can you tell me more about that?
Probably a better word is application. We all have the same information. We've all read the same books. The pilots who've been flying three or four years know just as much as Chrigel. They don't think they do, but they do. Chrigel is just better at applying what he knows. Chrigel has the discipline to always apply what he knows. The rest of us make mistakes, and sometimes we think we're cleverer than we are.

Discipline means applying what we know. For example, speed-to-fly. If we know there's a good climb in front of us, we should be on full bar, not on half bar. You may be on half speed because you're not too sure. You're not so certain. You might not reach it just in time. But actually you should just be flying full speed. You may not be flying full speed because you're not comfortable with your glider, which means that you need to work on your flying skills.

Some pilots are naturally extremely cautious when they fly cross country, and others are a bit gung-ho and push on a little bit too hard. There are pilots who will get to the top of the stack and push hard and go on a death glide and bomb out, and there are pilots like me who are always a little too conservative, and take one or two too many turns in the climb before goal, and someone a little more aggressive will beat me. The key is finding the sweet spot between the two and being disciplined to apply the right mix.

Discipline is about applying everything you know at every stage of the flight.

Russ after all these years, are you still really passionate about flying? And if so, what aspects?
My relationship with flying over the years is like a relationship. It has its ups and downs. Some days I'm not really into it and other days I'm really fired up. I really enjoy the testing work. Stalling, spinning, collapsing and all of that. I genuinely love that part. And I still really love competitions. I don't do a ton of cross-country flying just for fun on my own.

What separates the pilots like Honorin Hamard and Julien Wirtz and Xevi Bonet and yourself, the pilots who are so consistent at the very top level, from the rest?
They make fewer mistakes than everyone else. They hold their position really well. They climb very well, they glide very well and they make very good gaggle decisions. What's important in competitions is actually not making too many cross-country decisions. You want to dominate the gaggle and have other pilots out in front of you as markers. So that means being technically really good, but also having the discipline to dominate the gaggle and keeping yourself in a position to strike at the end, which is easier said than done.

Russell in Governador Valadares, Brazil. Photo: Nick Greece

Do you do anything before a comp to prepare mentally? Is there a certain headspace you try to get in?
I've tried the lucky socks. I've tried the lucky pants. I've tried being super-motivated. I've tried it all and it makes absolutely no difference whatsoever. For me the best thing is just to wake up in the morning and go fly. I try to see it as nothing more than that.

You have to be disciplined and focused for sure, but it doesn't help putting external pressure on myself or being too hard on myself. I think the most important thing is to be able to deal with the defeats and accept it. It's just a part of our sport. That's something that can be very demoralizing about flying, that there's a lot of luck involved. You could be flying really well, and yet you still do badly. You get a bad cycle or you miss the bottom of the climb. Whereas other days you might not be flying well and making a lot of mistakes blundering around the sky, and you catch a nice cycle that everyone else misses, and you win the day. It's just random like that. So I think it's best to just keep it simple and go flying.

When you gave your talk here in Sun Valley many pilots were quite surprised to hear that two-liners shouldn't be allowed to frontal, ever. You basically said if you're getting frontals on a two-liner you shouldn't be flying one.
I was quite surprised that wasn't common knowledge, because that had been the common teaching at that point for quite some time. Looking back on what I said, most

of it still stands. Regardless of the class of wing, two-liner, three-liner, whatever: if the glider starts to deflate, starts to frontal, the first thing you need to do is hit the brakes sharply to keep the nose open, and then let your hands up so it can recover and fly away. If you hit the brakes too hard and you go into a little stall that's no problem, just put your hands up and fly away. If you're flying a two-liner, you should have the skills to stall without hesitation any time you need it.

To keep a wing open, you usually just need to apply an abrupt change to the angle of attack. So on a two-liner you can stay on full bar through rough air by just being aggressive if need be on the B handles to a certain point. There's always a point where you'll have to come off bar and go to the brakes, and flying efficiently means learning where that point is on whatever glider you fly. These things take time to learn though. Paragliders are not easy machines to fly well. They're incredibly easy to fly, but incredibly difficult to fly well in turbulent air. You have to do the acro training and the SIVs and you have to fly in rough air. So in order to have the skills, you have to have subjected yourself to some experience of risk and danger.

What are the common things you see when it comes to accidents, especially for lower-hour pilots, and is it any different now than it was, say, ten years ago?
What's changed over the years is that we're flying now in conditions that we would have never considered before. The wings weren't fast enough, and they were too unstable. We were taught back then that if it was gusting from 5mph to 15mph, it was probably too strong. And now that's a good day! So the wings have got so much safer and better, but the sport hasn't gotten any safer because pilots are flying in much stronger air.

The most important thing for most intermediate pilots is ground handling. What gets people is trying to launch in strong conditions and they don't have the ground control. If you have good ground control skills, then when you're in tricky situations in the air, you'll be able to deal with everything much better. In fact, the only thing that the air can do to your glider is collapse it. So as long as you can deal with a frontal or a side collapse, the air can't do anything more to you. And the stuff that leads to a cascading event – the spiral, the autorotation, all of those types of things are not necessarily self-induced, but they're preventable with the correct input. What's great now is that there's a healthy attitude towards SIV and actually learning how to fly the glider.

A few years ago you'd see a pilot in the World Cup take a 60-70% side collapse and end up throwing their reserve. That just shouldn't happen, but it used to be quite a regular occurrence. People were too light or too aggressive with the inputs to their wing. They hadn't done enough training. There were plenty of completely avoidable accidents that just came down to poor piloting. But now the overall standard has improved, certainly at the World Cup level anyway. There are fewer reserve rides and fewer incidents now. The pilot quality is probably slightly lower in terms of cross-country flying skills, but the piloting skills are better.

One of your team pilots, Honorin Hamard, had a really amazing year. He flew huge world record triangles[1] in the Maritime Alps in France, and won the world

championship and the Europeans. What separates guys like Honorin from other elite pilots?

You can put a guy like Honorin in the same bracket as Chrigel. They have the balance of the geeky, technical side of flying along with the surfer kind of 'flow' side. This kind of pilot is totally wrapped up in flying, and treats it as his profession, and is into every facet of the game. The scary thing about Honorin is that he hasn't peaked. He's only 25 years old, and he's flying every day here as a test pilot, and he's only going to get better.

> **"What's changed over the years is that we're flying now in conditions that we would have never considered before."**

If you could rewind the clock to your 50-hour self, what advice do you wish you'd gotten?

I actually don't know. If there was a magical way to get through intermediate syndrome, say up through 500 hours without injuring yourself that would sure be valuable. And probably the best thing I could have done for my flying would have been to move to a better place to learn to fly. Learning on the South Downs in England, where it's very difficult to go XC and the opportunities to fly are few and far between wasn't the fastest way to learn.

Where is the best place in the world to learn safely and avoid the 'ground suck' crowd?

The ground suck crowd exists on every hill in the world. Some of them are wise and some of them are negative, and you have to learn to discern between the two. And the best place isn't something I know actually. You want a place that isn't rocky and is more forgiving, someplace with trees, as trees tend to be generally forgiving, and a place that has reliable conditions and nice air.

Round, square or delta (Beamer) shape reserve, and what weight range should we be on?

From what we've seen, the stability and sink rate is much better with squares compared to rounds. Round reserves work quite well, but they can often get quite unstable and oscillate. And it depends on what the glider does. If the lines become asymmetric in any way, then you can have quite a pendulum descent. So I'm

[1] Honorin set the FAI triangle world record twice in 10 days, flying a 306km FAI and then a 329km FAI, both from Col Agnel in the Maritime Alps on the border of France and Italy. This record was smashed on 2 June 2019 by Chrigel Maurer who flew a 343km FAI triangle in the Bernese Alps.

Late evening glide at the end of a 400km flight, Texas, USA. Photo: Nick Greece

convinced the square is a good way forward. The delta shape reserves are also very effective, if you can release the glider and you've got enough altitude to be able to steer them in the right direction. But if you have to throw very low and you're next to a cliff face or something, then a delta probably isn't the best option, as it will track with the wind. For acro pilots the deltas make a lot of sense because they're usually in clear space, but for cross-country pilots flying in the mountains, there are potentially disadvantages with the Beamer type reserves. But I think the squares address these issues. And definitely I think big is best. I've heard that a lightly loaded parachute can cause pendulum issues, but I like the idea of a big parachute when I have to use it, and coming down softly.

And two reserves?

I fly with two reserves all the time now. If we forget the situation of being really low and getting a big collapse, the most common situation where a pilot is going to need to deploy the reserve is a heavy, twisted cravatted spiral. In that configuration you're usually in an autorotation with a lot of force and it's terminal, so there's nothing you can do. I would say 50% of the reserves thrown in that situation go directly into the wing. So I'm very comfortable flying with two reserves and I wouldn't want to just fly with one.

The author exploring the magic lines of Morocco. Photo: Jody MacDonald

Some pilots have been taught that using speed bar and brakes at the same time is ok. Can you explain why it's not?
When you do both at the same time, you weaken the profile of the glider. You're giving the glider more camber, which makes a glider go more nose-down, which leads to more collapses.

Why is learning wingovers so important?
I love the wingover maneuver because it has everything. Pitch control, pressure control, roll control, timing, collapse-stopping – it has everything to learn the dynamics of a wing. The important thing with wingovers is doing them up high and away from the ground, because even super-experienced pilots can screw them up.

How important is it to learn stalls?
Ultimately having a good command of the stall can save your life. We're not playing golf here, are we? If you're not good at putting, it doesn't really matter. But if you're not good at stalling, it could kill you. I don't see the point in not being able to control the glider fully in terms of spin appreciation, spin control, collapse appreciation, collapse control, getting out cravats, being able to stall the glider if necessary, dealing with twists, being able to throw your reserve. So it's not absolutely important, you can go your entire flying career

without ever having to do a stall, that's for certain. But I don't think it's something that you should actively avoid for the sake of avoiding, or because you're scared of doing it. The more command you have of the wing, the less fear and the fewer gremlins you have on your shoulder, and the more enjoyment you can get from the sport.

What's your opinion on using a seatboard versus a hammock harness?
The difference isn't huge. For stalling and getting rid of twists and such, you have more control with a seatboard, but I think whatever you're comfortable with is fine. You can get good at those skills without a seatboard as well. The important thing is being able to ball up in a cascading event and keep your legs tucked up underneath you to keep you from getting twisted up. What I would say is important is to not change more than one piece of gear at a time, never change both the harness and the wing together.

How much does a pod harness help in terms of top speed and glide?
In terms of top speed not much at all, at least that I'm aware of. But in terms of glide there's about a point difference, but that depends a lot on being at the optimum angle. You of course want to have the perfect angle, but it's better to be slightly feet high than feet down if you err to one side.

What do you think of the technique of top landing by flapping hard?
It's a useful technique for landing in small places, but there are inherent dangers of course, and like everything it requires practice. You have to be very intimate with the stall point of your glider, because you can't look at your wing when you're doing it, and if you stall the glider low (asymmetrically or symmetrically) you can get into real trouble.

Do higher aspect gliders have a better sink rate than lower aspect gliders, or is increased performance just in top speed and glide?
Sink rate is better on high aspect gliders as a rule. You see that with competition wings; they not only glide better but they climb better, especially in broken lift. In broken lift the more efficient wing will cut through better and not lose as much height. But given a strong, tight, gnarly little core, a good pilot on an EN B wing will be able to outclimb a comp pilot, because they can maintain a tighter turn radius and stay in the strong lift.

How substantial is the performance difference of a large glider compared to a small glider? How much disadvantage do the smaller pilots have?
There's an advantage in speed and glide on the large gliders. You've got more surface area, you create more lift, and you've got better wing loading. And, as a general rule, the larger wings behave slightly better in the certification testing. That allows them to have a bigger speed range and more top speed. The smaller wings are more aggressive in collapses, and harder to get through certification. There's less relative wing loading on small gliders, and thus less speed. So yes, small people in paragliding, especially in competitive paragliding, have a disadvantage in speed, but they can climb better. The big boys push their buses around the outside of the thermal while the little guys squeak up through the middle. So you can gain in climbs. But it's difficult to make up in speed and glide.

HOW TO AVOID ACCIDENTS

Do we discuss safety too much? Maybe. Has it affected just about everyone in our sport? Almost certainly. Can we pursue flying and not get hurt? Absolutely.

It's interesting how many pilots talk about listening to that 'inner voice' that we all have. As Will Gadd says, if you're a pilot you're naturally an optimist: "You're going to huck off a mountain and think it's all going to work out!"

Read the following advice carefully. Come back to it often. Listen to that inner voice, be in the right frame of mind, avoid flying when you're distracted, and obey the golden rule: "There are old pilots and bold pilots, but there are no old bold pilots!"

"We're guests in the sky – we need to have respect. Anyone can enter a maneuver, but can you exit one? Ask the pros, read books, watch videos, have a plan A, but also a plan B and C. Slow down, take your time."
Xandi Meschuh

"Get fit. When I train pilots for the X-Alps, I focus on resilience. Flying means you've got to land, and landing wrong can be painful. Being fit and resilient means the difference between bouncing with a laugh, and going to the hospital."
Ben Abruzzo

"We all have an inner voice. Sometimes it only whispers, but you have to listen. Tune into the hair standing up on the back of your neck or the clench in your gut. Even if your buddies are all fired up to fly a hundred miles, sometimes it's not your day. That little voice is trying to keep you alive."
Matt Beechinor

"Practice acro. Before I got into acro, if I had to stall my glider or clear a cravat, it was a really big deal. But after you have some acro practice, these things don't even get your heart rate up."
Tom de Dorlodot

"When you have work or personal stress hanging over you, you're opening

"Fly straight on landing. Most of the accidents I've seen happen on landing, and are self-inflicted. Pilots turn close to the ground and spin their gliders. Fly straight and make friends with trees and bushes, don't get fixated on the field. It's counter-intuitive, but it's safer. The other one I see is pilots getting plucked on launch. When the wind is over 12km/h and you're on a steep slope and you're nervous about having that move, it's not the time to see if you do. Taking off when conditions are strong requires a lot of baby steps in kiting practice."
Rob Sporrer

"Learn to manage your mind better. Our minds do weird and wonderful things while we're flying. We'll suddenly think 'Are these carabiners going to snap?' or 'Why am I flying like a donkey?'

Chrigel Maurer has three modes: he's thermalling, planning or gliding. When he finds himself getting distracted, he asks himself which mode he's in and comes back to it. We should all think like that. When you're on take-off, assess conditions – only do that, don't get distracted. Then go through your pre-flight checklist. Don't listen to anyone else; keep it methodical. We still have big lessons to learn from commercial aviation."
Hugh Miller

yourself up to a lot more risk. Flying requires being fully present. If your life isn't going well, do something else to get the escape you need."
Gurpreet Dhindsa

"My instructor Chris Santacroce told me: 'Always be stoked for a sledder.' Even when I'm prepped on launch for a big flight and I've got high hopes, I think about this advice to check in with myself before every flight."
Willi Canell

"Accidents happen when pilots don't appreciate their own level of ability and push beyond it. If you're in doubt, take the easy option and do the safe thing. Overconfident pilots push the limits in two ways: they fly in too much wind, or they fly a glider beyond their skill level. What you're always trying to do is put the odds in your favor."
Bruce Goldsmith

"Any monkey can paraglide, and any monkey can teach any monkey to paraglide, but did your instructor set you up to make good decisions when you leave school? After a couple of years you'll know how to quantify the risk, you'll know if you're making good decisions. It's not about the technical skills in the beginning, it's really about creating a mindset and philosophy of good decision-making."
Chris Santacroce

"Fly in nice conditions on good days. If it's shitty go do something else! I get too scared to enjoy rough air."
Armin Harich

"Be happy to be inconvenienced. A lot of people get hurt because they want to land near a road just to save themselves from walking. Land in the best, safest place every time."
Nick Greece

"The buck stops with you. If you find yourself blaming your gear, someone else or conditions, you're wrong."
Tom Payne

"The only way to get very skilled is through a lot of practice. If you go ground handling in strong winds, you'll get very good at handling your glider in wind, but you'll get slapped around a little. Getting slapped is ok. You just don't want to get whacked!"
Antoine Laurens

The Coach

THOMAS THEURILLAT

Thomas Theurillat asks good questions.

Formerly a Swiss mountain guide, Thomas had just finished his psychology studies when Chrigel Maurer asked him to support him in his first Red Bull X-Alps race. The rest is history. Taught to fly by Chrigel, Thomas now heads a coaching company called 'OneDay', using solution-focused approaches. Essentially, he takes his clients out into the wilds and helps them transform their thinking, attitude and approach during an intense 24 hours.

Thomas coaches several pilots including Paul Guschlbauer, Patrick Von Känel, Sebastian Ospina, Tom de Dorlodot, Seiko Fukuoka and Yael Margelisch, as well as world-renowned adventure sailors, athletes and executives.

I contacted Thomas during the coronavirus pandemic, knowing it would be an interesting time not only to get his thoughts on the state of the world, but also to be a test-piece for his methodology.

One of my first questions was how he gives advice. Thomas cut me off before I got to the end of the sentence.

"Gavin, I don't ever give advice," he told me.

"How can I advise someone who knows much more about who they are than I do? I only ask questions. I never told Chrigel what I thought he should do; I just asked him questions and let him decide."

Thomas got into my head and waded around in places I hardly knew existed. The outcome was thrilling.

Thomas, can you tell us more about your coaching approach?
Whether in nature or in ourselves, there are two types of change. Change in sports, for example, is something like learning pull-ups, but if you stop training they go away. The same with learning a new language. If you stop speaking it, you soon forget the vocabulary. This is change, but it isn't permanent. But there are also deeper changes which we call a transformation. For example, if you learn swimming or if you become a parent and have a family or the world goes digital, this is a transformation on a second

level. It does not go back. You can't unlearn swimming. A caterpillar never goes to a flying school. There is a transformation and it's a butterfly. When you cook corn and it pops into popcorn, it never returns to being a kernel.

I think it's much more powerful to spend a whole day with someone and try to make a transformation instead of spending ten one-hour sessions to try to make a change. If our coaches can help a business leader or athlete to find the best version of themselves or to get to the next level, then we have a transformation. There is then a new approach and a new mindset. So that's the name of our approach and our product.

What does one day with 'One Day' look like?

It's a whole day of a hiking or other nature experience, with solution-focused coaching talks. There's an initial call three or four weeks before, which leads to homework for both parties, and then there's a follow-up call a month or two later where we assess how successful the transformation was. Before we go to the desert or the mountains, the clients are very well prepared for the day. They know their goal. We know what they want, what they don't want, and what their strengths are. During this day we try to find the new version for them or the new behavior that they seek.

How did you and Chrigel team up before the 2009 Red Bull X-Alps?

We didn't know one another. I was a Base jumper in Lauterbrunnen; my girlfriend was a test pilot for Advance, and he was flying for Advance in the same valley. I was finishing my Masters in psychology, and for me it was clear that I wanted to do something which really worked for my clients. 'Consulting' and 'coaching' often sound nice, but in the end there isn't much impact. I was giving a lot of thought to how I could really have an impact on improving people's performance, and when I met Chrigel the X-Alps seemed like an interesting project and a good prototype to test some of my theories. He had a dream, but he didn't really have a plan. And I had no clue about the X-Alps, but I asked some questions and we found out that maybe I could help him with his preparation. We never considered that I would become his supporter. It was a project where I learnt a lot about what worked and what didn't.

If I'm really honest, we didn't bring anything new to Chrigel's first campaign in 2009. The techniques I used were already well known in other sports; they just weren't being used in paragliding. In other sports, it's totally standard to work with a mental coach.

Chrigel has often said that a huge portion of his success is due to the coaching he got from you.

I think this is totally overrated, not true. Chrigel just needed to tweak the way he thought about challenges. Everyone was saying he was doing well. But what does that mean? I wanted to know what Chrigel looked like when he's performing at 100%.

If you ask an athlete: "How does it look when you're at 100%?", they'll respond that they need to do more of something or less of something else. But I don't accept more and less. I want to hear a number. For example, we asked what a perfect X-Alps day looks like when you perform at 100% in a given weather situation. Then you have a picture. I'm very, very convinced that if you can dream it, you can do it. But the dream has to be extremely specific. The first paper I made Chrigel write for me was what he wanted the story to be for himself when he reached Monaco.

You asked him to visualize what being in Monaco looked like before he did the race?
Yes. We call this a time jump. I also did it with Yael Margelisch, who flew 500km in Brazil in 2019 and beat the women's world record. I had her explain what she wanted to say after the record flight before she left for Brazil. If you really challenge people to explain their dreams, then it's very interesting to see how they will use their strengths. For example, I had Chrigel explain what a 'perfect' day in the X-Alps would be. He said: "I always want to use 80% of the day for flying. I want to be at launch 15 minutes before the thermals start on an east-facing slope. I want to have warm clothes for flying. I have the right food. I will change my socks every two hours…"

If you ask someone the right question and they can imagine the perfect day, then you can start preparing to make it happen.

> **"I think it's much more powerful to spend a whole day with someone and try to make a transformation instead of spending ten one-hour sessions to try to make a change."**

It's interesting to analyze success. In the US if someone is very good, he knows that he's very good. If someone is good in Switzerland, he's too shy to think about why he's good. So I ask a lot of athletes and also businessmen and women to make a list of their top 10 successes. For pilots, take one evening and analyze your ten best flights. Make it homework, something you lay out on a spreadsheet. Try to find a pattern. I know for example many pilots often fly their best if they are not home because they're on a holiday or are far away from work and their stress. Or it can be that they were technical flights in weak conditions, or big flights in strong conditions, or maybe they were during a competition. How you define 'best flight' is up to you.

When we looked at this list with Chrigel, it was very clear that his best flights were often alone. He doesn't fly as well when he's with other pilots. That's why we took the night pass on the first night in 2013, when the flying weather looked very good and we knew he would have a hard time shaking the better pilots. It's never a good idea to use the night pass early and get tired. That's stupid. But when you know that you're a good pilot when you're alone, we needed to get him out in front. To be successful you have to create a recipe with the ingredients available to a particular individual.

We understood with Chrigel that we have a certain mindset, certain equipment, and known strengths, so we put them together to achieve a high probability that he could perform his best. If you know this, then success becomes something like a recipe. If you have several good ingredients and you mix them in the right way, you get a nice cake. If you look at people who win repeatedly over several years, it's only because they have created a successful pattern. In my work, we try to write a very detailed book about the recipe. If you have a recipe, you can repeat it. If you don't have a recipe, you can't know the outcome and you will be nervous.

Psychological Tools

Cockpit of Success

HOW TO MOVE CONFIDENTLY FORWARD

What values help you to understand if you're primed for success or not?

WHAT'S MY ENERGY LEVEL?

WHAT'S MY OPTIMAL PERFORMANCE STATE?

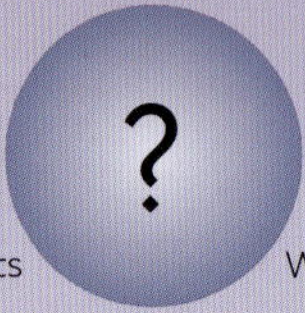

DO I SEE THE FULL PICTURE?

Circle of Control

PUT THE FOCUS IN MY REACH

How can I focus solely on what I can achieve?

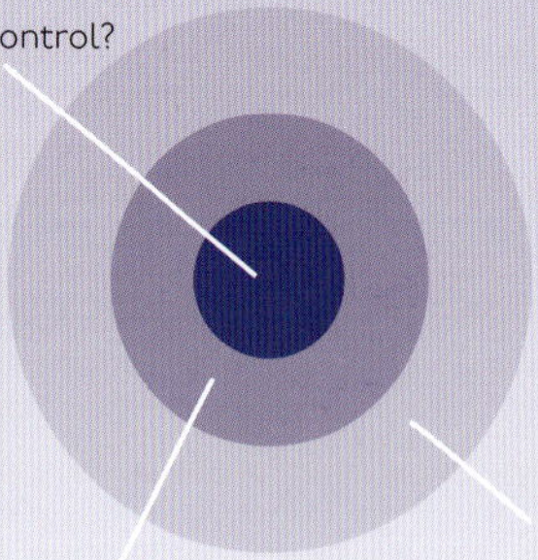

Time-Jump

LOOKING BACK IN ONE YEAR'S TIME...

What was the reason for doing it?

How did I get it done?

What did I achieve?

What am I most proud of?

Positive Spiral

What goals can I set to generate positive momentum?

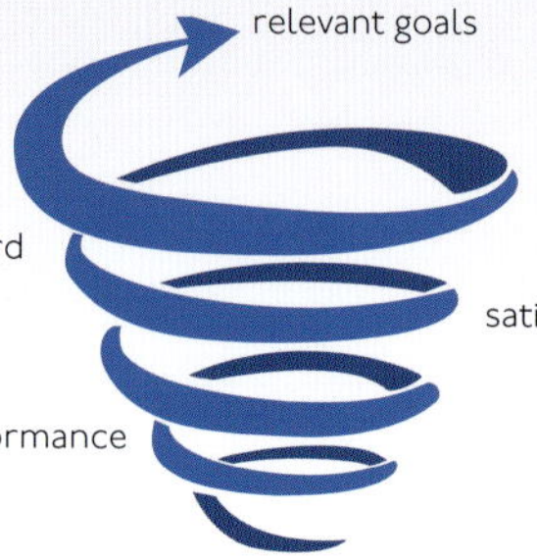

The Triangle of Change

Each change has three dimensions.

How clear am I on each?

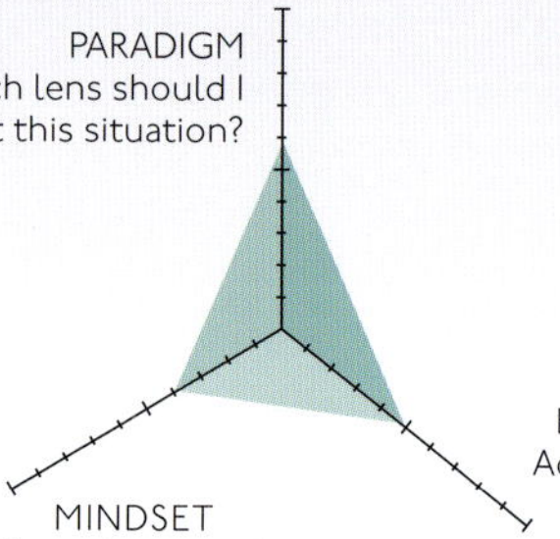

Can you tell me some other techniques we could all use?
The Covid-19 pandemic challenges us all to be the best versions of ourselves. But there are tools we can use to be as positive as possible. For example, one tool is called the helicopter view. It's just to imagine that you're sitting in a helicopter, or a satellite very high over your house, getting a picture of your life from above.

Gavin, if you sit now in a helicopter and you're 3,000m over your house, if you look down on yourself making the podcast and spending time with your family, what do you see?

It's been such a treat to be with my family so much. I've been spending hours in the kitchen. It's been really healthy for me, because I tend to be a pretty driven person and it's hard for me to slow down. From the helicopter view, I see calm.
Ok this is interesting. You're in a very challenging time in the world, and with the helicopter view you start talking with appreciation about your life and calm. Calm or calmness can be a good title for the month of April. Let's look at the rocket on the diagram, which we call the time jump. If you were to continue thinking like this when I call you in six months' time, what would you like to tell me then about this spring?

I'd like to tell you that I took advantage of the time, but being present is one of the hardest things I struggle with. Over the scope of my life the times that really stand out are the times when I've been fully in the moment. I wasn't thinking back, I wasn't thinking forward. So being in the moment.
I think this is very interesting. After one minute you're very clear what you want.

What I want and what I get are two different things sometimes, but that's what I would like to see at the end of September. Being present, things work better.
Okay. On a scale from 1 to 10, with 10 representing you having all the skills and the mindset and you're totally present, and 1 being the opposite, where are you at right now, today?

9. But that's not normally where I would be!
And why is it 9 and not 1? Why is it already so good?

I spent many years sailing around the world. I guess I'm used to external forces that you can't control very much. I'm used to things like storms, where ability and keeping calm are critical, but often attitude is your greatest weapon. I'm scared like everybody right now, but I know that there's very little I can do and I might as well enjoy what I can. I'm a 9 instead of a 1 because I'm just more here than I typically am. For my family, and for me. It's nice because there's nowhere else we can be.
And what can you do so you don't backtrack? That you don't get back to the old path? What can you do to stay on a 9 maybe for the rest of the year… or for the rest of your life?

I've thought about that a lot. I don't have a great answer, to be honest. I've tried mindfulness practice for years now and I really enjoy that, but I don't think that would keep me at a 9. Spending time outside is very good for slowing me down. That always brings me to the present. I think I need to continue playing with my daughter, sticking to the intermittent fasting, and having a bit more structure to my days.
So you make the day instead of the day makes you. And what would be a 10?

It's the exact same as when I'm training for the X-Alps. That is when I'm a 10. I love training so much and it's the most joyful I ever am. So maybe that's the answer. Focus.
So you need a goal which is bigger than the X-Alps or a goal that's not connected.

> **"Aiming to finish in a certain place in a competition will almost certainly be counter-productive."**

Yes. This has been the hardest thing about my three X-Alps campaigns - that they end!
We've just been through the 1 to 10 question. It's something Chrigel hates me for, but this is a very powerful, very simple, and maybe annoying tool because it is very specific. Everyone is between 1 and 10. We force you to think about where you are and how we can stabilize it if you are high, or how we can improve it if you are low.

Every human has a dream. You want to be thankful, and focused, and be working in the right direction. Maybe it's easier if the direction is a sporting competition, but you also can be like this without competition as long as you know what you want. I don't have to give you any advice. I just have to ask what is 9.1, and 9.2 and after the call you can go to your wife and tell her what we discussed. Then you have to keep yourself honest, by asking yourself once a day if your behavior is on track. I call this self-leadership.

So if you sail around the world or you go with all the daily hassles of work or you try to manage your family, you can ask yourself if your behavior is on track. When you're sitting in a car, you know how the car is performing. You know how much fuel remains and how much the motor turns per minute. You know it because you've done it so much. You don't have to think about it. If you look at a marathon – everyone in the race, thousands of people, they all know their heartbeat. If a runner is experienced, she feels her heartbeat. She doesn't need to look at her monitor to know how fast it's beating.

During any activity you can ask yourself: "How is my focus, how is my mindset about being thankful?" And the moment you start thinking like this, you get better at it. Ask yourself: are you in charge of the day or are your emails in charge of your day?

That was powerful. You told me you like to ask questions and don't give advice. Can you give an example?
Yes, of course. What's the most useful thing during this exercise we just did?

It made me think about where I am. I hadn't thought about where I was so much. It makes me think about a goal. If you'd asked me the same thing on the 1 to 10 scale three weeks after the X-Alps, I would've been more around a 1 or 2 maybe.
That's totally okay. If you are a 2, you can think about getting to a 2.1. It's totally okay wherever you are on the scale. Sometimes we have clients and we ask them: "Where are you between 1 and 10?" And they tell me they are minus one hundred. That's totally okay. Then we try to get to minus 99. I've been coaching athletes in really challenging situations like the X-Alps or a season in world cup ski racing, or business clients dealing with huge decisions or issues at their company. If you ask people questions like I just asked you there's a moment where they start thinking like this on their own.

Chrigel, for example, I remember I asked him once during the race, how are you? And he said 7. And then I thought, okay, I don't have to continue. I don't need to talk with him about 1 and 10. He was already thinking 10 would be chasing the perfect day, and 1 is he's lost control. This is the moment where I often stop coaching, because I can't add value anymore.

How much is Chrigel's focus on winning versus just making the next move?
I would like to explain it in a different way. Let's look at something like a marathon. If you do a marathon, you can make three goals. One is a ranking goal: to win the race or be top 10 or whatever. Ranking goals are useless. They don't help you.

The second is a performance goal. For example, "I will finish in four hours." A performance goal is something you can control. It's possible that a hundred other people will achieve the same performance goal, but it doesn't matter. In paragliding, it's like stating, "today I will stay airborne during my XC for five hours". Performance goals you can measure and they are useful.

Then there are process goals, which describe how you do it. For example, in a marathon you might say for the first 10k you will eat a banana and run with a heartbeat of 150. This type of goal often has the biggest impact. You told me about how you want to live in April. What you do in the morning before breakfast and what you do with your emails. These goals often come with a description of how you will do it. Having a good result is usually a good side effect of performing your best. When someone comes to me and says: "I want to win this," or: "We want to be the best company in this," I often say: "What kind of performance do you need for that?" For example, if you can travel 150km a day on average, you will win the X-Alps.

This is the performance you need to bring. If you sail 17.5 knots average for 78 days, you win the Vendée Globe (a round-the-world sailing race). If you can run 100m in 17 seconds for two hours, you can do a marathon in two hours. This is the performance required.

But to achieve this, you have to discover the **how**. How can you be sure that this happens? All the focus should be on the how of the process. Sometimes the world is too complex, the world is too difficult to describe the how because there are external factors.

More Psychological Tools

Helicopter-View

HOW WOULD I SEE MYSELF AND MY SURROUNDINGS FROM ABOVE?

What's different from this view?

What would I like to see for myself?

What advice would I give myself? (3-5 things)

Non-violent Communication

Clarity when talking and understanding

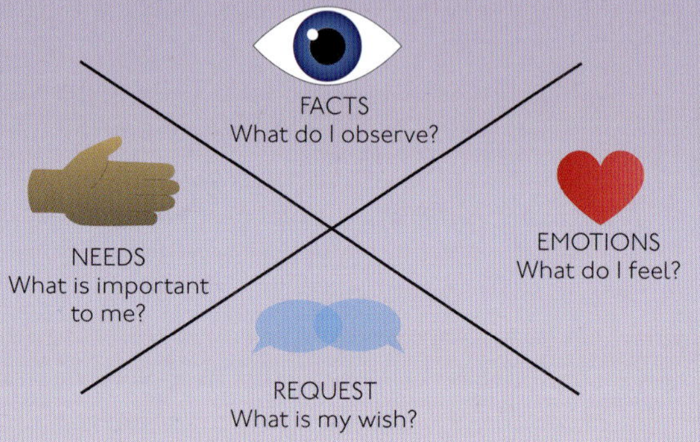

Solutions from 1 to 10

HOW ARE THINGS, FROM 1 TO 10?

If 10 is the maximum and 1 is the minimum, where am I right now?

Important:

A: Why it is not rated at 1?

B: What is different if I am one point higher?

C: If it's extremely difficult, what can I do to not make it worse?

Mental Hardness

How can I empower myself during challenging times?

How can I create or activate an effective backup plan?

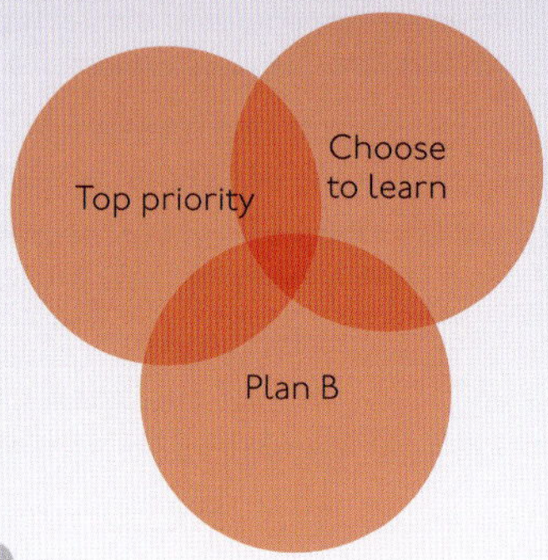

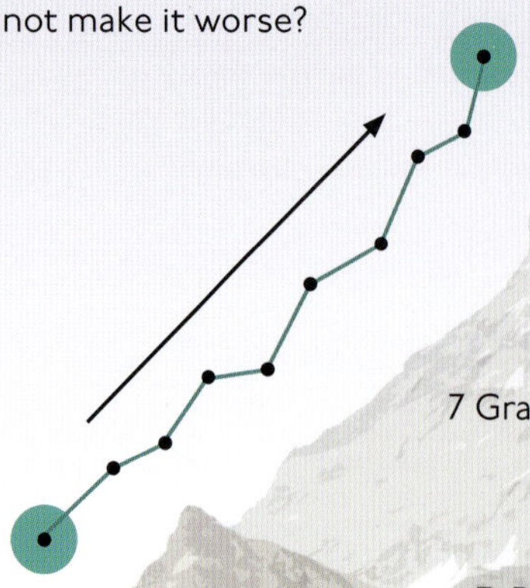

Step by Step Approach to the Top

7 Gratitude (satisfaction = reality/expectations)

6 Learning, optimising, developing

5 Doing & leading. Keep up the fire

4. Create and plan solutions

3. Do we need a new way of dealing with it?

2. Find inner strength and poise

1. Observe and accept. What is it? What's ok?

And for that it's very useful to have a mastery goal. When you master something, you'll know how to do the how right. If you look at the ancient martial arts, they only focus on the mastery goal because they have over a thousand years of experience. If they are a master, they will handle the how. If they handle the how they win the fight. When it comes to a difficult project like the X-Alps, what does mastery mean for Chrigel? It means that he can fly very well in difficult conditions, that he makes good strategic decisions, that he's at the right place at the right time, and he's achieved mastery during his preparation. The how is known and it's specific. If the how is good, the performance is good. So, we need to focus on the how. When you tell me about how to go from a 9 to a 10, it's about the how: the differences that make a difference.

Why have you kept your X-Alps team so small over the years?
If you have a big team, there's a big effort for the coordination of this team. If you have only two people, the communication is clear. There's no confusion between the two. If you're three, the complexity increases; just the time to communicate and coordinate goes up considerably. That's why we decided to keep our team small. You have to look at the benefits of more people, but also the costs. I think being agile and being very flexible and not having to please too many people is an advantage.

If you look at different sports, like sailing, the record for sailing around the world single-handed is 45 days, and only 43 days sailing with a crew. It's only two days faster. Mountaineering is the same. There are often huge teams assembled to climb 8,000m peaks: Sherpas to carry gear, expert support climbers to fix ropes, base camp managers to handle medical equipment, food, oxygen, garbage and media. These teams look nice, but often the outcome is not. In business we see the same. Bigger often isn't better. From a work psychology point this is a good question. What is a good size of team to complete a task? I'm not sure there's a hard answer, but you can't win in quality if you increase in quantity.

I've felt listless after the races. During the race you're on top of the metaphoric mountain, not just physically but mentally. You're enjoying it. It's fun. But you can't stay there forever. You have to come back down.
Musicians and surgeons experience the same thing. If you're on stage at a huge concert, or totally focused on a complicated operation, when it ends you feel empty. You lose the structure of the goal. Recovery is often connected with a bad mood. We know this from soldiers coming home from a tough mission. If the demand was very high, there's usually an opposite feeling of listlessness and agitation when it's over. I think it's very interesting and useful to use the theory of the flow channel to describe this. When you have the right mix between skills and demands, you're totally in the flow. Because the demands are so high in the X-Alps, and there are all the external factors like very little sleep, exciting flying, speed, risk, a lot of caffeine, physical effort, very high goals; for 250 hours you're in flow. Then you suddenly fall out of this flow channel. You feel useless because there's no goal anymore. Flow also makes you lucky. It can be like a drug.

The question is how do you handle life when you're not in flow? Everyone tries to get in flow but it's not possible to stay there. You're mindful and present because the circumstances in the X-Alps are extreme. It's somehow the opposite of meditation, but it has the same feeling. You're totally present in the moment because the circumstances require it.

I used to do a lot of Base jumping. When you're in the air you're very present. You see everything crystal clear. It's incredibly easy to get into flow doing something like this because of the external factors. The goal is to switch to this state of mind by having nothing. If you can get into that kind of focus or state of presence without flying in strong thermals but by just sitting there and focusing on your breath for example, you can easily switch. But we all know that switching from one state to another, this transformation, is the challenge.

Do you think one of the reasons that some people are so attracted to adventure sports is that we're no longer being hunted, or in danger like our ancestors?
I don't think so. I think these theories sound good, but they're not useful in explaining why some people pursue more risk than others. The same person with the same brain can show different behavior. I think we have this tendency in us, but it's more about what makes you happy in life. The challenge is if you want to be good at something, you have to spend all your time doing it. For example rock climbing. If you're a good rock climber, all your friends are rock climbers. Your partner is a rock climber. You live most of your life at Camp Four or somewhere like that. And then if you get injured or the weather is bad, then suddenly life is very empty. I think the challenge is to be good at something but also have something else in life which is fulfilling. We need several sources of happiness outside of our sport. But the challenge is, if you let yourself lose focus on your sport, maybe you don't perform as well!

Is there a risk for pilots who don't achieve satisfaction and joy outside of flow state?
That's a very good question. I think you can only have a good career if it's fun and gives you a lot of flow, because otherwise you can't spend so much time training and preparing. It has to be somehow intrinsically motivating. In psychology there's a formula for satisfaction, and it's very simple. Satisfaction is the reality of your achievements divided by your expectations. Why is this important? You can always increase reality. When you run fast, you can try to run faster, or when you fly a long flight, you can try to add kilometers or fly a route faster. But you can also simply reduce your expectation levels and be happier.

When we talk now about you and the coronavirus, the positive side of coronavirus is it reduces all our expectations. A lot of people will lose their jobs or lose a lot of money, but at the same time they reduce their expectations way more. In the end they have more satisfaction. I often ask athletes: "What's your satisfaction in a percentage?" And they tell me 85%, or 70%, or whatever.

Then it's a simple question: "Do you want to increase reality, which will be an endless game in your life, because there's always someone who is better? Or do you want to think about your expectations?"

This is why rich people are no more satisfied than poorer people, because satisfaction is only relative. Satisfaction is one thing divided by something else. If you have three million dollars but you expect four million, you're not happy. But if you're very poor in Africa and you have one kilo of rice, you're very happy. I hope our world will have time to think about this relationship, and have time to think about what is reality and what are our expectations and how we can find a better balance.

Let me ask you what may seem like a ridiculous question, but this is something that I constantly struggle with when it comes to flying. Flying gives me so much joy. And yet it's so selfish. In a sense it lacks purpose.
To me, this is three questions. One is what do you allow yourself: have you earned the right to play? This is one question you have to ask yourself. The second is, what kind of responsibility do you have? It's probably different for someone who has kids versus someone who doesn't, for example. Is your purpose in life to play, or is your purpose in life to produce something?

Being selfish here in Switzerland is seen as something negative. But I don't see it that way. When you sit in an airplane and there is a problem with the pressure, you have to put your mask on yourself first. Because if you don't have oxygen, you can't help anyone on your left or right. I think as long as everyone is happy on this planet and taking on the oxygen mask first, as long there are enough oxygen masks, then this is a very positive way of being selfish.

The point is: if you do something for your joy at the cost of others, then for sure it is negative. But if you go to Alaska to fulfil a dream and no one is paying the cost for you to be there, go for it! It will make the world a better place.

Thomas, back to Chrigel. Is it hard for him to stay motivated after winning six X-Alps?
You don't get happy by chasing numbers. It has to be something else. This is a good question for him to answer: "What's your purpose in this game?" I think it would be nice to be in a situation where he has to bounce back. To be a true master you get defeated and then win again. A good sportsman is not someone who is always winning. A good sportsman can handle a difficult situation, or coming second, with style. What Chrigel shows for me is not that he has a good ranking. He shows me that he has a good mindset and great performance.

How do you approach weaknesses?
Everyone has weaknesses. The question is what you do with your strengths. If you try to spend all your energy to reduce your weaknesses, then you get to average. I think you have to accept your weaknesses, learn to handle them and really focus on your strengths. If you have some strengths which are really strong, then you will be outstanding. If you look at exceptional people in the world in music or in art or in sports, no one asks them if they can spell well or if they can speak a certain number of languages or how they handle their weaknesses.

My philosophy focuses on people's strengths. We try to make them stronger. What is more interesting than weakness is anger. Anger is a place with huge potential, because if someone understands what makes them angry, then you have a shortcut to their needs. If someone understands their needs, then they can really flourish by achieving them. Often we are only angry about things which frustrate our needs. Some people think they're better off if they don't show their anger, but I always ask: "What makes you proud and what makes you angry?" If someone knows these two points, they can understand their values.

Someone who's a beginner is just doing something. Let's look at a new paragliding pilot. He's just going paragliding. But someone who's an expert adds preparation. He prepares for the flight, he spends the evening looking at the weather forecast and making a plan for the day, then he executes the flight, and after the flight he evaluates what can be improved. In every discipline, whether in business or sport or in life, someone who's an expert approaches things in a professional way. He prepares, he executes, and he takes time to reflect.

If you want to understand if someone is really an expert in something, you look at what they do after the event. If you look at good artists after a show, they drink a beer or a coffee and look at what was good. If you look at a good doctor, they make notes after the appointment. If you look at very good sailors, they clean the boat and create checklists of what needs to be changed and improved. When you win or get a prize in whatever you are doing, this is not the end of the project. The end of a project is maybe when every one of your sponsors has a hand-signed letter and a good presentation from the race.

How shall we leave this: do you have any last tips to share?
One piece of advice I could give is to look at the really big picture. Take one time in your career or in your hobby or your passion and have a look at the big picture. It can be the 1st of January or it can be the day after your 40th or 50th birthday. Just pick a time. If you have grandkids and if you're old and happy and you and your kids have kids, what would you like to tell them?

What you've done, what you haven't done, what have been the guiding stars or values in your life? If you think of the very big picture and ask yourself what you want to tell your grandkids it will make the questions you have today very simple. When you're old and telling your grandkids about your life, it's absolutely not important what you answered in this email you have in front of you or if you call someone back or not. Thinking about the very big picture can help you find out what your values are. Sailing at night with just the compass and the GPS, your steering can be very nervous because you're too focused on what's right in front of you. But if it's a clear night and you can see the stars and you steer by a point of light very, very far away, the steering is smooth, even if the seas are rough. I really recommend everyone takes some time to write down the big picture.

The other piece of advice I can offer is: often people in sports or in business, when it comes to performance, they think goals should be SMART (specific, measurable, achievable, realistic and time-limited). But there's something important missing from that, and that's the fun. Often goals are about discipline, about working hard, about trying more, about being tough. But to do well in the X-Alps, it has to be fun. For example, Paul Guschlbauer once had this quote on his vario, which read: "How much fun is it right now?" If you can do it with a smile, you'll do it better.

"Everyone knows goals have to be 'SMART'. But to do well, they have to be fun, too."
Photo: Tim Rochas / Niviuk

Pilots wait on launch in Verbier, Switzerland while others are enjoying the early thermals.
Photo: Martin Scheel / azoom.ch

HOW TO AVOID GROUND SUCK

"How do I avoid ground suck?" is one of the commonest questions from listeners of the podcast that I host, the Cloudbase Mayhem. Ground suck comes in two main forms. On a busy launch there's always that guy who sees problems everywhere. "It might get too windy!" "There's a chance of overdevelopment!" "Man, I don't like the look of this sky!" "Remember that one accident?" Beginner and intermediate pilots are invariably uber-excited to fly. That excitement is often multiplied by a lack of free time for flying, which puts pressure on them at launch. But this excitement and desire can exceed their ability. Thankfully, most people at this level in their flying career know that overconfidence can lead to problems. So they turn into bobble-heads on launch, trying to soak in every piece of information, and often get overwhelmed, eventually finding a million reasons not to launch, sometimes on perfectly good days.

Ground suck also happens once we're in the air. A common scenario goes like this: a cloud is developing on your planned course. You get on the radio to ask your friend what he or she thinks, and through a series of back-and-forth comms you talk one another out of the air. "I'm a little worried about that cloud!" "So am I!" "Let's get on the ground!" "Ok!" Nearly all of my biggest flights happened when I was totally alone, many of them on days that were not textbook good days. If I'd been flying with other people, I know for sure I would have flown more conservatively and landed early.

WARNING! This kind of ground suck should not be discounted as unreasonable. "Live to fly another day" is about the best advice I've ever received. In other words, some ground suck can be a very good thing. The trick is identifying when the ground suck is reasonable and should be acknowledged rather than disregarded.

If "that guy" is someone you know to be an excellent, safe pilot who makes great decisions and has a lot more skill than you do, that's not ground suck. That's being smart. But if you're in the van on the way up to launch and someone is going on and on about some terrible accident – steer clear. I have headphones handy for such scenarios every time I fly.

Fear is a very good thing. It keeps us alive. But there's a fine line between a healthy amount of fear and too much, and if you launch at busy sites, there are always going to be some people around who maybe should have stayed home that day. They want their fear to be justified; they want people on their team. They can very quickly sap your reserve of courage. The pilots who are hungry AND capable are confident on launch. These folks should be your mentors. They're easy to identify. They have their gear out first; they move swiftly and aren't bumbling around. They haven't forgotten anything, and their smiles read "this is going to be a good day!" They pull their wings up with authority, and never blow launches. They're the folks who are being watched on satellite tracking long after everyone else has landed.

One of my guests on the show, Mads Syndergaard, has been a frequent contributor to Cross Country magazine, and even wrote a book about racing paragliders called Flying Rags for Glory, which I highly recommend. He talks about 'priming' your mind for success. At its core, priming means simply putting good things in instead of bad. That doesn't mean being stupidly optimistic and avoiding the danger signs. The best way to prime your head for success is to develop solid skills, so you become one of those pilots on launch who are clearly totally in control. They're relaxed, they're having fun, and they're ready to SEND.

A recurring theme that I hear from the best pilots in the world is that to excel and learn, you've got to surround yourself with the kind of pilot you want to become. Now if you want to become an X-Alps pilot and you ruck up with me somewhere in the Swiss Alps on a super-marginal day when it's blowing cross on launch, and overdevelopment is inevitable, just because I ping off doesn't mean you should! We've got a devil on one shoulder and an angel on the other. Learning who to listen to is one of the many, many skills that human flight requires. Train, train, and train some more, and you'll find that ground suck becomes a thing of the past.

Gavin McClurg

Red Bull

The Positive Power of Negative Thinking

WILL GADD

Will Gadd doesn't believe in positive thinking. Quite the opposite: he thinks it can be lethal.

"What could go wrong here?" is a question that's kept Will safe through decades at the frontiers of flying. Will was the first to break the 400km barrier, pioneering the 'Texas dry line' convergence route and setting a world record in 2002. Soon after, he notched up wins in the US and Canadian nationals. Will's mountaineering achievements – particularly his ice climbing firsts – have made him a North American household name.

When I first knocked on Will's front door in Canmore, Alberta, I felt like I was about to meet a celebrity. I put my hand out to shake his, but Will pulled me into a big bear hug. We were meeting a day before we embarked on one of the boldest adventures either of us had ever attempted: a 700km vol-biv route across the Canadian Rockies to the US border, completed 100% in the air. The route includes huge sections of unlandable terrain, where there are more grizzly bears than people.

Several years on, Will remains one of my biggest heroes. Before I met him, for years I'd followed his climbing, kayaking and flying career, and read his gifted writing. I was about to embark on a big-budget, high-risk, highly unpredictable, rather ridiculous expedition with someone I barely knew whom I had to completely rely on. And vice versa. The expedition took eighteen days, a lot of it spent locked down in our tents waiting for the weather. That's a lot of time to get to know someone and witness how a true expert operates in the mountains. Spending time with Will is a delight. He's humble, inspiring and always instructive. No other person has had a more positive impact on my flying and changed the way I manage risk. Here's why.

Will, how did you get into flying?

I was a sports reporter in Colorado. I went to cover the 1995 US paragliding nationals in Aspen, and I was blown away. I already did all the other mountain sports – skiing, kayaking, mountain running – and a lot of my friends had gotten into paragliding, so I went for a tandem with John Yates. It's all been downhill from there – or uphill, depending on how you look at it!

"In society right now there's this heavy emphasis on the positive power of positive thinking. I think that's bullshit. It's just going to get you killed."

On our traverse of the Rockies, you had me pegged pretty quickly as a 'pathological optimist', which is a way of operating that drives you nuts. Why is that – what is it about 'the positive power of negative thinking' that so appeals to you?
Everybody involved in mountain sports is kind of an optimist to begin with. You think: "I'm going to fly off this mountain and it's all going to work out!" Now that's pretty optimistic to begin with.

I do a lot of ice climbing. It's the same. People who climb frozen waterfalls and think everything's going to be great are inherently optimistic. It's an act of optimism, no matter how you look at it, just to do something like that.

But right now in our society, there's this heavy emphasis on the positive power of positive thinking. Just believe in yourself, dream it and do it. And I think it's all bullshit. When it comes to adventure sports, it's just gonna get you killed.

In my view, a useful tool for surviving these sports, or anything risky in life – starting a new business or whatever – is to try to figure out what can go wrong and why. You need to use your imagination to break it down into chunks and then solve the mini dilemmas. Then when you go out and do something in life, you've got justified confidence, not just a sort of 'I've got this' belief that you can do anything.

YouTube has a lot of videos of people who really thought they could do it, and you don't want to be that guy! You want to be the guy who's going to do something that is cool and out there. But first you're going to break every little chunk down, and use the best tools you have at your disposal to figure out, in sometimes gruesome detail, everything that can go wrong and why, and work through it.

What that allows me to do is eliminate my major fears. When I'm standing on launch and the wind's a bit cross-on and gusty, I still do that same thing. Even after 20 years of flying, I break it down. I think, what are the issues here? Can I deal with them or not? And then if I'm still afraid, I pack up and go home. I run away a lot. I'm into the positive power of negative thinking, and it's served me really well for a long time.

You had an incident in the inaugural 2003 X-Alps that I'd love for you to recount. You had to greatly reduce your desired level of margin on a particularly wild day, and it altered how you approach competitions.
Well, I had a few incidents in the X-Alps, as probably everyone does in that race! First, I launched on a really windy day in the lee of Mont Blanc, but that was okay, it was manageable. I got destroyed a few times, but I climbed out and got high. But as the day

advanced, I got blown by the wind that was coming over Mont Blanc and down into the Aosta Valley, and that really isn't a place you want to be. It's full of power lines and dams and towns, and it's mayhem in there for a paraglider.

I was flying along downwind at about 45km/h and thinking everything was ok, but then I looked down a few hundred meters and all the trees were totally bent over. At that time I didn't have much experience with really strong valley winds, because we don't get them in the Rockies and most other places I fly. I knew there'd be valley wind, but I totally underestimated it. I started getting blown backwards up the valley at an incredible speed, dodging power lines and taking massive collapses. It was a horrifying few minutes. I didn't feel I'd been pushing it hard that day, but then suddenly I'm in a situation that was way out of control. I could have easily been killed. Eventually I managed to sort of crash beside a sewage plant. To be honest, crashing into the sewage pond would have been a better option. But I landed, or crashed, really, on grass and rolled down the hillside. The guy who ran the sewage plant watched me on my way down. He wasn't a pilot, but it was obviously a pretty traumatic situation with the wing balling up left, right and center. Sure, there was some skill happening to keep the wing open enough to control the collapses and get to the ground, but there was a lot of luck too. The guy gave me a beer, and I sat on the grass and realized that not only did I have some things to learn about flying in the Alps, but also competing in that style of competition was leading me to make bad decisions. So that was my last X-Alps!

You chased distance records and competitions for a long time. You set a world record, and your North American distance record in Texas held for over 10 years, and several of your state records set nearly two decades ago still stand. Tell me about that period in your life.

For me, doing interesting things is about as good as it gets. If I'm fired up and interested in something, that's where I operate the best. Whether it's paragliding or ice climbing or kayaking, I'm a happier person in those environments doing something cool. With records and paragliding, I was just really curious to see how far can we fly? I didn't really care too much about setting records – I wanted to see how far we could go. It began in the '90s, just seeing if we could get over the next mountain range. Our gear was primitive by today's standards, but the principle is the same: get up high, go on glide, how far can you get? A lot of the things I did were firsts, but I didn't think about being the first, I just thought it was cool to chase it and see what happened! I wanted to learn and learn and learn.

Were there any "Aha!" moments along the way, things that really gelled in that period?

I was obsessed with flying. I'd had a pretty successful career as a climber, but I wanted something different in paragliding. The first time I flew, I basically quit competition climbing the same day. I immediately got stoked and flew every day that I could. That's what I wanted to do. If I couldn't fly, I'd go ground handle in ridiculous conditions, and I learned something every single day.

I progressed not because I'm any good as a pilot, but because I'm quite good at going at it as hard as I can. I flew every day in the winter, even though there wasn't a thermal to be seen. If there was any hope of turning a circle, I was out on the hill, and there was

Will Gadd in action ice climbing near the summit at 19,000 feet on the glacier ice on Mount Kilimanjaro in Tanzania, Africa. Photo: Christian Pondella/Red Bull Content Pool

a bunch of pilots back then that had the same mentality. We weren't competitive, we were very supportive of one other. We knew it was risky and we watched out for each other, but it was hardcore about who was in the air at the end of the day! We fought hard for that. We were motivated to max it out.

There was never a discussion about whether or not to go cross country. Somebody was going. It wasn't a competition per se, but we were all trying to do the coolest thing you could with the day, and stay in the air longer and fly farther than anyone else. That really structured my attitude toward paragliding. You do the most with what you've got. I don't think I've gotten any good at these things because I was talented at them, but I obsessed about them and restructured my life radically so I could go fly at nearly every opportunity.

How do you keep such a high stoke for the sport after all these years?
Paragliding is a complicated sport. Just when you think you've got it figured out, you learn something new. I flew in wave the other day and wound up at a ridiculous altitude above the Rockies. And I'm thinking: how does that happen after 20-something years of flying on a day when I didn't think there were any significant winds aloft? I'm flying in my local valley, a place I know intimately and have flown a million times, and I'm on the moon! I realize I'm a hazard up there!

It's intensely interesting on a small scale. Why are the thermals here today? How does it work? Why is it working like that when it wasn't yesterday? And on a big scale, why am I getting beamed out today? It's endlessly complicated and interesting. That's the real reward of paragliding: solving these intensely complicated questions and understanding them. There are things you didn't know you didn't know that make it engaging in a way that very few other sports are. So yeah, I'm fired up!

You've maybe just answered my next question: why is it worth the risk?
Everybody who flies should be able to answer that question. And the answer shouldn't be: "I can do it safely." Everybody makes mistakes, and in paragliding those errors are maybe going to put you in the hospital or kill you. Everybody's answer is going to be different. It's not like one size fits all. For me answering the question helps me make better decisions. Not only in paragliding, but in ice climbing or mountaineering or guiding or whatever I'm doing.

The answer to that question was different for me when I was younger. When I was younger, it was simply: "This is the coolest thing ever and I'm going to go do it!" And I was broadly okay with dying doing it. That's how it works when you're young.

I think that's not a bad state to be in, actually. If you're a person like I was, you're either going to pursue a life of crime or do really cool things. I wasn't the kind of person who was going to make it in an office environment. I'm not trying to denigrate people who do that, but I need more positive things to do with my life. Paragliding and climbing are beautiful and wonderful, but my approach has changed. I'm not willing to take on the same level of risk these days. I do recognize that all of these sports can and may ultimately kill me. And I'm still okay with that. But I've definitely backed down. I want to be back at the dinner table tonight, and that's helped me work with the risk.

These sports are magic, but they also have a very dark side, and you have to recognize that and realize that accidents can and will happen to me and my friends. In total it's worth it, but no single day is worth getting destroyed for. I walk down a lot from my local site. If something is wrong, or I just can't figure it out and nothing makes sense, I don't become the human probe and huck myself out there.

You've just had an amazing year. You pulled off Helmken Falls, one of the hardest mixed routes ever done; we did The Rockies Traverse; you climbed some of the last ice on Kilimanjaro; and you climbed the spray ice on Niagara Falls. These were all projects that took years to plan and were massive undertakings from a media perspective as well as a training perspective. Talk to me about contentment, as I imagine living those kinds of highs also has corresponding lows?
I think you need different things at different points in your life. That was an amazing year from a sheer accomplishment perspective, and I'm probably unlikely to have one like it again. You just can't live at that level over and over again, and trying to live there probably isn't very healthy. I've had some other years where I tried really hard and nothing worked. I've had years where you just get beat down.

I think it's important to have cool things to look forward to, but know that some of them aren't going to work out like you want. You have to be where you are and get up and keep going forward. Nothing's guaranteed in life. I have zero financial backing from family or anything like that. I've spent a lot of my life washing dishes and pounding nails, and every time I get to do one of these trips, I think to myself: man, I won! I think it's good to have a future goal, but it's also good to be where you are and relish what you have right now. In fifty years, or really in two weeks, nobody is going to give a shit what we've done. Everything we're doing is transitory. My philosophy is: if you're not stoked with where you are, then change it.

"My philosophy is: if you're not stoked with where you are, then change it."

You've lived a very public life. What are the benefits and pitfalls of sponsorship and being such a public persona?

Well, first of all I've hung out with people who actually are famous. Those people can't walk anywhere. They can't do anything in public. That's a crazy life. I'm in no danger of getting stopped on the street – by comparison I'm a nobody! But as far as sponsorship goes, the key distinction that's helped me to understand where I'm at and keep things both ethical and rewarding is that I get sponsorship to do things. I don't do things to get sponsorship. For example, I really wanted to climb the last ice on Kilimanjaro, and Red Bull said no at least six times to that project. In the end I cobbled together plane tickets from one company and got a bit of help from another, and finally the trip came together. It turned out to be super successful when you look at it from what the sponsors want: marketing and awareness and content. But I really wanted to do that trip. If I had an unlimited bank account, I wouldn't need sponsorship, I'd just go do these things. But I don't; I've got to make it work economically. I need sponsorship to do things, and they need things from me to make it work for them. But if you're thinking of doing something cool to get more sponsorship, then it hasn't worked. The moments in my life where I've found myself in that situation and let it get away from me, I've pretty quickly realized I'm bullshitting myself and I'm not taking the right approach.

Do you have a favorite flight, one that really stood out?

I don't think there's any one flight; it's just the experience of flying for all these years and getting to see the world from that perspective. That's what I love as much as anything: flying a paraglider and seeing the rivers I paddle and the mountains I climb all laid out below in a pretty slow-speed event. I fly over these mountains in jets all the time, and it just zaps by. I never really understood the scope of the US until I flew across it on a paramotor. We took something like 30 days to fly across the US, and I've got an idea of what it looks like all the way from Ventura, California, to Kitty Hawk, North Carolina.

What's the most common thing you've seen in all your years of flying and being in the mountains that leads to most accidents?

A desire to see things differently than how they are. There's a Buddhist idea of trying to see things as they are, instead of what you want to happen or think should happen or you've been told is going to happen. We all get to the hill with preconceptions. It's Saturday, I'm off work, the forecast is good, and I'm psyched to be heading up the hill. But at the top it's a bit snarky and messy, but you still think it's going to be great. The forecast is good and this is the only day you've got to fly.

What I see with accidents is people wanting the world to adapt to them rather than adapting to the world and seeing it for what it is. We also have to be honest and realistic with our own skills. I'm not Chrigel Maurer. I can't do what he does. I have to leave a margin. I try to always leave a little more room than I think I absolutely need, because I'm likely to screw it up a little. Everybody who flies or participates in any of these sports is going to screw it up. You have to have enough margin that you can recover from wherever you are.

Then very rarely you might feel this is important enough that you're going to gamble. And if you've made that decision and screw it up, then I've got no sympathy for me or anybody else that stacks it in. It's not a tragedy. You've made the gamble, and you need to know when you're making that gamble.

We've both done a ton of paddling. I've noticed paddlers seem to pick up flying really fast. Any theories on that?

The way you fly a paraglider is pretty much identical to how you paddle a kayak. Neither sport has a stop button: you can't just stop playing like you can in most sports. They're both really committing. In a kayak, you're often dealing with things you can't directly see. You have to feel and understand the dynamics of invisible forces and have a theory about how they work. You can't see what's going on with the water or the air. If a paddler says: "I want to get into paragliding," I always think it'll probably work out pretty well. But if a climber wants to get into paragliding, that may be an uphill road. Kayaking is a very 'flow' sport. Same as Alpine ski racing. If a skier wants to get into flying, it will probably go pretty well, that makes sense. But if you're a triathlete, maybe not so much. Our brains are wired different ways depending on what we do for sports.

Will Gadd takes a break after top landing during the Rockies Traverse with Gavin McClurg.
Photo: Pablo Durana.

THREE TOOLS TO SURVIVE PARAGLIDING AND HIGH-RISK SPORTS

Know that the consequences of flying are always inherently very high. I've done CPR on days with perfect easy mellow conditions. Flying is always high consequence, and if you know this then you may respect it more and fly like you want to live.

Expect error: We all make errors. If you're squeaking the last meter out of a long glide going over a ridge in the lee just above rocks, you haven't left any margin. Most of the time flying close to the edge doesn't benefit you very much, so you might as well leave 100m over the trees, so you can take a deflation and either recover or throw the reserve. Over and over again I've been glad I left a little more altitude above the ground than I thought I really needed. When you screw up a circle or take a big hit, it sure is great not to hit the ground, plus you get to keep flying.

Good conditions are good. Not sort of good, maybe good, but clearly good. Push on these days. Don't push on marginal days. If it's windy and you can't get high, then that's not the day. Do what you can, but save the big pushes for when conditions are solid.

This isn't a survival tool, but always max what you can so you learn the most. Get the most out of every single day, even if that means just seeing if you can come into the LZ and hit the landing spot perfectly, ten times in a row. Or glide to the next field. Stay up 30 minutes longer…

WILL'S PRE-FLIGHT CHECK LIST

- Does it make sense to fly?
- Given what I see, what would be cool to do? Do I have the maps, coms, bivvy gear that I might need?
- Talk over the day with any interested pilots. Even if I'm just going ridge soaring, what's the coolest thing I could do?
- Be ready early, before anyone else if possible, so I can launch when I want to
- Where are my shoes? I won the US Paragliding Nationals but had to borrow some shoes on the last day
- Food and water? I always fly XC with enough food and water for 24 hours
- Reserve system ok? I've had reserves fall out a few times
- Sunscreen
- Pack up harness with all gear. Water hose: make sure it's closed up. I forget that a lot
- Organize instrument deck, batteries, cameras, etc
- Line-check glider. For real. I've had days ruined by one stupid knot
- Watch the sky. Still make sense to fly?
- Check all connection points. I've launched without leg straps
- Unzip and unhook waist belt on pants so I can pee easily in the air. Been doing this for 25 years, works
- Does it still make sense to fly?
- Check straps, etc. I always turn the same way. I roll my kayak mostly that way too
- Launch, usually first, if I think it's ok to stay up
- Have a ripping fucking flight!

Photo: Luc Hentsch / Niviuk

USING THREAT AND ERROR MANAGEMENT

Pilot error is the cause of nearly all accidents. Things in our environment can trip us up – but they aren't often easily identifiable. Threat and Error Management (TEM) is a safety concept used in the airline industry. Its premise is that a chain of threats can lead to pilot errors. If we get better at identifying them, we'll have fewer accidents. This interview with commercial airline pilot Jonathan Smith is both training for the mind, and training to stay alive.

Let's start with the basics. What is 'Threat and Error Management', and why does it matter?

In 1994, psychologists at the University of Texas were focusing on human factors and safety in aviation, using detailed accident statistics. They understood that pilot error causes most accidents, but they knew it had to be something more than just pilot error – because pilots don't intentionally make mistakes. They concluded that things in our flying environment can trip us up and lead us down the road to errors. They called those things threats, but not threats like a mugger in the park. Threats to flight safety can be anything from weather, to new equipment, to dehydration or hypoxia. They're everywhere. Sometimes we expect them, sometimes we don't. They found that threats that we're not aware of tend to have their way with us, but threats that we're expecting, we can mitigate. Those can be managed effectively and prevent an error from occurring. It's not a chain of errors that causes an accident, but a chain of threats that leads to errors. You're much better off managing the threat and not having an error.

So that's where the TEM cone symbol comes from. Describe that graphic, where we go from threats to errors to an 'Undesired Aircraft State' (UAS)?

The cone can be divided into three sections. The top section is the biggest one. That's the threat or threats – there's often more than one. In the middle are the errors. The one at the bottom, the one that happens the least but is the most consequential, is the undesired aircraft state. You're always trying to keep things at the top. If you can manage the threats first, everything works great. If you miss something and you mismanage a threat, then it

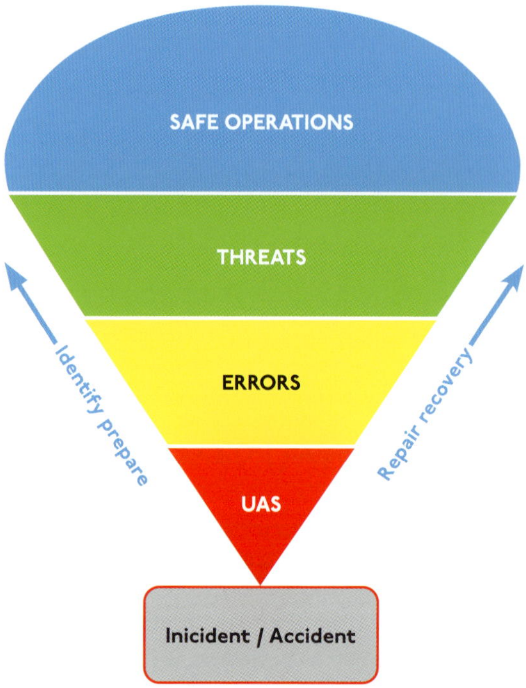

As pilots, we're always aiming to keep things in the top of this cone. TEM helps us review incidents and work forwards and backwards through these stages to identify where improvements in processes and operations are needed to make flying safer

may work down to an error. When that happens, you need to recognize it and repair it. If you do then you go back to managing threats and everything is fine. But if you don't then it could progress down to an undesired aircraft state.

In our case that could be a stall or an asymmetric collapse, or a simple vector into terrain. You need to correct that. If you don't, you could have an accident. The cool thing about TEM is that it's an effective tool for forensics. If you're confused about how and why an accident happened, you look at the accident and work backwards. Unfortunately, in our sport we often stop at the error. The error is sometimes obvious. "He stalled his wing 20ft off the ground," for example. We conclude that we shouldn't do that. But that's only the error that caused the undesired aircraft state. We need to go back farther in time and find the threat that led to the error. If we focus on the threats when we fly and learn to manage them effectively, we reduce errors tremendously.

A few years back one of my mentors, Matt Beechinor, had an incident that sounds like it fits TEM perfectly. This was before paragliders were using oxygen regularly, and for some reason Matt got hypoxic at a much lower altitude than he'd experienced in the past. Something physiologically was different with him that day. His awareness was triggered when he called his flying partner on the radio, and the partner responded that he sounded like a four-year-old, that he wasn't making any sense. But he felt fine. Then

he started to lose all the feeling in his arms. He immediately went into a spiral dive and landed without incident because he recognized the threat and took action before it became an error. That's classic TEM, correct?

That's exactly how it works. Where Matt could possibly improve would be to do more hypoxia training so he could mitigate the threat before it became debilitating. I was in the Air Force for 25 years and every five years we had to go into a hypobaric chamber, which is the opposite of a hyperbaric chamber where they add pressure to divers who have ascended too fast. A hypobaric chamber sucks the air out to simulate high altitudes. Everyone experiences hypoxia in different ways. Some people's minds wander, others get kind of punch-drunk, others get drowsy. The training helps you recognize the symptoms and increases your threat awareness. A definitive way to reduce threats is to fly with other people. Matt got an early tip that he was in trouble because his flying partner told him he didn't sound right.

The important thing to remember with threats is that they can pile onto one another. Performance can decrease because of things like dehydration, fatigue, hypoxia, distraction and hunger. You might be fine on one day when you're a bit dehydrated, but add some fatigue from a bad sleep and suddenly your threats spike.

How do they teach commercial pilots to identify threats?

A lot of the checklists and procedures and call-outs that we have in the airlines are built-in threat mitigation. You have to have defensive measures in place to prevent threats from causing problems. So a lot of threat mitigation is built into our procedures. It's inevitable that commercial pilots have a much greater likelihood of making an error than free-flight pilots, because there are so many more things to do. Thankfully most mistakes are inconsequential, but they're still mistakes. In free flight, we don't have nearly as many procedures. We don't usually have much airspace to deal with. What checklists we have are the ones that we make up ourselves. So there aren't as many errors to make, but when a paraglider does make an error, it's usually not inconsequential. Usually it has to be dealt with and corrected. There's no such thing as a perfect flight.

Would you say commercial pilots are equipped better than free-flight pilots to recognize threats?

Yes. The airlines make threat and error management part of the culture. Every airline pilot is well versed on what a threat is and what to do with one when it surfaces. They're aware that they lead to errors, and they understand how that process works. The best way to stop an accident is to disrupt that process. I think in those terms we're better equipped than free-flight pilots. But that's something we can change. If free-flight pilots understand how the process works, they're going to have better tools to prevent the chain from threats to an undesired aircraft state.

What are the tools?

Number one is to take care of the threats. If you do that, the threats won't lead to errors. There are four things that you can do to mitigate a threat. We call them the threat mitigation toolkit.

> **Good judgement is the result of experience, and experience is the result of bad judgement.**
> **Mark Twain**

First, avoid it. If you can, just don't let it get in your way. For example, turbulence or rotor. Avoid it. If it's a bad day to fly, don't fly. Sometimes it's hard to do that, because it looks like it might be okay and then you commit to flying and now you're in the air. Our next mitigation tool is passive safety. In this category are things like protective clothing, a good helmet, a harness with excellent protection and the level of the glider you fly. Then we have defensive safety, which is action you take immediately prior to a threat that gives you more margin. For example, a strong torpedo launch and a torpedo landing so you're in an athletic stance when the ground is close and our only defense is a good PLF if we have a collapse. Or having some weight shift away from the hill when you're ridge soaring just in case you take a hit, so you don't spin into the terrain. The fourth tool is active and reactive safety. In turbulence, when you take a collapse you have to react to it. If you put a lot of weight on active and reactive safety, you don't want too many threats that reduce your ability to perform. Let's use you as an example. Let's say it's the sixth day of the X-Alps and you've had some hard days without much sleep. You've got to fly on a ratty day in a lot of lee, where you're going to be relying a lot on your reactions to keep the wing open. The number of threats you'll be mitigating is incredibly high, which will impact your ability to perform.

What we don't want to do is encounter threats with surprise and confusion. Threat mitigation goes a lot better if we are aware and we have a plan.

You use the analogies of Sun Tzu's The Art of War and also chess to describe decision-making in free flight. Kelly Farina talks about it in his book Mastering Paragliding from the offensive standpoint. You talk about it from the defensive.
People talk about cross-country paragliding like chess because you have to think two, three, four moves ahead, and moving forward typically entails being on the offense. If you're going to get from point A to point B you have to piece all the little moves together. But good chess players have to play solid defense or they get in checkmate, and so do we. In Kelly's book there's a diagram of progression that looks like a pyramid. The base is the foundation where you have to build skills before you can move up. That's offense: training, progression, learning, leaving your comfort zone and striking out.

But if you flip it upside down it becomes defense – the symbol that we use for threat and error management. Above the pyramid is safe flight. The top third of the pyramid is the threats that you have to mitigate. The middle is the error. If you can't manage the error, you get an undesired aircraft state. If you can't correct that, you have an accident or an incident. It's the whole thing upside down. They say the best defense is a good offense. That's true if I'm playing you and you're playing me in the same game, but that's not the chess we're talking about. The chess we play is against, or preferably with, mother nature. We're not up against an equal opponent.

A parallel I see with flying is backcountry skiing. A lot of the risk that we encounter in the backcountry is hidden. We might have a buried persistent slab avalanche problem, and at the end of the day we get back to our car and we feel we've mitigated the risk really well, when in fact we might have just gotten lucky. We didn't get caught in an avalanche, so we're positively reinforced for making a bad decision. In other words, the mistake we made might not even be known, or it might be a really inexpensive mistake. I think this kind of thing happens to us all the time in free flight. We don't even recognize the threat. Or we do, but we deal with it by getting lucky rather than skill. How do we use TEM more effectively to know how close we are to going over the edge?

One of the big disadvantages we have in paragliding is often the threat is something that you can't see. If we had special glasses that allowed us to see what we're actually flying in, I'm pretty sure most people wouldn't fly. It would be terrifying. We have to anticipate and react to an invisible element. The TEM model doesn't make the invisible visible; it just gives us a framework to better identify and mitigate hazards.

Statistically, most accidents happen launching and landing, and then way down the list is something happening in the air. How can we use TEM to help us in what commercial airline pilots call the critical phase of flight?

In the airlines, when we're below 10,000ft, or in approach mode, which is below 1,000ft, we transition to something called the sterile cockpit. All you can talk about is what's going on with this airplane and things that are pertinent to this flight. The reason is you're fairly close to the ground and you've got a high density of air traffic, so you have to be very alert. We call this the critical phase of flight, where errors can have much higher consequences.

How many accidents have we all seen because a pilot is distracted on launch? They haven't clipped in, they haven't clipped their helmet, they haven't done their leg straps, they haven't checked their reserve handle, etc. Someone died this year in Colombia when he didn't attach his leg straps.

This is where TEM comes in. Consider take-offs and landings as a critical phase of flight. Eliminate as many external threats as possible. Some of the internal threats are insidious. Especially the ones that affect you more toward the end of the flight because you're tired or you're dehydrated. You probably didn't start out that way, but at the end of the flight those things become more prevalent. It's really hard to recognize those, because they're internal and they come up gradually.

When we come in to land, we should have a sterile cockpit approach. Ask yourself: "How am I right now? What's my state? What am I dealing with as far as threats go?" Assess both the external and internal threats. Are there dust devils? Are other pilots having any trouble? Is the wind gusty? I always advocate people fly with radios because they allow you to receive input on threats. Flying with others and flying with a radio are two great ways to increase your threat awareness.

Let's use your example of a pilot not clipping in and having an accident. If we use the TEM framework and start with the accident and work backwards, we easily see the error: the pilot didn't clip in. But stopping there is a disservice to everyone. If you don't take it to the next level and explain what it was that caused the pilot to make the error, whether it was a distraction or they were in a hurry or they were unfamiliar with a new harness or one of many possible threats, we don't learn how to avoid the mistake in future.

I threw my reserve over the desert when doing acro training, and it wasn't attached. The night before I switched all my gear, I was super-tired, I was sick, my back was killing me, I was working in bad light, I didn't want to wake up my girlfriend. There was a litany of threats there that added up, and I got really lucky to walk away.

Here's the thing about the airlines. If there's an accident or an incident, it gets looked at very closely. A panel of experts finds out what mistakes were made, and why they were made, and the threats are identified. Then they turn it around. They'll change the way we do our training or they'll change the checklist or they'll change a procedure. They'll give us built-in threat mitigation through their findings, and the end result is they'll change the way we fly. The chance of that accident happening again is radically reduced.

If the investigation reveals that it was just somebody who made a mistake and they can't identify a threat, it's just that a pilot screwed up, they'll send the pilot back to training and get them straightened out. But if they find an error and uncover a threat that caused it that could trip up other pilots, they'll institute some kind of threat mitigation throughout the entire operation. But no one's going to do that for us. We don't have anyone looking at our accidents and doing investigations and uncovering all this information. It's up to us to do that. And we can.

After a few people forgot to clip in, they started teaching the launch checklist that most pilots in the world use. If we don't do the checklist because we forgot it or we were in a hurry, we've made an error. It might be inconsequential, but it's still an error. And it may not matter that day, but one day it might. Now you're thinking like we do in the airlines.

One of my X-Alps supporters, Reavis, has a 'three things rule'. If he forgets three things before he launches, he has to sit down and take stock of where he is mentally. They can be really minor things. Maybe he's forgotten to plug his phone into his external battery, or forgotten to zip up his glove pouch. But at three mistakes he has a rule to stop and take a step back. We all need something that triggers a red flag, something that helps us identify if we aren't quite with it.

He's capturing the threat at the error level. He's using TEM on the fly.

Can you describe the difference between TEM and risk management?

Risk management is when a meet director at a comp decides if it's safe enough to put pilots in the air and have a task. TEM is what pilots use once we're in the air. Sometimes we're tired, but we still decide to fly. That's risk management. The important thing is to realize it and understand that it's going to lower your level of performance, and any other threat may be harder to mitigate. Let's say it's a 15km/h wind day in the mountains and you know it's going to require some leeside flying. Maybe that's okay when you're on your game, but if you're tired maybe that's not the day to do it. Risk management is important. We use it in the airlines and everyone should use it. If you have to manage something, you should be able to define it. If something goes wrong and it doesn't affect anything, there's no risk. If there's a very small chance of something going wrong and there's a massive amount of loss if it does, that's a risk. Risk management is the choice to fly or not that day. In some cases, if you accept a large amount of risk and you decide to fly and you're aware of that risk, then you change the way you fly, and you bring what's necessary, but you have to do that consciously and be perfectly aware of what you're doing. Risk management is the big picture.

Once you commit to flight it's very difficult to manage risk, in my opinion. Risk is a cocktail of threats and errors, and you're much better off keeping your eye on the ball and focusing on individual threats when you're actively flying. We're dealing with a very dynamic environment. And there's a huge spectrum of external and internal threats. If there's something obvious like a massive cumulonimbus cell, it's time to land immediately. But if you're a little bit tired, a little bit dehydrated, there's a little bit of turbulence, you've got a new wing, all these little threats combined equal risk, but it's not obvious risk and therefore much harder to identify. When we're in the air TEM is much more effective at dealing with risk.

Everyone who participates in free flight at some point is most likely going to have a really scary incident. Can TEM help us with overcoming fear and anxiety?
I think fear is a very difficult thing to work with sometimes. If your fear comes from something you don't understand, it can be debilitating. But if you can determine exactly what it is that you're afraid of, you can find methods to mitigate the fear. Understanding fear helps it disappear. Having a plan helps keep irrational fear at bay. TEM is structurally a plan. Fear isn't a bad thing. Fear is good. It's self-preservation. Fear is essentially threat awareness or perceived awareness.

Because of your commercial background and your intimacy with TEM, do you find you're using it naturally?
At first I didn't. We all have crossover experiences that we bring with us when we fly. For example, your kayaking experience has given you the ability to read water, which is similar to how air flows. I'm sure your ability to read water translates into your ability to read air even though you can't see it. You can imagine it. Your time on a boat and sailing around the world probably got you into a number of situations where you had to make safety assessments and deal with threats and not let them get the best of you.

The biggest crossover I've gotten from my job is TEM. I think it's something everybody can use even if you barely understand it. As long as you recognize that threats that aren't managed often lead to errors, and you need to be aware of the threat and you need to have a plan to deal with it, you're already miles ahead of pilots who aren't looking at things that way. It's basically defensive flying. It gives us something to focus on and I think it could have a huge positive impact on our community.

FINAL THOUGHTS

Early on in our flying careers, the wonder of flight is like a new lover that you can't get enough of. But, as in good relationships, as time passes the urgency fades and the love deepens. How do we maintain a healthy relationship with flying? How do we stay balanced? How do we deal with burnout or avoid the trap of more? More distance, more records, more results…

"There's nothing better in life than to be a beginner again. I don't care about being good at something, I care about learning."
Jeff Shapiro

"I think the very first flight I had was the best of my life. But the sport is so much more than flying. Flying is the part of the iceberg that you see. The rest is what you can't see. It's discovering a new country, new cultures, and spending time with the amazing flying community. When you fly in New Zealand, it's not the same as flying in France or Patagonia or South Africa. It's a different sport everywhere, but pilots are welcoming and friendly no matter where you go, and that keeps it interesting."
Tom de Dorlodot

"Everything has an expiration date, even something like flying that gives us so much pleasure. If we squeeze any sport or activity too much, there's no more juice. If that happens, we have to take a different approach. It's confusing: suddenly we don't get the same feeling that the sport once gave us, and there's a huge risk if you keep pushing distance or maneuvers to try to find the same joy. It's better to change our perspective. Maybe rather than competing or trying to operate at the top end, you can instruct new pilots, or get into acro if you're a cross-country pilot or vice versa. Find a new aspect of the sport, and it's like learning all over again. And learning is exciting."
Veso Ovcharov

"I love how small paragliding makes you feel. It's such a great lesson in humility. It's like sailing in the middle of the ocean; it makes you feel totally insignificant.

"It's hard to think of something cooler than spending time with real characters from all over the world all sharing this stupid addiction. As horrible as my accident was for me, and as horrible as it was for my wife and daughters to go through, I was adamant that I wasn't going to give up paragliding. Hearing that was a bit of a shock to my wife, but I wasn't prepared to live a diluted version of my life and future when such an important part of it is paragliding."
Guy Anderson

"For a long time I've been trying to describe the headspace that cross-country paragliding puts me into. I call it "the alien world", because I feel so alien when I land. After a six or eight-hour flight, it takes me a while to come back to earth and want to talk with people again. I want to stay in the alien world for a while, and enjoy the feeling that I can only get from flying. I think it's like meditation, because you've had to stay in such a heightened state of focus for long periods. The longer I fly, the deeper I get into this head space. And I really enjoy it, because I have an extremely busy mind and I can't control my thoughts completely. Flying is one of the few places where I have a calm mindset and I can truly focus on only one thing."
Matt Beechinor

When you're really high in the mountains of Pakistan or the Alps and playing with this thing that looks like a toy, it's amazing. If you respect the mountains, they'll bring you home."
Tom de Dorlodot

"My goal is to stay out of an office. I want to be out in nature. Flying is the portal to nature and if I can make a living from flying, I don't have to be in an office, and that keeps me passionate."
Ondrej Prochazca

"You know, nothing's guaranteed in life. There were a lot of years before all the sponsors came along that I spent washing dishes and pounding nails, so every time I get to do one of these trips, it feels like I've won."
Will Gadd

"I've gone through huge waves in passion over the years. In the early days we had a crazy number of fatal accidents in hang gliding that made me step way, way back. I got really tired of seeing my friends die. I decided to either quit or figure out how to keep it safe. So I decided to go from a high-performance glider to a school glider for a long time. And I've done that kind of thing several times in my career, where I go from pushing at the leading edge of the sport to playing around at the recreational end. I competed passionately for over a decade because it was fun; I do all of this because it's fun. Whenever it hasn't been fun, I back off, because what's the point if it isn't fun?"
Kari Castle

"I used to be a lot more goal-oriented than I am now. I have a calmer passion for the sport these days, and I'm more into the process rather than the results. That allows me to enjoy my surroundings more than when I was so obsessed. I turn down a lot more days that I would have definitely flown when I was so hungry. A lot of those days were pretty ridiculous [strong and dangerous], and because it all worked out, I wouldn't want to change anything. The experience I got from those flights was incredibly valuable and that now benefits all the recreational flying I do, but I'm appreciating it more now because there's less pressure."
Dustin Martin

"It can be dangerous to be in the air when you don't want to be. We all go through periods of less motivation to fly,

and that's ok. I don't worry about times when I'm not as excited to fly. I know it will come back and I don't force it."
Christian Ciech

"I chased distance and cross-county competitions for a long time, but I realized I was often going to the same places and flying with the same people, and often we weren't flying at all but sitting around in the rain. I needed to make a change. For the past twenty years or so my key to staying excited about this sport is to do it all. I instruct, do maneuvers clinics, fly tandems, fly hang gliders and paragliders, build winches, I've gotten really involved in Project Airtime, I fly drones, and I manage our business [Superfly Paragliding]. Each of these things is super rewarding, because it doesn't get redundant and it keeps me engaged and interested. As long as there's change and things are a little different every day, I'm smiling."
Chris Santacroce

"Learn to recognize when you're too tired to keep flying. Often the adrenaline masks tiredness, but when you're tired you have to stop. Competitions can really tire your mind, and when you're tired it's very easy to make costly mistakes."
Annalena Hinestroza

"If it's not good, don't go paragliding. Scary paragliding sucks. Getting scared can be just as damaging as getting hurt. I'm not saying don't push it, but push it when it feels good. Push it when it feels right. The reason we all love it so much is because in everything else we do we can space out and be thinking about other things. But when you're flying, all you're thinking about is flying. Keeping the glider open, finding your next thermal, finding the best glide. Because we know that if we make a bad decision we can get hurt or die. And that's a big part of the fun – the focus and clarity you get."
Nate Scales

"The highs are often the ultimate highs, and the lows for some are truly the ultimate lows. After witnessing a serious accident, I suffered PTSD and had to work through it to regain my joy of flying. I think we all need to be more candid about the impact it can have on us."
Nick Greece

"The advice I wish I'd gotten when I got into this sport is to not change a thing about who you are. Approach the sport exactly like you would any other sport. Don't allow yourself to be talked down to, but don't allow yourself to be pushed, either. Be hyper-aware of being independent, and stand true to your gut instincts. Women tend to be a little more intuitive and more aware of their gut instinct. Listen to it. Women have to be careful about competitions in a way that men typically don't. There are so few women competing that you can make your national team for some countries with very little experience. But you can't shortcut experience, and if you're suddenly flying high-level comps, you need to be aware of the potential pressure and keep flying at your level."
Isabella Messenger

Gavin arriving in Monaco at the end of the Red Bull X-Alps 2015
Photo: Kelvin Trautman / Red Bull Content Pool

Nick Greece, Matt Beechinor and Gavin McClurg soar Hurricane Ridge, Utah during the filming of 500 Miles to Nowhere. Photo Jody MacDonald

AN ADVANCED PILOT'S FIRST AID KIT

When putting together a kit, make sure you can confidently use every item. The kit needs to balance weight and bulk, with the capacity to treat common but minor injuries, and rare but very serious injuries.

CORE KIT

- Permanent marker and notepad (1)
- Rolltop dry bag
- Rubber gloves x 2 (2)
- Fabric plasters (3)
- Steri-Strips 3mm/6mm x 75mm (4)
- Gauze swabs (sterile, pack of 5) (5)
- Absorbent field dressing ('Battlefield'/'Israeli') (6)
- Zinc oxide tape 2.5cm (7)
- Ibuprofen 200mg x 2 and acetaminophen (paracetamol) 500mg x 2 (8)
- Small knife or non-sterile thumb scalpel (9)
- SAM splint (10)

This kit is recommended by Dr Matt Wilkes, an expedition doctor, mountaineer and pilot, and trainer in adventure first aid and wilderness medicine.

OPTIONAL ADDITIONS

- Water purifying tablets (11)
- Additional SAM splint
- Triangular bandage (non-sterile, non-woven) (12)
- Hemostatic gauze (13)
- Needle and syringe (14)
- Aspirin 300mg single dose (15)

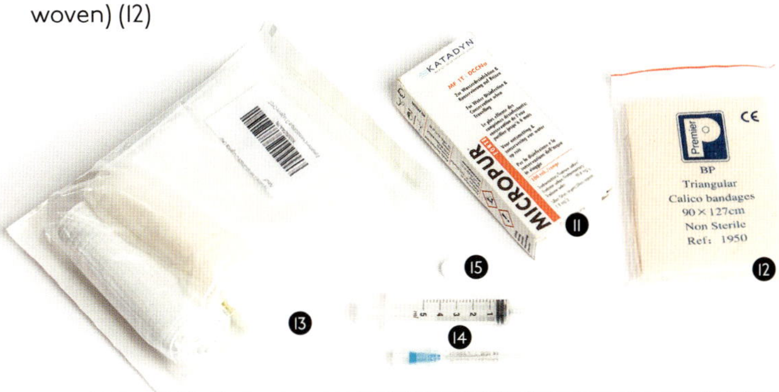

NOTES

- Gloves – you need two pairs, as these sometimes tear or may need to be changed if contaminated
- Plasters and Steri-Strips are for wound closure
- Swabs help to pack or clean a wound
- Field dressing helps effectively apply direct pressure to a wound
- Zinc oxide tape is to support joints
- Painkillers – these are uncontrolled drugs, legal worldwide. Use half doses for adults under 50kg. Avoid ibuprofen in asthmatics, or if there is heavy bleeding.
- SAM splint – we recommend storing underneath the seat or in the back of the harness.
- Permanent marker – it's good practice to make notes, including mechanism of injury, changes in condition and treatments given. Take a photograph of your notes, then send them to hospital with the casualty.
- Purification tablets - if water is clean enough to drink, it's clean enough to wash a wound. High volumes of clean water are much more effective than small alcohol wipes in decontaminating wounds.
- Triangular bandages are useful to support joints, and to assist with pelvic binding
- Hemostatic gauze – highly effective at stopping bleeding, but expensive
- Needle and syringe – can help with wound cleaning, when used as a 'pressure washer'
- Aspirin 300mg – the commonest cause of the death in the mountains is a heart attack. A single dose of aspirin can help somebody having a heart attack. Do not use in any casualty where bleeding is suspected.

PILOT SELF-ASSESSMENT

An honest appraisal of your skills and aptitudes will help you discover what you need to work on.

SELF-APPRAISAL

First, rate yourself 0-10 for each of the sub-categories, with 0 being 'not at all able' and 10 being 'world champion level'. For example, if your light wind launches are consistently good but you struggle in light backwinds, you might give yourself a 5.

TECHNICAL

Pre-flight checks and equipment maintenance

Launching in light winds
Launching in strong winds

Climbing in light conditions
Climbing in strong conditions

Dealing with side collapses, including spin recovery
Dealing with front collapses
Stalling and back flying

Understanding of competition rules and tasks
Setting tasks on your instruments

Using your instruments effectively
Calculating best glide with your instruments

Ability to find good lifty lines while gliding
Understanding speed-to-fly for best task performance and best glide

MENTAL

Ability to focus well over long flights
Ability to spot clues quickly (pilots/birds/smoke)

Ability to deal with failure and continue unaffected
Ability to deal with success and continue unaffected

Confidence in sometimes feeling afraid but managing and continuing

Self-confidence not to be pushed around by others (on launch/in air etc)

PHYSICAL

Physical fitness for flying (arms, shoulders, core, legs) over long tasks
Physical fitness for carrying equipment for 2-3 hours
Flexibility: able to perform maneuvers (eg stall) without pulling muscles

YOUR FRIEND'S APPRAISAL

Give this sheet to a friend who you fly with a lot, who knows you well, and who you can trust to be honest in giving you feedback. Ask them to repeat the exercise thinking about you from their perspective, scoring you from 0-10 in the same way. Also ask them to write answers to the questions about the qualities that make a really good competition or XC pilot, and to rate you on those, too.

TECHNICAL

Pre-flight checks and equipment maintenance

Launching in light winds
Launching in strong winds

Climbing in light conditions
Climbing in strong conditions

Dealing with side collapses including spin recovery
Dealing with front collapses
Stalling and back flying

Understanding of competition rules and tasks
Setting tasks on your instruments

Using your instruments effectively
Calculating best glide with your instruments

Ability to find good lifty lines while climbing
Understanding of speed-to-fly for best task performance and best glide

Another physical quality that the very best XC/competition pilot (delete as appropriate) that I know has, is:

I would rate my friend's skill in this area as... (0-10)

MENTAL

Ability to focus well over long flights
Ability to spot clues (pilots/birds/smoke) quickly

Ability to deal with failure and continue unaffected
Ability to deal with success and continue unaffected

Confidence in sometimes feeling afraid but managing and continuing
Self-confidence not to be pushed around by others (on launch/in air etc)

Another mental quality that the very best XC/competition pilot (delete as appropriate) I know has, is:

I would rate my friend's skill in this area as... (0-10)

PHYSICAL

Physical fitness for flying (arms, shoulders, core, legs) over long tasks
Physical fitness for carrying equipment for 2-3 hours
Flexibility: able to perform maneuvers (eg stall) without pulling muscles

Another physical quality that the very best XC/competition pilot (delete as appropriate) that I know has, is:

I would rate my friend's skill in this area as... (0-10)

After you've completed the exercise, follow the following process.

1. Look for any big inconsistencies between your self-generated scores and your friend's. Ask for honest feedback to add clarity.
2. Discuss the qualities that your friend thinks are important for you to progress to be an even better pilot. Are they meaningful to you?
3. Next, circle one item from each of Technical, Physical and Mental that you want to work on. This might include one of the additional qualities that your friend has added.

For each item, answer the following questions.

TECHNICAL

My goal is
(Eg my goal is to improve my back-flying)

How would you have improved if you had moved up 2-3 numbers (eg from a 4 to a 6)? (Eg I would be able to back-fly consistently from side collapses)

How will you be able to know you have achieved this progress?

Who else will know?

When will you have achieved it by?

What do you now need to do to help you progress? Write down the steps you need to take: what, where and when (and how often).

1
2
3
4
5

MENTAL

My goal is

How would you have improved if you had moved up 2-3 numbers (eg from a 4 to a 6)? (Eg I would be able to back-fly consistently from side collapses)

How will you be able to know you have achieved this progress?

Who else will know?

When will you have achieved it by?

What do you now need to do to help you progress? Write down the steps you need to take: what, where and when (and how often)

1
2
3
4
5

PHYSICAL

My goal is
(Eg my goal is to improve my shoulder strength)

How would you have improved if you had moved up 2-3 numbers (eg from a 4 to a 6)?

How will you be able to know you have achieved this progress?

Who else will know?

When will you have achieved it by?

What do you now need to do to help you progress?

1
2
3
4
5

KORTEL DESIGN
Design & Innovation since 1999 ...
www.korteldesign.com

porcher

ABOUT THE AUTHOR

Gavin McClurg is no stranger to adventure and exploration. Following his paragliding expedition across the Canadian Rockies, he was named a 2015 National Geographic Adventurer of the Year alongside Will Gadd. Gavin then went on to become the first person to traverse the full length of the Alaska Range by foot and paraglider, unsupported, the following year. It was an expedition that took 37 days to complete.

Gavin is the owner and founder of Offshore Odysseys, a global kitesurfing, surfing and sailing expedition where he pioneered hundreds of kitesurfing locations and dozens of flying sites in over 90 countries. He has twice circumnavigated the world by sail, living at sea for 13 straight years, including short-handed roundings of both of the notorious capes - Horn and Good Hope.

In 2004 Gavin learned to ground handle in New Zealand and got the flying bug bad and has been chasing it ever since. Gavin moved from living on a sailboat in Morocco to Sun Valley, Idaho in the summer of 2012 because he'd heard it was one of the best places in the world to fly big air.

The next summer Gavin broke the North American foot-launch record - a flight of 387km from Bald Mountain, Idaho across six mountain ranges into Montana. The record held for eight years. Gavin became the first American to complete the Red Bull X-Alps, a race by foot and paraglider across the Alps from Salzburg to Monaco in 2015. In ten days Gavin flew 1,560km, walked 498km and scaled the height of Everest four times (120,000 vertical feet). He competed again in 2017 and 2019, and as this was going to press was in training for the 2021 race, his fourth.

Gavin started the Cloudbase Mayhem podcast in 2014 and plans to continue it for many years to come. Gavin lives in Sun Valley, Idaho with his wife and daughter because "it has the best backcountry skiing and big air flying on Earth!"

ABOUT THE PILOTS

Guy Anderson (UK) has won silver at the FAI Paragliding European Championships, is a multiple British champion, a world record holder, and a winner of the XContest

Ben Abruzzo (USA) is a sports coach and committed pilot, and has trained and supported the author in all his Red Bull X-Alps campaigns

Matt Beechinor (USA) holds multiple site records and can come off the bench and beat pretty much anyone

Maxime Bellemin (France) is an accomplished Paragliding World Cup pilot, French team performance coach, and author of Performance Paragliding

Bill Belcourt (USA) is the Yoda of paragliding, one of the most respected pilots and alpinists in North America and former head of research and design for Black Diamond Equipment

Fabien Blanco (France) is co-owner and founder of Flyeo Paragliding School. He's a leading SIV instructor, former professional acro pilot and mountain guide

Théo de Blic (France) has been ranked No 1 in the FAI Acro World Rankings since 2017 to the time of publication. He's won numerous acro contests, including the French Championships

Willi Canell (USA) is a river guide and adventure seeker who took to flying like syrup to pancakes. He has competed in the X-Pyr and Red Bull X-Alps

Kari Castle (USA) has won more championships in hang gliding and paragliding than anyone! 14 national hang gliding championships, and six or seven (she can't remember!) in paragliding. She's won the FAI Women's Hang Gliding Championships and set multiple distance records

Jon Chambers (UK) is a two-time Red Bull X-Alps competitor, finishing fifth in 2011 and fourth in 2013

Christian Ciech (Italy) is one of the most consistent and successful competition hang glider pilots in history. He's a test pilot for Icaro, and multiple FAI Hang Gliding World Champion

Josh Cohn (USA), also known as the "Josh Bot", has multiple US national titles under his belt, won a Paragliding World Cup task in his teens, and holds many site distance records

ABOUT THE PILOTS

Gurpreet Dhindsa (India) is a multiple Indian National Champion, Paragliding World Cup pilot and paragliding instructor

Tom de Dorlodot (Belgium) has competed in the Red Bull X-Alps eight times (and counting). He has flown widely in the Karakoram and Himalaya and is a filmmaker, Red Bull sponsored athlete and sailor

Aaron Durogati (Italy) has won the overall Paragliding World Cup multiple times and is a veteran Red Bull X-Alps participant

Max Fanderl (Canada) is a four-time Red Bull X-Alps competitor and flying instructor

Kelly Farina (Italy) is the author of Mastering Paragliding, an instructor, and former British team pilot

Will Gadd (Canada) is a professional adventure athlete, former world paraglidiing world record holder, National Geographic Adventurer of the Year, Red Bull X-Alps competitor and whitewater paddler

Phil Glutz (Switzerland) is an Australian-born transplant to the Alps, professional tandem pilot and a very lucky individual

Till Gottbrath (Austria) has nearly 40 years of accident-free flying experience and runs PR for Nova Paragliders

Nick Greece (USA) was the first pilot to fly over 200 miles in the USA. He is a multiple US National Champion and has represented the US in multiple FAI Paragliding World Championships

Joanna Di Grigoli (France) is a Paragliding World Cup pilot and has represented Venezuela multiple times at the FAI Paragliding World Championships. She has won the Women's class in XContest and flew 400km to set a new South American women's record in Brazil in 2016

Bruce Goldsmith (France) is a former FAI Paragliding World Champion, many-time British champion and designer and managing director at BGD

Greg Hamerton (UK) is an instructor, coach, producer of amazing tutorial videos, and X-Pyr competitor

Armin Harich (Germany) is co-founder of Skywalk Paragliders and the first person to fly over 300km in Germany (on a low-level EN B!). Armin has flown over 40 years without a single accident

Annalena Hinestroza (Germany) is a veteran competition pilot and has competed for Germany at FAI World Championship level. She's won the women's class in the German Championships twice.

Adel Honti (Hungary) is one of the top-ranked female pilots in the world

Marko Hrgetic Hrga (Mexico) is a Czech veteran of the Paragliding World Cup, instructor, and Red Bull X-Alps competitor

Bernhard Kalin (Switzerland) is a paragliding instructor, professional speed pilot, and Base jumper

Christina Kolb (Germany) is the FAI Women's Acro World Champion, a bivvy pilot, and one of the few women in the world to perform the infinite tumble

Antoine Laurens (France) is one of our sport's greatest adventurers. He crossed the Indian and Nepalese Himalaya by paraglider and was one of the members of the Sierra vol-biv to the Oregon border with the author in 2012

Max Marien (USA) is a veteran instructor, acro pilot and tandem pilot

Dustin Martin (USA) flew 761km in Texas in July 2012 to set the hang gliding distance world record and is a multiple US hang gliding champion, and also a distance-hungry paraglider pilot

Chrigel Maurer (Switzerland) has won multiple Paragliding World Cups, is a former acro champion, winner of six Red Bull X-Alps and dozens of other hike-and-fly races, and currently holds the world-record FAI triangle. The most accomplished mountain pilot on Earth

Xandi Meschuh (Austria) is an acro and SIV instructor and designer for Icaro Paragliders

Isabella Messenger (Germany) has been a professional tandem pilot in Nepal and Germany for over a decade, and is an accomplished competition and acro pilot

Hugh Miller (UK) is a former FAI World Air Games champion, British champion and national XC league winner, and is a course tutor in post-graduate psychology

Nick Neynens (New Zealand) is a huge fan favorite in the Red Bull X-Alps and one of the most prolific vol-biv pilots the sport has ever seen

Cody Mittanck (USA) is an accomplished acro pilot, regularly top-ten in the Paragliding World Cup, holds multiple site and state records and Red Bull X-Alps competitor

Russ Ogden (France) is one of the most consistent podium finishers on the Paragliding World Cup circuit and has had frequent spells as World No I in the World Pilot Ranking System (WPRS). Ozone test pilot and many-time British team pilot

Veso Ovcharov (Bulgaria) is the first Bulgarian to master the infinite tumble. He holds multiple acro records and has recently become an exceptional big distance XC pilot

Caroline Paul (USA) is the first female firefighter in San Francisco, an Olympic luge competitor, pilot, professional speaker and author of four books

Tom Payne (Switzerland) is a veteran Paragliding World Cup pilot who has several site records. He competed in the 2009 Red Bull X-Alps and supported Jon Chambers twice

John Pendry (UK) has won both the FAI Hang Gliding World Championship and FAI Paragliding World Championship, one of only three pilots to do so (the other two being Judy Leden and Rob Whittall)

Ondrej Prochazka (Czech Republic) is a professional acro pilot, who holds numerous records, including the Esfera record (off-axis infinite tumble)

Honza Rejmanek (USA) is a Czech-born five-time Red Bull X-Alps competitor, multiple site record holder, meteorologist, former professional dirt bag, and father-son tandem vol-biv expedition pilot

Mitch Riley (USA) has his hand in just about every aspect of paragliding and is a professional wanderer who regularly clocks up 500+ hours flying in a year. He is a veteran instructor, Red Bull X-Alps competitor, and World Cup regular

Alex Robé (Austria) is a multiple winner of the world XContest and continues to be one of the names at the top of XContest on the huge days in the Alps

Dominic Rohner (Switzerland) is a former paragliding school owner and site record holder near his home in Zurich. Dominic can be found chasing big distance around the globe

Rafael Saladini (Brazil) has broken the open-distance world record multiple times and scooped several Paragliding World Cup wins too

Jocky Sanderson (UK) has coached several national teams, meet-directed international competitions, won bronze in the FAI Paragliding World Championships, and continues to be one of the world's most respected SIV and XC instructors

Chris Santacroce (USA) is a former Red Bull Air Force athlete for all things flying – hang gliding, paragliding, paramotoring, Base jump and skydiving. He is one of the most influential instructors and personalities in US free flight

Nate Scales (USA) is a flying legend

Jeff Shapiro (USA) is a professional hang glider, paraglider and wingsuit pilot. He is also a Base jumper, gear designer, writer, rock and ice climber and a damn good dad

Wolfgang Siess (Switzerland) is a professional tandem hang-glider pilot, adventurer extraordinaire, high-level comp pilot, proximity speed pilot and filmmaker

Michael Sigel (Switzerland) is a Gin test pilot, Swiss open-distance record holder and one of the youngest competition pilots in history to win the PWCA Superfinal

Jonathan Smith (USA) is a commercial airline pilot and free-flight enthusiast

Rob Sporrer (USA) is owner of one of the largest flight schools in the world, an accomplished comp pilot and ground-breaking US-based instructor

Reavis Sutphin-Gray (USA) is a weather expert, computer guru, paragliding gypsy, XC crusher and the author's brain and strategy supporter in the Red Bull X-Alps

Mads Syndergaard (Denmark) has over 20 years' competition experience and is the author of Flying Rags for Glory

Pál Takáts (Hungary) is the inventor of multiple acrobatic maneuvers, a Paragliding World Cup cross-country ace, and two-time competitor in the Red Bull X-Alps

Thomas Theurillat (Switzerland) is a mountain guide and sports and personal coach. He was Chrigel Maurer's supporter in his first four wins of the Red Bull X-Alps and heads up OneDay coaching, training some of the world's most accomplished athletes and business people

Larry Tudor (USA) is one of the most famous big-distance hang glider pilots in the history of the sport and is still chasing it on paragliders today.

Mark Watts (UK) is one of the most successful pilots in UK history. The only British pilot who's won a PWC, the British Championship, the UK XC League, and to have held the UK open distance record

Dr Matt Wilkes (UK) is an emergency-care physician, expert on high altitude risk and has headed up comprehensive studies on free flying physiology and effective use of safety equipment

AUTHOR'S THANKS

This book has been made possible only through the generous time given freely by our community of exceptional free flight pilots, and the thousands of regular listeners who tune in to the Cloudbase Mayhem. Thank you to each and every one of you. A special thanks is owed to Myles Connolly, our tireless podcast editor, and the amazing team at Cross Country – Hugh, Marcus, Charlie, Ed and Andrew – for believing in this project and giving it life.

PROFILE PICTURE CREDITS

Page	Pilot	Photographer
8	Gavin McClurg	Marcus King
16	Adel Honti	Mátyás Pődör
28	Alex Robé	Birgit Steinberger
38	Armin Harich	Andrea Simon
46	Bruce Goldsmith	Freyja Goldsmith
58	Chrigel Maurer	Marcus King
70	Cody Mittanck	Cody Mittanck
82	Dustin Martin	Steven Grezlak
92	Honza Rejmanek	Harald Tauderer / Red Bull Content Pool
106	Jeff Shapiro	Christopher Gibisch
120	Jocky Sanderson	James Mills
130	Kelly Farina	Kelly Farina
140	Maxime Bellemin	Antonin Michaud-Soret / ahstudio.fr
150	Nick Neynens	Harald Tauderer / Red Bull Content Pool
160	Pál Takáts	Marcus King
170	Rafael Saladini	Marcus King
182	Russ Ogden	Marcus King
194	Thomas Theurillat	Thomas Ulrich
210	Will Gadd	Christian Pondella / Red Bull Content Pool
240	Gavin McClurg	Gavin McClurg

UNITS

We all talk the language of free flight, but some of us speak a different dialect when it comes to numbers. Throughout this book we've stuck to describing distances and heights how the pilot has described them in the original Cloudbase Mayhem interview, using metres and kilometres or miles and feet, sometimes both. Here's a quick conversion table!

1m = 3.28ft
100m = 328ft
1,000m = 1,093 yards
1km = 0.62 miles
100km = 62.14 miles
10ft = 3.05m
1,000ft = 304.8m
1 mile = 1,609m (1.6km)
100 miles = 160.94km

0.5m/s = 98.5 ft per minute
1m/s = 197 ft per minute
2m/s = 394 ft per minute
3m/s = 591 ft per minute
5m/s = 984 ft per minute
10m/s = 1,969 ft per minute

1km/h = 0.54 knots = 0.62mph
1 knot = 1.15mph = 1.85km/h
1mph = 0.87 knots = 1.61km/h

10km/h = 5.4 knots = 6.2mph
15km/h = 8.1 knots = 9.32mph
32km/h = 17.3 knots = 20mph
50km/h = 27 knots = 31.07mph

Wherever your journey takes you, enjoy the ride.
Photo: Jody MacDonald